Taste of Home

AMERICAN SUMMER

COOKBOOK

AMERICAN SUMMER
COOKBOOK

TASTE OF HOME BOOKS • RDA ENTHUSIAST BRANDS, LLC • MILWAUKEE, WI

International Standard Book Numbers
Retail: 978-1-61765-929-4
DTC: 978-1-61765-969-0

LOCC: 2019950034
Component Number: 115800514S

Executive Editor: Mark Hagen
Senior Art Director: Raeann Thompson
Assistant Art Director: Courtney Lovetere
Designer: Arielle Jardine
Senior Editor, Copy Desk: Dulcie Shoener
Copy Editor: Ann Walter

Cover Photography
Photographer: Grace Natoli Sheldon
Senior Set Stylist: Melissa Franco
Senior Food Stylist: Shannon Roum

Pictured on front cover:
All-American Hamburgers, p. 146;
Mama's Warm German Potato Salad, p. 41; and
Marinated Mozzarella & Tomato Appetizers, p. 18

Pictured on title page:
Red, White & Blue Summer Salad, p. 45

Pictured on back cover:
Grilled Green Beans, p. 71;
Star-Spangled Lemon Icebox Pie, p. 312;
Grilled Lemon Chicken, p. 205; and
Summertime Fun Cookies, p. 228

Printed in U.S.A.
1 3 5 7 9 10 8 6 4 2

DIG INTO SUMMER!

Turn here for summer's best food, flavor and fun! Serve up everything from juicy burgers and savory steaks to frosty treats and desserts made brilliant with fresh berries. You'll find hundreds of the season's best beverages, appetizers, main courses, sides and desserts in this incredible collection.

AT-A-GLANCE ICONS

🕐 **FAST FIX:** Prepare these recipes, start to finish, in 30 minutes or less.

5i **5 INGREDIENTS:** These dishes call for just a few staples, excluding water, salt, pepper, oils and optional items.

❄️ **FREEZE IT:** What's more refreshing than a frosty treat? Stock the freezer with these specialties.

🍲 **SLOW COOKER:** Put your favorite kitchen tool to work with dishes that simmer to perfection on their own.

THIS ULTIMATE GUIDE TO SUMMER INCLUDES:

- 253 no-fuss recipes that celebrate the tastiest time of year and 170+ tips, hints and timesavers

- Complete party menus for hosting impressive get-togethers all season long

- More than 400 full-color photos and complete nutrition facts with every recipe

- An entire section of Instant Pot and air-fryer dishes perfect for keeping the kitchen cool

- 140 recipes that use 5 ingredients or are table-ready in as little as half an hour

- A grilling guide for perfect flame-broiled fare every time, and handy reference charts regarding summer produce

Take a bite out of the best season of the year! It's never been more delicious than with **American Summer Cookbook.**

CONTENTS

More ways to connect with us:

SHOPTASTEOFHOME.COM

SUMMER'S CLASSIC

APPETIZERS & BEVERAGES

From pool parties and backyard barbecues to church picnics and pregame tailgates, summer snacking is a snap when you take advantage of all the refreshing flavors this season has to offer.

BEAT THE HEAT BY JAZZING UP WARM-WEATHER COOLERS

Give ho-hum beverages a makeover with these easy ideas and garnishes.

KEEP IT COOL. Frost a glass by placing it in the freezer 15-30 minutes before using. Fill with ice and cold beverages.

SWEET OR SASSY? Coat the rim of a glass with sugar or salt. Invert the glass, dip the rim in water, then dip it into a plate of salt, sugar or colored sugar.

ADD A POP OF COLOR. Attach seasonal fruit—pineapple wedges or whole strawberries—to the rim of the glass. Cut a slit partway through the fruit so it will rest on the rim without falling.

CURLS ARE IN. For colorful citrus curls, use a citrus stripper to remove a long continuous strip of peel. Tightly wind the strip around a straw and secure the end with waterproof tape. Let stand at least 20 minutes. Remove the tape and slide the curl off the straw for a garnish.

MAKE A STAR STATEMENT. Skewer a slice of star fruit and place it vertically into a clear drink. Or use a small cookie cutter to cut decorative shapes from slices of melon. Thread a few pieces onto skewers for cocktail stirrers.

TRY A WEAVE. Weave a long, wide strip of citrus peel onto a skewer accordion-style. If desired, add a piece of fruit or mint to the top for extra color.

SAY IT WITH CHOCOLATE. Melt dark chocolate and carefully place in a small resealable plastic bag. Make a small snip off a corner. Squeeze to pipe chocolate designs on waxed paper; let them stand until set. Be careful, though—if the design is too thin, it is more likely to break. Use garnishes to top iced coffee, shakes and other chilly sippers.

THE ESSENTIAL SUMMER BAR

A well-stocked bar doesn't need to be extensive—a handful of liquors and mixers, garnishes and a few tools. Add specialty items based on individual recipes. And make sure you have ice!

MUST-HAVE LIQUORS:
Rum • Bourbon or whiskey • Gin • Vodka •Tequila • Brandy

BEYOND THE BASICS:
Bitters • Orange liqueur (Cointreau or Grand Marnier) • Amaretto • Coffee liqueur (Kahlua) • Irish cream liqueur • Flavored vodkas & rums • Vermouth

SUMMER FRUIT, VEGGIES & HERBS:
Citrus fruits • Stone fruits and berries • Herbs (mint, rosemary & basil)

WINES:
White • Red • Rosé • Champagne or sparkling white wine • Port

MIXERS:
Club soda • Tonic water • Cola, ginger ale & lemon-lime soda • Fruit juices • Simple syrup • Grenadine syrup

THE TOOLKIT:
Cocktail shaker and strainer • Jigger • Muddler • Bottle/wine opener • Peeler • Citrus press • Straws • Cocktail skewers or picks

GLASSES & MORE:
Highball (Collins) • Lowball (rocks) • Champagne flute • Martini (cocktail) • Margarita • Wineglass • Pitcher • Ice bucket

← MUDDLE A DRINK
Place ingredients such as citrus or berries in a glass. Add a small amount of sugar or bitters. With a muddler, gently crush and bruise the ingredients until they release their aromas. A wooden spoon handle is a good stand-in if you don't have an actual muddler.

BLOODY MARY

We think horseradish makes this one of the best Bloody Mary recipes in the world. Without the horseradish, you will have a more traditional drink, and without the alcohol, you'll have a Virgin Mary. Serve it with your favorite garnish.
—Taste of Home *Test Kitchen*

Takes: 10 min.
Makes: 1 serving

- ¼ tsp. plus ⅛ tsp. celery salt, divided
- 1½ to 2 cups ice cubes, divided
- 2 oz. vodka
- 1 cup tomato juice, chilled
- 1 Tbsp. lemon juice
- 1½ tsp. lime juice
- ¾ tsp. Worcestershire sauce
- ½ tsp. prepared horseradish, optional
- ⅛ tsp. pepper
- ⅛ tsp. hot pepper sauce

OPTIONAL GARNISHES
Celery rib, pickle spear, green and ripe olives, cucumber slice and/or cooked shrimp

1. Using water, moisten rim of a highball glass. Sprinkle ¼ tsp. celery salt on a small plate; dip rim into salt. Discard remaining celery salt from plate. Fill a shaker three-fourths full with ice. Place the remaining ice in prepared glass.
2. Add vodka, juices, Worcestershire sauce, horseradish if desired, pepper, remaining celery salt and pepper sauce to shaker; cover and shake until condensation forms on exterior, 10-15 seconds. Strain into prepared glass. Garnish as desired.

1½ cups: 180 cal., 1g fat (0 sat. fat), 0 chol., 1110mg sod., 12g carb. (7g sugars, 1g fiber), 2g pro.

BLOODY MARY BAR

Set a buffet of fixin's and let guests jazz up their own bloody.

- Put out an assortment of flavored salts and seasonings to rim glasses.

- Set the bar high with add-ons such as beef sticks, bacon, cheese, deviled eggs or even soft pretzels.

- Include a bottle of hot pepper sauce for those who need extra heat.

- Don't forget the sudsy beer chasers!

🕐 5️⃣

BASIL CITRUS COCKTAIL

This irresistible cocktail is not only fruity and fantastic, but it's low in calories, making it perfect for swimsuit season.
—Taste of Home *Test Kitchen*

Takes: 10 min.
Makes: 1 serving

- 6 fresh basil leaves
- 1½ to 2 cups ice cubes
- 2 oz. white grapefruit juice
- 2 oz. mandarin orange juice
- ¾ oz. gin
- ½ oz. Domaine de Canton ginger liqueur

1. In a shaker, muddle basil leaves.
2. Fill shaker three-fourths full with ice. Add the juices, gin and ginger liqueur; cover and shake until condensation forms on outside of shaker, 10-15 seconds. Strain into a chilled cocktail glass.

1 serving: 136 cal., 0 fat (0 sat. fat), 0 chol., 0 sod., 14g carb. (7g sugars, 0 fiber), 1g pro.

SLAW-TOPPED BEEF SLIDERS

To ease prep time and avoid extra cleanup on these colorful, hearty appetizers, use bagged coleslaw mix and bottled slaw dressing. When I was working full time, I also relied on the easy sliders for make-ahead meals.
—*Jane Whittaker, Pensacola, FL*

Prep: 20 min.
Cook: 6 hours.
Makes: 1 dozen

- 3 cups coleslaw mix
- ½ medium red onion, chopped (about ⅔ cup)
- ⅛ tsp. celery seed
- ¼ tsp. pepper
- ⅓ cup coleslaw salad dressing
SANDWICHES
- 1 boneless beef chuck roast (2 lbs.)
- 1 tsp. salt
- ½ tsp. pepper
- 1 can (6 oz.) tomato paste
- ¼ cup water
- 1 tsp. Worcestershire sauce
- 1 small onion, diced
- 1 cup barbecue sauce
- 12 slider buns or dinner rolls, split

1. Combine coleslaw, onion, celery seed and pepper. Add salad dressing; toss to coat. Refrigerate until serving.
2. Sprinkle roast with salt and pepper; transfer roast to a 5-qt. slow cooker. Mix tomato paste, water and Worcestershire sauce; pour over roast. Top with onion. Cook, covered, on low 6-8 hours or until meat is tender.
3. Shred meat with 2 forks; return to slow cooker. Stir in barbecue sauce; heat through. Serve beef on buns; top with coleslaw. Replace tops.

1 slider: 322 cal., 12g fat (4g sat. fat), 67mg chol., 726mg sod., 34g carb. (13g sugars, 3g fiber), 20g pro.

HOW MUCH IS ENOUGH?

Whether hosting a backyard bash, bridal shower or family reunion, it's key to have enough appetizers for the crowd. Keep these guidelines in mind when planning your party.

Cocktails before dinner: Plan on 3-4 different appetizers and about 4-5 pieces per guest.

Open house buffet: Serve 4-5 types of appetizers and about 4-6 pieces per person.

Light dinner of finger foods: Consider 6-8 different appetizers and roughly 14-16 servings per guest.

CRUNCHY VEGETABLE DIP

This new recipes was a big hit with my family. Dig into it as an appetizer or sandwich spread.
—*Dottie Miller, Jonesborough, TN*

Prep: 15 min. + chilling
Makes: 16 servings

1 pkg. (8 oz.) cream cheese, softened
1 Tbsp. mayonnaise
1 Tbsp. lemon juice
½ tsp. salt
⅛ tsp. pepper
¾ cup grated carrots
½ cup diced celery
½ cup diced green pepper
⅓ cup chopped green onions
Assorted crackers and fresh
vegetables

In a bowl, beat the first 5 ingredients until smooth. Stir in vegetables. Refrigerate, covered, 2-3 hours. Serve with crackers and vegetables.

2 Tbsp. dip: 60 cal., 6g fat (3g sat. fat), 14mg chol., 129mg sod., 2g carb. (1g sugars, 0 fiber), 1g pro.

HONEY HYDRATOR

Stir up a pitcher of this refreshing drink, naturally sweetened with honey.
—*National Honey Board, Firestone, CO*

Takes: 5 min.
Makes: 8 servings (1 cup each)

- ½ **cup lukewarm water**
- ½ **cup honey**
- ½ **tsp. salt substitute or ¼ tsp. salt**
- 2 **cups cold orange juice**
- 5 **cups cold water**

Place water, honey and salt substitute in a pitcher; stir until blended. Stir in juice and cold water. Refrigerate until serving.

1 cup: 94 cal., 0 fat (0 sat. fat), 0 chol., 76mg sod., 24g carb. (23g sugars, 0 fiber), 0 pro.
Diabetic exchanges: 1½ starch.

GRILLED PEACH & PINEAPPLE SANGRIA

I grill fresh peaches and pineapple slathered in cinnamon butter and use them to make a refreshing summer sangria. I also like to add slices of grilled lemon and lime to drop in the glasses for a citrusy boost of flavor.
—*Heather King, Frostburg, MD*

Prep: 25 min. + chilling
Makes: 8 servings

- 1   bottle (750 ml) sauvignon blanc or other white wine
- 2   cups lemonade
- ½   cup orange liqueur
- 1   Tbsp. butter, melted
- 1   Tbsp. sugar
- 1   tsp. ground cinnamon
- 3   medium peeled peaches, pitted and halved
- ¼   fresh pineapple, peeled and cut into 4 slices

1. Make sangria by combining the wine, lemonade and liqueur. Refrigerate. Meanwhile, in a small bowl, combine melted butter, sugar and cinnamon. Mix well.
2. Brush butter mixture over cut side of peaches and all over pineapple slices. Grill fruit, covered, on a greased rack over medium direct heat 4-5 minutes. Turn the peaches and pineapple. Grill 4-5 minutes more. Remove from grill.
3. Cut each peach half into 5 or 6 slices and each pineapple slice into 5 or 6 pieces. Add three-fourths of fruit to sangria, reserving remainder. Refrigerate at least 2 hours.
4. Before serving, thread several pieces of reserved fruit onto appetizer skewers. Pour sangria over ice; serve with fruit skewers.

¾ cup: 206 cal., 2g fat (1g sat. fat), 4mg chol., 20mg sod., 25g carb. (21g sugars, 1g fiber), 1g pro.

COCONUT CHICKEN & SHRIMP

I was looking for an easy-breezy snack, so I created this recipe based on two fast-food staples. It quickly became a family favorite, particularly alongside the dipping sauce..
—Susan Seymour, Valatie, NY

Prep: 30 min.
Cook: 5 min./batch
Makes: 6 servings

- 1 cup all-purpose flour
- 1 cup lime-flavored seltzer water
- 1 tsp. ground ginger
- 1 tsp. salt
- 1 tsp. pepper
- 2½ cups sweetened shredded coconut
- 1¼ cups panko (Japanese) bread crumbs
- 1 lb. uncooked shrimp (31-40 per lb.), peeled and deveined
- 2 boneless skinless chicken breasts (6 oz. each), cut into ¾-in. cubes
  Oil for deep-fat frying
  Salt and pepper to taste, optional

MAUI MUSTARD
- 1 can (8 oz.) crushed pineapple, well drained
- ½ cup red pepper jelly
- 3 Tbsp. stone-ground mustard

1. In a shallow bowl, whisk together the first 5 ingredients. In another shallow bowl, combine coconut and panko. Dip shrimp in batter to coat. Dip in coconut mixture, patting to help coating adhere. Repeat with the chicken.

2. In an electric skillet or deep fryer, heat oil to 350°. Fry shrimp, a few at a time, until golden brown, 3-4 minutes. Drain on paper towels. Repeat with chicken. If desired, sprinkle lightly with salt and pepper.

3. For mustard, mix together pineapple, pepper jelly and stone-ground mustard. Combine shrimp and chicken; serve with Maui mustard.

1 serving: 659 cal., 31g fat (14g sat. fat), 123mg chol., 735mg sod., 69g carb. (39g sugars, 4g fiber), 29g pro.

In the mood for just seafood? Skip the chicken and use more shrimp.

MARINATED MOZZARELLA & TOMATO APPETIZERS

This party hit was inspired by a dish I enjoyed at a restaurant. It's best served chilled and should marinate for a bit. My daughter likes to put the mozzarella on her antipasti platters at backyard barbecues.
—*Mary Ann Lee, Clifton Park, NY*

Prep: 15 min. + marinating
Bake: 5 min.
Makes: 16 servings

- ½ cup Italian salad dressing
- 2 Tbsp. minced fresh basil
- 2 Tbsp. minced fresh chives
- ½ tsp. coarsely ground pepper
- 2 cartons (8 oz. each) miniature fresh mozzarella cheese balls, drained
- 2 cups cherry tomatoes
- 12 slices French bread baguette (½ in. thick), cut into quarters
- 2 tsp. olive oil
- ⅛ tsp. salt

1. Preheat oven to 450°. Combine salad dressing, basil, chives and pepper. Add the cheese and tomatoes; toss to coat. Refrigerate, covered, at least 3 hours to let flavors blend.

2. Meanwhile, toss baguette pieces with oil and salt; arrange on a baking sheet. Bake until toasted, 4-5 minutes. Cool completely. Just before serving, add toasted bread to cheese mixture; toss to combine. If desired, thread tomatoes, cheese and bread on skewers for serving.

¼ cup: 119 cal., 8g fat (4g sat. fat), 22mg chol., 171mg sod., 5g carb. (2g sugars, 0 fiber), 6g pro.

MARGARITA CHICKEN QUESADILLAS

Quesadillas have never tasted so good as when they are filled with slightly sweet onions and peppers and topped with lime butter and salt, the perfect balance of sweet and savory. This version is ideal for a summer party—or a great way to bring a little bit of warm-weather fun to chilly winter nights.
—*Stephanie Bright, Simpsonville, SC*

Prep: 35 min. + marinating
Bake: 10 min.
Makes: 16 wedges

- 4 boneless skinless chicken breast halves (5 oz. each)
- ¾ cup thawed frozen limeade concentrate
- 1 large onion, sliced
- 1 medium sweet orange pepper, julienned
- 1 medium sweet yellow pepper, julienned
- 1 Tbsp. canola oil
- ¼ tsp. salt
- ¼ tsp. pepper
- 4 flour tortillas (10 in.)
- 1 cup shredded Monterey Jack cheese
- 1 cup shredded cheddar cheese

- 2 Tbsp. butter, melted
- 1 Tbsp. lime juice
- 1 Tbsp. chopped fresh cilantro Lime wedges, optional

1. Place chicken in a large bowl. Add limeade concentrate and toss to coat. Cover bowl; refrigerate for 6 hours or overnight.

2. In a large nonstick skillet, saute the onion and sweet peppers in oil until tender; season with salt and pepper. Remove and set aside; wipe out skillet. Drain chicken and discard the marinade.

3. Grill chicken, covered, on a greased rack over medium heat or broil 4 in. from the heat for 5-8 minutes on each side or until a thermometer reads 170°. Cut chicken into ¼-in. strips; set aside. On half of each tortilla, layer Monterey Jack cheese, chicken, pepper mixture and cheddar cheese; fold over.

4. Combine butter and lime juice; brush over the tortillas.

5. In same skillet used to cook vegetables, cook quesadillas over medium heat until cheese is melted, 2-3 minutes per side. Keep warm in oven while cooking the remaining quesadillas. Cut each chicken quesadilla into 4 wedges. Sprinkle with cilantro; serve with lime wedges if desired.

1 wedge: 204 cal., 9g fat (4g sat. fat), 37mg chol., 288mg sod., 18g carb. (8g sugars, 1g fiber), 12g pro.

5i
BLACKBERRY LEMONADE

Here's a special beverage that's perfect when blackberries are in season. It has a tangy, refreshing flavor.
—*Rich Murray, Nevada, MO*

Prep: 20 min. + chilling
Makes: about 1½ qt.

- 4   **cups water, divided**
- 1   **cup sugar**
- 1   **cup lemon juice**
- 1   **Tbsp. grated lemon zest**
- 1   **cup blackberries**
- 1   **to 2 drops blue food coloring, optional**

1. In a large saucepan, bring 2 cups water and sugar to a boil. Boil for 2 minutes, stirring occasionally. Remove from the heat. Stir in the lemon juice, zest and remaining water; cool slightly.

2. In a blender, combine 1 cup of lemon mixture and the blackberries; cover and process until blended. Strain and discard the seeds. Pour blackberry mixture and remaining lemon mixture into a pitcher; stir well. Add food coloring if desired. Refrigerate until chilled. Serve in chilled glasses over ice.

1 cup: 152 cal., 0 fat (0 sat. fat), 0 chol., 1mg sod., 40g carb. (35g sugars, 2g fiber), 0 pro.

PEACHY JALAPENO GUACAMOLE

Fresh jalapenos and summer-ripe peaches give this creamy guacamole so much flavor. It's got a little kick, but I love that it's not so spicy it burns my taste buds!
—*Colleen Delawder, Herndon, VA*

Takes: 15 min.
Makes: 1½ cups

2 **medium ripe avocados, peeled and cubed**
2 **Tbsp. lime juice**
½ **tsp. kosher salt**
½ **tsp. ground cumin**
¼ **tsp. pepper**
1 **medium peach, peeled and finely chopped**
1 **jalapeno pepper, seeded and minced**
2 **Tbsp. finely chopped red onion**
   Tortilla chips

Mash avocados with lime juice, salt, cumin and pepper. Gently stir in peach, jalapeno and red onion. Serve with tortilla chips.

¼ cup: 90 cal., 7g fat (1g sat. fat), 0 chol., 164mg sod., 7g carb. (2g sugars, 4g fiber), 1g pro. **Diabetic exchanges:** 1 fat, ½ starch.

Leave the seeds in the jalapeno pepper for extra heat.

SWEET GINGERED CHICKEN WINGS

Whenever I prepare this tasty recipe for a get-together, it disappears fast. I first tasted the delicious chicken wings 11 years ago when I attended a class on cooking with honey. Now, I even use the wings as a no-fuss main course.
—*Debbie Dougal, Roseville, CA*

Prep: 10 min.
Bake: 1 hour
Makes: 2 dozen

- 1 **cup all-purpose flour**
- 2 **tsp. salt**
- 2 **tsp. paprika**
- ¼ **tsp. pepper**
- 24 **chicken wings (about 5 lbs.)**

SAUCE

- ¼ **cup honey**
- ¼ **cup thawed orange juice concentrate**
- ½ **tsp. ground ginger**
  Minced fresh parsley, optional

1. Preheat oven to 350°. Line 2 baking sheets with foil; coat with cooking spray.

2. In a shallow dish, combine the flour, salt, paprika and pepper. Add chicken wings, a few at a time; toss to coat. Divide wings between prepared pans. Bake 30 minutes.

3. In a small bowl, combine honey, orange juice concentrate and ginger; brush over the chicken wings. Bake until the juices run clear, 25-30 minutes.

4. Preheat broiler. Broil wings 4 in. from heat until lightly browned, 1-2 minutes. If desired, sprinkle with parsley.

1 chicken wing: 134 cal., 7g fat (2g sat. fat), 29mg chol., 225mg sod., 8g carb. (4g sugars, 0 fiber), 10g pro.

WATERMELON CUPS

This lovely appetizer is almost too pretty to eat! Sweet watermelon cubes hold a refreshing topping that showcases cucumber, red onion and fresh herbs.
—Taste of Home *Test Kitchen*

Takes: 25 min.
Makes: 16 appetizers

16 seedless watermelon cubes (1 in.)
⅓ cup finely chopped cucumber
5 tsp. finely chopped red onion
2 tsp. minced fresh mint
2 tsp. minced fresh cilantro
½ to 1 tsp. lime juice

1. Using a small melon baller or measuring spoon, scoop out the center of each watermelon cube, leaving a ¼-in. shell (save pulp for another use).
2. In a small bowl, combine the remaining ingredients; spoon into watermelon cubes.

1 piece: 7 cal., 0 fat (0 sat. fat), 0 chol., 1mg sod., 2g carb. (2g sugars, 0 fiber), 0 pro.

SWEET ONION PIMIENTO CHEESE DEVILED EGGS

For my mother's 92nd birthday, we had deviled eggs topped with pimientos as part of the spread. They're timeless and always in good taste.
—Linda Foreman, Locust Grove, OK

Takes: 15 min.
Makes: 1 dozen

- 6   hard-boiled large eggs
- ¼   cup finely shredded sharp cheddar cheese
- 2   Tbsp. mayonnaise
- 4   tsp. diced pimientos, drained
- 2   tsp. finely chopped sweet onion
- 1   tsp. Dijon mustard
- 1   small garlic clove, minced
- ¼   tsp. salt
- ⅛   tsp. pepper
     Additional diced pimientos and shredded sharp cheddar cheese

Cut eggs lengthwise in half. Remove yolks, reserving whites. In a bowl, mash yolks. Stir in cheese, mayonnaise, pimientos, onion, mustard, garlic, salt and pepper. Spoon or pipe into egg whites. Sprinkle with additional pimientos and cheese. Refrigerate, covered, until serving.

1 stuffed egg half: 67 cal., 5g fat (2g sat. fat), 96mg chol., 128mg sod., 1g carb. (0 sugars, 0 fiber), 4g pro.

HOT DOG SLIDERS WITH MANGO-PINEAPPLE SALSA

For parties, we shrink down lots of foods to slider size, including these quick hot dogs. Pile on the easy but irresistible fruit salsa for a burst of fresh flavor.
—Carole Resnick, Cleveland, OH

Takes: 30 min.
Makes: 2 dozen (2 cups salsa)

- 3   Tbsp. lime juice
- 2   Tbsp. honey
- ¼   tsp. salt
- 1   cup cubed fresh pineapple (½ in.)
- 1   cup cubed peeled mango (½ in.)
- ¼   cup finely chopped red onion
- 2   Tbsp. finely chopped sweet red pepper
- 12 hot dogs
- 12 hot dog buns, split

1. In a small bowl, whisk lime juice, honey and salt until blended. Add the pineapple, mango, onion and pepper; toss to coat.
2. Grill hot dogs, covered, over medium heat or broil 4 in. from heat until heated through, 7-9 minutes, turning occasionally.
3. Place hot dogs in buns; cut each crosswise in half. Serve with fruit salsa.

1 slider with 1 Tbsp. salsa: 146 cal., 8g fat (3g sat. fat), 13mg chol., 361mg sod., 15g carb. (5g sugars, 1g fiber), 5g pro.

SLIDERS TO THE RESCUE

Not sure what to serve at the next party? Think sliders! These appetizers are popular for several reasons—they're quick and easy, they travel well, they're hearty and you can customize them.

Whip up the hot dog sliders at left or try the beef sliders on page 13. You can also create your own masterpiece with deli meats, cheeses, prepared meatballs and pasta sauce, cooked taco meat and shredded lettuce, hot chicken nuggets and barbecue sauce or whatever you might have on hand. Get creative and let the summer snacking begin!

MINIATURE CORN DOGS

Fun-sized corn dogs add a little wow to any party. Kids and adults love them equally, so expect them to disappear fast.

—Deb Perry, Bluffton, IN

Prep: 25 min.
Cook: 5 min./batch
Makes: about 3½ dozen

- 1 cup all-purpose flour
- 2 Tbsp. cornmeal
- 1½ tsp. baking powder
- ¼ tsp. salt
  Dash onion powder
- 3 Tbsp. shortening
- ¾ cup 2% milk
- 1 large egg
- 1 pkg. (16 oz.) miniature smoked sausages
  Oil for deep-fat frying
  Spicy ketchup

1. In a small bowl combine the flour, cornmeal, baking powder, salt and onion powder; cut in shortening until crumbly. Whisk milk and egg; stir into flour mixture just until moistened. Dip the sausages into the batter.

2. In a cast-iron or other heavy skillet, heat oil to 375°. Fry sausages a few at a time until golden brown, 2-3 minutes. Drain on paper towels. Serve with ketchup.

1 mini corn dog: 68 cal., 6g fat (1g sat. fat), 11mg chol., 136mg sod., 2g carb. (0 sugars, 0 fiber), 2g pro.

STRAWBERRY MELON FIZZ

Experimenting in the kitchen's fun for me. I came up with this by combining two different recipes—one for a melon-ball salad and one for a sparkling beverage.
—*Teresa Messick, Montgomery, AL*

Takes: 30 min.
Makes: 10 servings

- 2 **cups sugar**
- 1 **cup water**
- 5 **fresh mint sprigs**
- 1 **qt. fresh strawberries, halved**
- 2 **cups cubed honeydew**
- 1¾ **cups cubed cantaloupe**
  Ginger ale or sparkling white grape juice

1. In a large saucepan, combine the sugar, water and mint; bring to a boil. Reduce the heat; simmer 10 minutes. Remove from heat; allow to cool completely. Discard mint.
2. Combine strawberries and melon. Just before serving, fill tall glasses with fruit and drizzle each with 1 Tbsp. syrup. Add ginger ale to each glass.

1 serving: 194 cal., 0 fat (0 sat. fat), 0 chol., 7mg sod., 49g carb. (46g sugars, 2g fiber), 1g pro.

SUMMER'S TOP

SALADS & DRESSINGS

Memorable summer menus aren't complete without garden-fresh sidekicks that complement any entree. See how easy it is to toss together a hit that rounds out any warm-weather meal.

TOSSING UP SUMMER GREENS

The variety of salad-suitable greens seems endless! Some of the most common are listed below, but bok choy, mustard greens, kale, spinach and Swiss chard are great options, too.

TYPE	DESCRIPTION
LETTUCE	
ICEBERG	Has a round, compact head with pale green leaves. Mild-flavored, crispy iceberg lettuce is what's known as a crisphead lettuce.
BOSTON OR BIBB	Butterhead lettuces have small, loosely formed heads with tender, silky-soft leaves. Bibb lettuce has a sweet, subtle flavor. Boston lettuce has a mild, sweet flavor.
LEAF OR LOOSELEAF	Has leaves that branch out from a stalk. Green and red leaf lettuces are flavorful with crisp, curly-edged leaves. The red leaf variety has red-tipped leaves.
ROMAINE OR COS	Has a long, cylindrical head with large, crisp, green outer leaves. The leaves taste slightly bitter.
SALAD GREENS	
ARUGULA	Is also known as rocket. It is a tender, bitter green and offers a distinct peppery, mustard flavor.
BELGIAN ENDIVE	Has white leaves with pale yellow-green tips. Its bitter leaves are crunchy.
CURLY ENDIVE	Is also known as chicory, and has curly leaves that are tough, chewy and bitter. Curly endive is best used as an accent flavor in a salad. Its strong flavor mellows when cooked.
ESCAROLE	Has slightly bitter, firm, lettuce-like leaves.
FRISEE	Gets a feathery appearance from its delicate curly leaves. This mildly bitter green ranges in color from yellow-white to yellow-green.
RADICCHIO	Has satiny, red, bitter-tasting leaves.
SPINACH	Has a soft bite and a mild, goes-with-anything taste.
WATERCRESS	Has delicate, small, deep green leaves with a peppery, slightly bitter bite.

WASHING AND STORING

- For iceberg lettuce, cut out the core with a paring knife or plastic lettuce knife. Or grasp the head in your hand and hit the core area against the countertop; lift out the core. Rinse the head under running water and drain, core side down, in a colander in the sink.

- Before using lettuce leaves, wash in cool water and dry well. Just before serving, tear leaves into bite-sized pieces or cut with a lettuce knife. (Metal knives will cause the lettuce edges to brown.) Keep greens refrigerated until serving.

- Remove and discard any brown, wilted or damaged outer leaves. Cut off or cut out core from lettuce. Separate leaves, except for iceberg.

- Greens such as arugula or escarole may be sandy or dirty, and should be swished in a clean sink or bowl of cold water. Lift greens out, allowing the sand and grit to sink to the bottom. Repeat in clean water if necessary. Rinse other greens gently in cool water.

- Greens need to be dried; they do not keep well in the refrigerator if they are wet. Pat them dry with a clean towel or paper towel. A salad spinner is an easy way to remove the water (fill only half to two-thirds full). Greens can also be stored in some salad spinners.

- To crisp the greens, store in a covered container or plastic bag and chill for at least 30 minutes before serving. Place a piece of paper towel in the bottom of the container or bag to absorb any excess moisture. Store in the refrigerator crisper drawer for about 1 week.

COMMON SALAD INGREDIENTS

Here are some of the basic building blocks of a classic green salad.

AVOCADOS

Most avocados have buttery texture and rich, slightly nutty flavor. The two most common avocados are Hass and Florida.

The *Hass avocado* is grown in California, weighs about ½ pound, has a pebbly skin that goes from green to black as it ripens, and is available year-round.

The *Florida avocado* is grown in Florida, is larger than the Hass, and has a shiny medium-green skin that doesn't change color as it ripens. It has more water and, ounce for ounce, less fat and fewer calories. It is available from early fall through winter.

Choose avocados that are heavy for their size and have no blemishes. If the avocado is hard, it will need to ripen before using. If it yields to gentle pressure, it is ready to slice. If the avocado has a small dent after pressing, it's too soft to slice but is suitable for mashing. If there is a large dent after pressing, it is overripe and the flesh is likely spoiled.

To ripen avocados, place them in a brown paper bag and leave at room temperature for a few days. To hasten ripening, add an apple or banana to the bag.

Store ripe avocados in the refrigerator for up to 3 days. Brush cut avocados with lemon or lime juice to help prevent the flesh from darkening. Place in an airtight container and eat within 2 days.

CUCUMBERS

The most popular cucumber is just classified as the common cucumber. It was bred to have a thicker skin than other cucumbers to protect it during shipping. This cucumber generally has a waxed coating on the skin to keep it fresher longer.

The *Kirby cucumber* is shorter and has bumpy skin. Originally used for pickling, it can be used in place of the common cucumber in recipes.

The *English cucumber*, also known as burpless or hothouse, is narrow and about 2 feet long. This seedless cucumber is sold wrapped in plastic.

Select firm cucumbers with round ends. Avoid those with soft spots, bulging middles or withered ends. Store unwashed cucumbers in the refrigerator's crisper drawer for up to 1 week. Avoid cold areas of the refrigerator where the cucumber might freeze. Wash cucumbers before using. Peel waxed cucumbers and seed if desired.

RADISHES

The most commonly available radish is the red radish, which is round or oval. Radishes have a peppery flavor that can range from mild to fiery.

White icicle radishes have a flavor similar to the red but are elongated and carrot-shaped. The Japanese *daikon radishes* are large white radishes that can weigh around 2 pounds.

Select firm, well-formed radishes. Avoid those that have cracks or blemishes. Store in the refrigerator crisper drawer for 1 week. Store daikon radishes for only 3 days. Wash or scrub with a vegetable brush before using.

TIPS FOR SUCCESSFUL SALADS

- Select a dressing that pairs well with the lettuce. Sturdy lettuce (iceberg or romaine) can stand up to a thick, creamy dressing like blue cheese or Thousand Island. A delicate lettuce like Bibb or Boston should be tossed with a light vinaigrette.

- Add the dressing just before serving or let each person add his or her own.

- Experiment with a combination of fresh flavors (mild, sweet lettuce with bitter greens), textures (buttery and tender with crisp and crunchy) and colors (shades of green, red and white). Make your salads appeal to the eye as well as the palate.

- Homemade oil and vinegar salad dressing can be shaken together in a jar or container with a tight-fitting lid. The mixture will separate; shake well again before serving.

- Homemade salad dressings made with olive oil will thicken in the refrigerator. Remove them 30 minutes before serving to allow the olive oil to warm.

BASIC VINAIGRETTE

You can modify a basic vinaigrette to create unexpected new flavors. Here are a few suggestions:

- Substitute fruit-, herb- or wine-flavored vinegar for distilled white or cider vinegar.

- Use citrus juice to replace all or part of the vinegar.

- Instead of canola oil, use a nut-flavored oil or add a drop or two of dark sesame oil.

- Try adding some fresh herbs.

GARDEN BOUNTY PANZANELLA SALAD

When my sister gave me fresh tomatoes and basil, I made this traditional bread salad. The longer it sits, the more the bread soaks up the seasonings.
—*Jannine Fisk, Malden, MA*

Prep: 15 min.
Cook: 20 min.
Makes: 16 servings

¼ cup olive oil
12 oz. French or ciabatta bread, cut into 1-in. cubes (about 12 cups)
4 large tomatoes, coarsely chopped
1 English cucumber, coarsely chopped
1 medium green pepper, cut into 1-in. pieces
1 medium sweet yellow pepper, cut into 1-in. pieces
1 small red onion, halved and thinly sliced
½ cup coarsely chopped fresh basil
¼ cup grated Parmesan cheese
¾ tsp. kosher salt
¼ tsp. coarsely ground pepper
½ cup Italian salad dressing

1. In a large skillet, heat 2 Tbsp. oil over medium heat. Add half of the bread cubes; cook and stir until toasted, about 8 minutes. Remove from pan. Repeat with remaining oil and bread cubes.
2. Combine bread cubes, chopped tomatoes, cucumber, peppers, onion, basil, cheese, salt and pepper. Toss with dressing.

1 cup: 131 cal., 6g fat (1g sat. fat), 1mg chol., 310mg sod., 18g carb. (3g sugars, 2g fiber), 3g pro. **Diabetic exchanges:** 1 starch, 1 vegetable, 1 fat.

STRAWBERRY SALAD WITH POPPY SEED DRESSING

My family is always happy to see this fruit and veggie salad, and not just during the summer. When fresh strawberries aren't in season, I substitute mandarin oranges and a handful of dried cranberries.
—*Irene Keller, Kalamazoo, MI*

Takes: 30 min.
Makes: 10 servings

- ¼ cup sugar
- ⅓ cup slivered almonds
- 1 bunch romaine, torn (about 8 cups)
- 1 small onion, halved and thinly sliced
- 2 cups halved fresh strawberries

DRESSING
- ¼ cup mayonnaise
- 2 Tbsp. sugar
- 1 Tbsp. sour cream
- 1 Tbsp. 2% milk
- 2¼ tsp. cider vinegar
- 1½ tsp. poppy seeds

1. Place sugar in a small heavy skillet; cook and stir over medium-low heat until melted and caramel-colored, about 10 minutes. Stir in the almonds until coated. Spread on foil to cool.

2. Place romaine, onion and strawberries in a large bowl. Whisk together dressing ingredients; toss with salad. Break candied almonds into pieces; sprinkle over salad. Serve immediately.

¾ cup: 110 cal., 6g fat (1g sat. fat), 1mg chol., 33mg sod., 13g carb. (10g sugars, 2g fiber), 2g pro. **Diabetic exchanges:** ½ starch, 1 vegetable, 1 fat.

Turn this potluck salad into something heartier. Grill 2 pounds boneless skinless chicken breasts, slice and add to the salad for an easy main dish.

 BASIC BUTTERMILK SALAD DRESSING

When serving salad to a crowd, this easy recipe comes in handy. It makes a full quart of creamy, delicious dressing to toss with your favorite greens and veggies.
—*Patricia Mele, Lower Burrell, PA*

Takes: 5 min.
Makes: 32 servings (1 qt.)

2 cups mayonnaise
2 cups buttermilk
1 Tbsp. onion powder
1 Tbsp. dried parsley flakes
1½ tsp. garlic powder
½ tsp. salt
½ tsp. celery salt
¼ tsp. pepper

Whisk together all ingredients. Refrigerate, covered, until serving.

2 Tbsp.: 98 cal., 10g fat (2g sat. fat), 2mg chol., 155mg sod., 1g carb. (1g sugars, 0 fiber), 1g pro. **Diabetic exchanges:** 2 fat.

 POTLUCK ANTIPASTO PASTA SALAD

I love trying new recipes, and this one for pasta salad tops all other varieties. With beans, cheese, sausage and vegetables, it's a hearty complement to any meal. You'll love the vinaigrette that makes good use of fresh basil.
—*Bernadette Nelson, Arcadia, CA*

Takes: 30 min.
Makes: 18 servings

1 pkg. (16 oz.) penne pasta
1 can (15 oz.) garbanzo beans or chickpeas, rinsed and drained
1 medium sweet red or green pepper, julienned
2 plum tomatoes, halved lengthwise and sliced
1 bunch green onions, sliced
4 oz. Monterey Jack cheese, julienned
4 oz. part-skim mozzarella cheese, julienned

4 oz. brick or provolone cheese, julienned
4 oz. thinly sliced hard salami, julienned
3 oz. thinly sliced pepperoni
1 can (2¼ oz.) sliced ripe olives, drained
1 to 2 Tbsp. minced chives
BASIL VINAIGRETTE
⅔ cup canola oil
⅓ cup red wine vinegar
3 Tbsp. minced fresh basil or 1 Tbsp. dried basil
1 garlic clove, minced
¼ tsp. salt

1. Cook pasta according to package directions; rinse with cold water and drain. In a large bowl, combine the pasta, beans, vegetables, cheeses, meats, olives and minced chives.
2. In a small bowl, whisk the vinaigrette ingredients. Pour over salad; toss to coat. Cover and refrigerate. Toss before serving.

1 cup: 248 cal., 18g fat (5g sat. fat), 24mg chol., 431mg sod., 13g carb. (2g sugars, 2g fiber), 9g pro.

To keep pasta from sticking together when cooking, use a large pot with plenty of water. Add a little cooking oil if desired (this also prevents boiling over).

GREEN GODDESS SALAD DRESSING

It's no trick to fix this time-honored dressing at home. Made with fresh ingredients, it is excellent. I think it's a real treat compared to store-bought dressing.
—*Page Alexander, Baldwin City, KS*

Takes: 10 min.
Makes: 16 servings (2 cups)

- 1   cup mayonnaise
- ½   cup sour cream
- ¼   cup chopped green pepper
- ¼   cup packed fresh parsley sprigs
- 3   anchovy fillets
- 2   Tbsp. lemon juice
- 2   green onion tops, coarsely chopped
- 1   garlic clove, peeled
- ¼   tsp. pepper
- ⅛   tsp. Worcestershire sauce

Place all ingredients in a blender; cover and process until smooth. Transfer to a bowl or jar; cover and store in the refrigerator.

2 Tbsp.: 119 cal., 12g fat (2g sat. fat), 11mg chol., 108mg sod., 1g carb. (0 sugars, 0 fiber), 1g pro.

TOMATO, AVOCADO & GRILLED CORN SALAD

With ripe tomatoes, fresh basil and grilled corn, this colorful salad tastes just like summertime! Try it for yourself.
—*Angela Spengler, Niceville, FL*

Prep: 20 min.
Grill: 10 min. + cooling
Makes: 8 servings

- 1   medium ear sweet corn, husks removed
- 3   large red tomatoes, sliced
- 3   large yellow tomatoes, sliced
- ¾   tsp. kosher salt, divided
- ½   tsp. pepper, divided
- 2   medium ripe avocados, peeled and sliced
- ¼   cup olive oil
- 2   Tbsp. red wine vinegar
- 1   Tbsp. minced fresh basil, plus more for garnish
- ⅓   cup crumbled feta cheese

This dish is spectacular with fresh heirloom tomatoes, and all that flavor means you can use less salt.

1. Grill corn, covered, over medium heat 10-12 minutes or until lightly browned and tender, turning occasionally. Cool slightly. Cut corn from cob.

2. Arrange tomatoes on large serving platter. Sprinkle with ½ tsp. salt and ¼ tsp. pepper. Top with avocado slices. Whisk together the oil, vinegar, basil and the remaining salt and pepper; drizzle half over the tomatoes and avocado. Top with grilled corn and feta; drizzle remaining dressing over top. Garnish with additional chopped basil.

1 serving: 164 cal., 13g fat (2g sat. fat), 3mg chol., 237mg sod., 11g carb. (4g sugars, 4g fiber), 3g pro. **Diabetic exchanges:** 2 fat, 1 vegetable, ½ starch.

LEMON VINAIGRETTE

Add a spark of citrus to your salads with this quick and easy vinaigrette. Try it over a fresh spinach salad or use it to jazz up a side dish of roasted veggies.
—*Sarah Farmer, Waukesha, WI*

Prep: 5 min.
Makes: 4 servings (½ cup)

2 Tbsp. fresh lemon juice
2 tsp. Dijon mustard
¼ tsp. salt
⅛ tsp. coarsely ground pepper
6 Tbsp. extra virgin olive oil

In a large bowl, whisk together the first 4 ingredients. Slowly add olive oil while whisking constantly.

2 Tbsp.: 183 cal., 20g fat (3g sat. fat), 0 chol., 208mg sod., 1g carb. (0 sugars, 0 fiber), 0 pro.

For the best results, start with all the ingredients at room temperature.
If the oil is cool or cold, it is much more difficult to form the emulsion.

KHMER PICKLED VEGETABLE SALAD

I grew up as a missionary kid in Cambodia, and most of my favorite foods have a Southeast Asian background. Locals love eating this pickled salad for breakfast, but I like it for lunch or dinner as a side with chicken satay.
—*Hannah Heavener, Belton, TX*

Prep: 25 min. + chilling
Cook: 5 min.
Makes: 16 servings (¾ cup each)

2 medium daikon radishes
   (about 1¼ lbs. each),
   peeled and thinly sliced
4 cups shredded cabbage
   (about ½ small)
1 large cucumber, thinly sliced
2 medium carrots, thinly sliced

1 cup cut fresh green beans (2 in.)
½ medium red onion, thinly sliced
1 piece fresh gingerroot
   (1 in.), thinly sliced
2 Thai chili or serrano peppers,
   halved lengthwise, seeded if desired
2 cups rice vinegar
¾ cup sugar
2 tsp. salt
2 Tbsp. chopped fresh cilantro

1. Place first 8 ingredients in a large nonreactive bowl. Place vinegar, sugar and salt in a 2-cup or larger glass measure; microwave until warm, 2-3 minutes. Stir until sugar is dissolved. Stir into vegetables. Refrigerate, covered, for at least 1 hour before serving.
2. To serve, sprinkle with cilantro. Serve with a slotted spoon.

¾ cup: 99 cal., 0 fat (0 sat. fat), 0 chol., 794mg sod., 25g carb. (22g sugars, 2g fiber), 1g pro.

TANGERINE TOSSED SALAD

My mother taught me how to cook when I was a young girl. The sweet tangerines and crunchy caramelized almonds make this one of my favorite recipes.
—*Helen Musenbrock, O'Fallon, MO*

Prep: 40 min.
Makes: 6 servings

- ½ cup sliced almonds
- 3 Tbsp. sugar, divided
- 2 medium tangerines or 1 navel orange
- 6 cups torn lettuce
- 3 green onions, chopped
- 2 Tbsp. cider vinegar
- 2 Tbsp. olive oil
- ¼ tsp. salt
- ¼ tsp. pepper

1. In a small skillet, cook and stir the almonds and 2 Tbsp. sugar over medium-low heat for 25-30 minutes or until the sugar is melted and the almonds are toasted. Remove from the heat. Peel and section the tangerines, reserving 1 Tbsp. juice.

2. In a large bowl, combine the lettuce, onions, tangerines and almonds. In a small bowl, whisk the vinegar, oil, salt, pepper, reserved juice and remaining sugar. Pour over salad; toss to coat.

1 cup: 138 cal., 9g fat (1g sat. fat), 0 chol., 105mg sod., 14g carb. (11g sugars, 3g fiber), 3g pro. **Diabetic exchanges:** 2 fat, 1 vegetable, ½ starch.

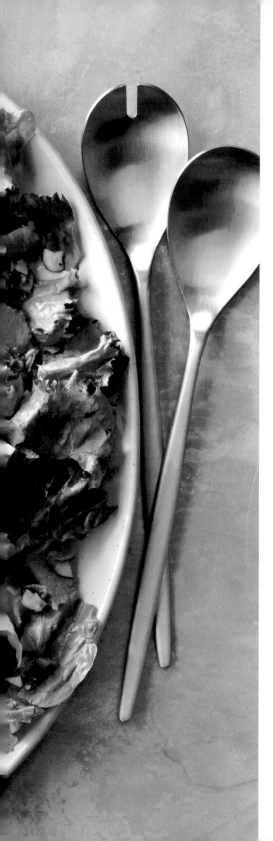

MAMA'S WARM GERMAN POTATO SALAD

My grandmother, Mama, made this potato salad for every family gathering at her home. It was truly her specialty. She never wrote it down, so I had to re-create the recipe from memory. Years later, it's just about right.
—*Charlene Chambers, Ormond Beach, FL*

Prep: 20 min. • **Cook:** 30 min.
Makes: 12 servings

- 3 lbs. small red potatoes
- ⅓ cup canola oil
- 2 Tbsp. champagne vinegar
- 1 tsp. kosher salt
- ½ tsp. coarsely ground pepper
- ½ English cucumber, very thinly sliced
- 2 celery ribs, thinly sliced
- 1 small onion, chopped
- 6 bacon strips, cooked and crumbled
- 1 Tbsp. minced fresh parsley

Place potatoes in a large saucepan; add water to cover. Bring to a boil. Reduce heat; cook, uncovered, until tender, 18-21 minutes. Drain; cool slightly. Peel and thinly slice. Whisk oil, vinegar, salt and pepper. Add potatoes; toss to coat. Add remaining ingredients; toss to combine. Serve warm.

¾ cup: 163 cal., 8g fat (1g sat. fat), 4mg chol., 246mg sod., 20g carb. (2g sugars, 2g fiber), 4g pro. **Diabetic exchanges:** 1½ fat, 1 starch.

SPINACH-ORZO SALAD WITH CHICKPEAS

The first version of this salad was an experiment in mixing together some random ingredients I had on hand. It was a success, and several people at the party asked for the recipe...which meant I had to try to make it again! It's healthy, delicious and perfect for warm-weather days.
—*Glen White, Kissimmee, FL*

Takes: 25 min.
Makes: 12 servings

- 1   can (14½ oz.) reduced-sodium chicken broth
- 1½ cups uncooked whole wheat orzo pasta
- 4   cups fresh baby spinach
- 2   cups grape tomatoes, halved
- 2   cans (15 oz. each) chickpeas or garbanzo beans, rinsed and drained
- ¾   cup chopped fresh parsley
- 2   green onions, chopped

DRESSING

- ¼   cup olive oil
- 3   Tbsp. lemon juice
- ¾   tsp. salt
- ¼   tsp. garlic powder
- ¼   tsp. hot pepper sauce
- ¼   tsp. pepper

1. In a large saucepan, bring broth to a boil. Stir in orzo; return to a boil. Reduce heat; simmer, covered, until al dente, 8-10 minutes.
2. In a large bowl, toss spinach and warm orzo, allowing spinach to wilt slightly. Add tomatoes, chickpeas, parsley and chopped green onions.
3. Whisk together dressing ingredients. Toss with salad.

¾ cup: 122 cal., 5g fat (1g sat. fat), 0 chol., 259mg sod., 16g carb. (1g sugars, 4g fiber), 4g pro.

PASTA SALAD 101
Dive in to flavor with a refreshing pasta salad. Mix up your own specialty with these easy steps.

- Cook pasta according to recipe or box directions. Rinse pasta in cold water to halt the cooking process. (Pasta continues to cook after it is removed from boiling water.) Drain well.

- Add a variety of mix-ins, paying particular attention to flavors, colors and textures.

- Stir in a cup (or more) of dressing. Note that pasta will absorb dressing as it sits.

- Add zesty accents such as bacon bits, lemon zest, toasted nuts or even curry powder.

WARM GREEN BEAN & POTATO SALAD

The combination of green beans and red potatoes, sometimes known as green beans Pierre, is one of my go-to dishes. It's terrific with chicken as well.
—*Preci D'Silva, Dubai, AE*

Takes: 30 min.
Makes: 10 servings

1	lb. small red potatoes, quartered
¼	cup olive oil
2	Tbsp. white wine vinegar
½	tsp. salt
⅛	tsp. each garlic powder, ground mustard and pepper
⅛	tsp. each dried basil, parsley flakes and tarragon
1	lb. fresh green beans, cut into 2-in. pieces
2	medium tomatoes, coarsely chopped
2	Tbsp. chopped onion

1. Place red potatoes in a large saucepan; add water to cover. Bring to a boil. Cook, uncovered, for 10 minutes. Meanwhile, in a large bowl, whisk the olive oil, white wine vinegar and seasonings.
2. Add green beans to potatoes; return to a boil. Cook until the vegetables are tender, 3-5 minutes longer. Drain; add to dressing and toss to coat. Stir in tomatoes and onion. Serve warm.

¾ cup: 100 cal., 5g fat (1g sat. fat), 0 chol., 125mg sod., 12g carb. (2g sugars, 3g fiber), 2g pro. **Diabetic exchanges:** 1 vegetable, ½ starch.

CAESAR DRESSING

Looking for a new and different salad dressing that you can whisk up in minutes for special occasions? You can't miss with this light, savory Caesar blend. It really dresses up summer's freshest greens!
—Taste of Home *Test Kitchen*

Prep: 15 min. + chilling
Makes: 13 servings (1⅔ cups)

- ⅔ cup reduced-fat mayonnaise
- ½ cup reduced-fat sour cream
- ½ cup buttermilk
- 1 Tbsp. red wine vinegar
- 1 Tbsp. stone-ground mustard
- 1½ tsp. lemon juice
- 1½ tsp. Worcestershire sauce
- ⅓ cup grated Parmigiano-Reggiano cheese
- 2 anchovy fillets, minced
- 2 garlic cloves, minced
- ½ tsp. coarsely ground pepper

In a small bowl, whisk the mayonnaise, sour cream, buttermilk, vinegar, mustard, lemon juice and Worcestershire sauce. Stir in the cheese, anchovies, garlic and pepper. Cover and refrigerate for at least 1 hour.

2 Tbsp.: 71 cal., 6g fat (2g sat. fat), 10mg chol., 205mg sod., 3g carb. (2g sugars, 0 fiber), 2g pro. **Diabetic exchanges:** 1 fat.

RED, WHITE & BLUE SUMMER SALAD

Caprese and fresh fruit always remind me of summer. In this salad, I combine traditional Caprese flavors with summer blueberries, peaches and added prosciutto for saltiness, creating a balanced and flavor-packed popular dish.
—*Emily Falke, Santa Barbara, CA*

Takes: 25 min.
Makes: 12 servings

- ⅔ cup extra virgin olive oil
- ½ cup julienned fresh basil
- ⅓ cup white balsamic vinegar
- ¼ cup julienned fresh mint leaves
- 2 garlic cloves, minced
- 2 tsp. Dijon mustard
- 1 tsp. sea salt
- 1 tsp. sugar
- 1 tsp. pepper
- 2 cups cherry tomatoes
- 8 cups fresh arugula
- 1 carton (8 oz.) fresh mozzarella cheese pearls, drained
- 2 medium peaches, sliced
- 2 cups fresh blueberries
- 6 oz. thinly sliced prosciutto, julienned

1. In a small bowl, whisk first 9 ingredients. Add the cherry tomatoes; let stand while preparing salad.
2. In a large bowl, combine the arugula, mozzarella, peach slices, blueberries, and prosciutto. Pour tomato mixture over top; toss to coat. Garnish with additional mint leaves. Serve immediately.

1 cup: 233 cal., 18g fat (5g sat. fat), 27mg chol., 486mg sod., 10g carb. (8g sugars, 2g fiber), 8g pro.

White balsamic vinegar keeps the colors bright in this sweet-salty salad.

KANSAS CUCUMBER SALAD

Cucumbers are my very favorite garden vegetable, so I use this recipe often. I got it from a friend years ago. I've heard this refreshing dish keeps very well in the refrigerator, but it goes so fast around our house, I've never found out for myself!
—*Karen Ann Bland, Gove City, KS*

Prep: 10 min. + chilling
Makes: 8 servings

- 1 cup Miracle Whip
- ¼ cup sugar
- 4 tsp. cider vinegar
- ½ tsp. dill weed
- ½ tsp. salt, optional
- 4 medium cucumbers, peeled and thinly sliced
- 3 green onions, chopped

In a large bowl, combine Miracle Whip, sugar, vinegar, dill and, if desired, salt; mix well. Add cucumbers and onions; toss. Cover and chill for at least 1 hour.

⅔ cup: 122 cal., 7g fat (1g sat. fat), 2mg chol., 201mg sod., 12g carb. (10g sugars, 2g fiber), 2g pro.

MACARONI COLESLAW

The term coleslaw is derived from the Dutch word *koolsla*, literally translated as "cabbage salad." The term has evolved to refer to many types of crunchy, shredded vegetable salads that hold up well after being dressed.

My friend Peggy brought this coleslaw to one of our picnics, and everyone liked it so much, we all had to have the recipe as soon as possible.
—*Sandra Matteson, Westhope, ND*

Prep: 25 min. + chilling
Makes: 16 servings

- 1 pkg. (7 oz.) ring macaroni or ditalini
- 1 pkg. (14 oz.) coleslaw mix
- 2 medium onions, finely chopped
- 2 celery ribs, finely chopped
- 1 medium cucumber, finely chopped
- 1 medium green pepper, finely chopped
- 1 can (8 oz.) whole water chestnuts, drained and chopped

DRESSING
- 1½ cups Miracle Whip Light
- ⅓ cup sugar
- ¼ cup cider vinegar
- ½ tsp. salt
- ¼ tsp. pepper

1. Cook macaroni according to package directions; drain and rinse in cold water. Transfer to a large bowl; add the coleslaw mix, onions, celery, cucumber, green pepper and water chestnuts.
2. In a small bowl, whisk the dressing ingredients. Pour over salad; toss to coat. Cover and refrigerate for at least 1 hour.

¾ cup: 150 cal., 5g fat (1g sat. fat), 6mg chol., 286mg sod., 24g carb. (12g sugars, 2g fiber), 3g pro. **Diabetic exchanges:** 1 starch, 1 vegetable, 1 fat.

FRUITS & BERRIES

Few foods represent summer like ripe, juicy fruits and berries. Turn to this section to see how easily the season's freshest produce dresses up everything from savory entrees to sweet sensations.

GUIDE TO FRUIT

	HOW TO BUY	HOW TO STORE	HOW TO PREP
APRICOTS	Select apricots that are plump and fairly firm, not hard, and are orange-yellow to orange in color. Avoid apricots that have blemishes or soft spots or that have a pale yellow or greenish yellow color.	Store firm apricots at room temperature. Once the fruit yields to gentle pressure, store it in the refrigerator for 2-3 days.	Rinse apricots under running water. Remove the pit by running a paring knife around the natural seam and gently twist the apricot in half. The pit should lift out easily.
BANANAS	Select plump bananas that are free from bruises. The banana skin goes from green to yellow to yellow with speckles to black, depending on ripeness and how the banana is stored.	Store at room temperature until ripe, then store in the refrigerator or freeze. The skin will turn black in the refrigerator. Brush cut bananas with lemon, lime, orange or pineapple juice to prevent browning.	Bananas don't require any special preparation prior to eating or using in a recipe. Use firm bananas with yellow skins and green tips for cooking. Use firm but ripe bananas for salads, and use ripe bananas for baking.
BERRIES	Select berries that are plump; avoid those that are bruised, mushy or moldy. Avoid packages that have juice-stained bottoms.	Berries are fragile and highly perishable. Store unwashed berries in their container for 1-2 days. To freeze, wash berries and drain well; arrange in a single layer on a parchment-lined baking sheet. Once frozen, transfer to a freezer container. Freeze up to 1 year.	Gently but thoroughly wash berries before using. Eat them on their own or follow a recipe's directions for slicing, chopping or pureeing.
CHERRIES	Cherries should be firm and show no blemishes, cuts or bruises. Look for ones that have their stems attached, as this increases the amount of time they will keep. If you want sweet cherries, choose darker ones. Avoid any that look especially small or have soft spots.	Store unwashed cherries, with stems intact, in an airtight container in the refrigerator for 4-10 days. To freeze, wash, drain and pit cherries. Arrange in a single layer on a parchment-lined baking sheet. Once frozen, transfer to freezer container. Freeze up to 1 year.	Wash cherries and remove the stems before eating or using in a recipe. For a quick way to pit cherries, place one at a time on the lip of an empty soft drink bottle. Use a chopstick to push the pit through the cherry and into the bottle.
CITRUS FRUIT	Select citrus fruit that is firm, feels heavy for its size and has a bright color. Avoid fruit with bruises or wrinkles. Weather conditions during the growing season can affect the thickness of the peel.	Store most citrus fruit at room temperature for about 3 days. For longer storage, store in the crisper drawer in the refrigerator for 2-3 weeks. Juice or grated zest may be frozen for up to 1 year.	Citrus fruits don't require any special preparation prior to eating or using in a recipe. Follow the recipe's directions if juicing or grating is required.
DATES	Select dates that are plump with a smooth, shiny skin.	Store dates in the refrigerator in an airtight container for up to 2 weeks. Remove the pits before using.	To prevent sticking when slicing or chopping dates, spray your scissors or knife with cooking spray. Dates can be eaten on their own or added to salads, stews or other recipes.
FIGS	Select plump, firm fruit that is heavy for its size and gives slightly when gently pressed. Avoid bruised, soft fruits or those with a sour aroma. Handle carefully, as figs bruise easily.	Store unwashed figs in the refrigerator and use within 2 days. Dried figs can be stored in an airtight container for up to 6 months.	Handle figs with care. Rinse under running water and gently pat dry before cooking or eating raw.
GRAPES	Select grapes that are plump and firmly attached to the stem, with good color for their variety. Avoid grapes that have bruises, soft spots or mold.	Grapes are delicate and bruise easily. Store unwashed grapes in the refrigerator in a perforated bag for about 1 week. Grapes can also be frozen and stored in an airtight container.	Run under running water. Drain well and gently pat dry before using.
KIWIFRUIT	Select plump fruit that yields to gentle pressure. Avoid fruit with soft spots or a shriveled skin. Firm fruit will still need to ripen.	Store unripened kiwifruit at room temperature. To speed the ripening process, store in a paper bag with an apple or banana. Once ripened, store in the refrigerator for 2-3 days.	To eat, just cut in half and scoop out the fruit with a spoon. Or peel the skin and cut the flesh into slices or cubes. Do not add fresh kiwifruit to gelatin salads or desserts. It contains an enzyme that prevents gelatin from setting up.
KUMQUATS	Kumquats look like miniature oval oranges. Select fruit that is completely orange with firm and glossy skin. Avoid fruits that are bruised, soft or shriveled.	Store unwashed kumquats in the refrigerator for about 2 weeks. Wash before using.	Rinse kumquats under running water. The peel is edible so you don't want any traces of pesticides or dirt on the outside. Remove the seeds if desired. They're not poisonous; however, they have a bitter taste similar to orange seeds.

	HOW TO BUY	HOW TO STORE	HOW TO PREP
MANGOES	Select plump fruit with a sweet, fruity aroma. Avoid very soft or bruised fruit. The skin of a ripe mango is green to yellow in color with a tinge of red. It should yield slightly when pressed and have a fruity aroma at the stem end.	Store unwashed mangoes in the refrigerator away from other fruits and vegetables with strong aromas. Keep green mangoes at room temperature, out of direct sunlight, until ripened.	Wash before using. Peel and remove stone before eating. Mangoes can be eaten whole, sliced, chopped or pureed. Heat destroys their flavor, so only warm slightly at most.
MELONS	Select melons that are heavy for their size and have no cracks or dents in the skin. A ripe melon should have a fruity, pleasant aroma. Avoid melons that are bruised or have a strong aroma, which indicates they are overripe.	Store underripe melons at room temperature for 2-3 days. Store ripe melons in the refrigerator for 1 week. Store cut melon in an airtight container in the refrigerator.	Cut melon in half and remove seeds. Cut into cubes or wedges, or use a melon baller or ice cream scoop to shape fruit into balls. Serve chilled if desired. Note that chilling sometimes diminishes the flavor.
NECTARINES & PEACHES	Select nectarines and peaches that are firm but yield a bit to gentle pressure. They should be bright with skin free of discoloration, soft spots or bruises. Choose fruits with defined clefts, as this indicates they are mature and sweeter.	Both nectarines and peaches can be stored unrefrigerated for up to 4 days, depending on how ripe they were when you bought them. Keeping peaches at room temperature offers a fuller, more intense flavor.	Give the fruit a light rinse; scrubbing will remove its delicate skin. Fully slice the fruit lengthwise. Take the two halves and twist—a ripe peach will come apart in two halves, exposing the pit, which you can then pluck out.
PAPAYAS	Papayas are available year-round. Select papayas that have a golden-yellow skin. Ripe fruit will give slightly when gently pressed and have a sweet aroma. Avoid bruised, soft or shriveled fruit.	Store ripe fruit in the refrigerator for 3-4 days. Store fruit that has slightly green skin or firm fruit at room temperature until ripened.	Cut papaya in half and scoop out seeds. Use a small sharp knife to cut away peel. Slice or chop flesh or press for juice.
PEARS	Select pears that are plump. Avoid those with bruises, soft spots or cuts. For some varieties, the color of the skin will change as the pear ripens. Select firm pears for baking. For eating, select pears that give slightly when gently pressed.	Store unwashed ripe pears in the refrigerator for 3-5 days, away from other fruits and vegetables with strong aromas. To ripen pears, place in a paper bag at room temperature for 2-3 days. Freeze for up to 1 year.	Wash before using. Peel if desired and eat whole, sliced or chopped. When preparing pears for a reicpe, brush the cut flesh with lemon juice to prevent browning. Pears that are slightly underripe work best for cooking.
PERSIMMONS	Select plump, slightly firm fruit with smooth, glossy skin (the cap end should still be attached). Avoid fruit that is bruised or has cuts in the skin.	To ripen, place fruit in a paper bag at room temperature for 1-3 days. Store ripe fruit in the refrigerator for up to 3 days.	Wash before using. To eat fresh, peel, core and slice. Or cut the top off and spoon out the pulp.
PINEAPPLE	Select pineapple that is plump and looks fresh, is slightly soft and has a sweet fragrance. Avoid fruit with dry or brown leaves, bruises and soft spots.	Best when eaten right away. Do not store whole fruit in the refrigerator. Refrigerate cut fruit in an airtight container for up to 3 days.	Using a large chef's knife, cut off the crown of the fruit. Stand pineapple upright and and cut off the rind and base. Cut the fruit into slices, cubes or wedges.
PLUMS	Select plump fruit with a chalky bloom. Ripe plums will give slightly when gently pressed and have a fruity aroma. Avoid plums that are hard, bruised, soft, squishy or shriveled.	Store unwashed ripe plums in a paper bag in the crisper drawer of the refrigerator for 3-5 days. To ripen, place in a paper bag at room temperature for 1-3 days.	Wash before using. Using a sharp knife, cut along the seam of the dimple and twist the fruit in half. Remove the stone, then chop or slice the flesh.
QUINCE	Select fruit that is heavy for its size, has smooth skin and is fragrant. Avoid fruit that looks shriveled. Handle quinces gently, as they bruise easily.	Store at room temperature for a few days. Store unripened fruit at room temperature until they are fragrant. For longer storage, wrap each quince in an airtight container and refrigerate for up to 2 months.	Peel and core before using. Cooking mellows the flavor and turns the white flesh pink. Try quinces in cooked apple dishes in place of a portion of the apples called for. Quinces can be poached, baked or simmered.
RHUBARB	Look for thin stalks that are red or pink in color. Thicker stalks impart an especially sour taste, as do greener ones. Look for a smooth texture, and avoid stalks that are rough or pitted, as well as those with wilted leaves.	Fresh stalks don't last long, but sealing them in an airtight container will help them retain their moisture. They'll last 3-5 days in the refrigerator's crisper drawer. Or, freeze them up to 1 year. Cut into 1-in. pieces for best results when thawed.	Thoroughly wash rhubarb under cold running water. Then cut off the ends near the root base, and remove the leaves by cutting off the tops of the stalks.
STAR FRUIT	Select fruit with glossy, golden yellow skin. Choose fruit with wider-spaced ribs, which are said to be sweeter than fruit with narrower ribs. Avoid fruit with browned ribs.	Refrigerate unwashed ripe fruit for up to 2 weeks. Store at room temperature until it becomes yellow and develops a fruity fragrance.	Wash before using. Cut into slices. The skin is edible and doesn't need to be peeled. Star fruit is good for eating on its own, for adding to salads and desserts, or for garnishes.
WATERMELONS	Look for a round, dark green watermelon that feels heavy for its size. Also, be sure there's a yellow spot on the fruit's underside. This "ground spot" indicates that the melon was ripe when it was picked, ensuring sweetness.	Store in a cool, dark place or in the refrigerator, if possible. Store cut melon, in an airtight container, in the refrigerator for up to 1 week.	Wash the outside of the melon to remove any dirt, then slice the melon lengthwise. Continue slicing to get the desired number of pieces. Remove the rind by slicing along the edge where the white of the rind meets the red flesh of the melon.

MANDARIN-BERRY STEAK SALAD

It's hard to believe this satisfying entree salad comes together so quickly. We love it with sirloin steak, but try it with cooked chicken breasts or even pork. You'll also want to whisk together the vinaigrette for salads all summer long.
—Taste of Home *Test Kitchen*

Takes: 25 min.
Makes: 4 servings (1 cup vinaigrette)

3   Tbsp. olive oil
¼   cup cider vinegar
¼   cup orange juice
2   Tbsp. minced fresh parsley
2   Tbsp. honey
1   garlic clove, minced
1   tsp. chili sauce
½   tsp. salt
8   cups torn romaine
½   lb. cooked beef sirloin steak, sliced
3   cups sliced fresh strawberries
1   small red onion, sliced
1   can (11 oz.) mandarin
     oranges, drained

½   cup chopped pecans toasted
2   oz. fresh goat cheese, crumbled

In a small bowl, whisk the first eight ingredients; set aside. Divide romaine among four plates; top with steak, strawberries, onion, oranges, pecans and cheese. Serve with vinaigrette.

1 serving: 926 calories, 69g fat (12g saturated fat), 118mg cholesterol, 549mg sodium, 39g carbohydrate (28g sugars, 8g fiber), 45g protein.

GOLDEN BEET & PEACH SOUP

We had a bumper crop of peaches from our two trees this summer and I've been having fun experimenting with different recipes. After seeing a beet soup recipe in a cookbook, I changed it up a bit to include our homegrown golden beets and to suit our tastes.
—Sue Gronholz, Beaver Dam, WI

Prep: 20 min.
Bake: 40 min. + chilling
Makes: 6 servings

2   lbs. fresh golden beets, peeled
     and cut into 1-in. cubes
1   Tbsp. olive oil
2   cups white grape peach juice
2   Tbsp. cider vinegar
¼   cup plain Greek yogurt
¼   tsp. finely chopped fresh tarragon
2   medium fresh peaches,
     peeled and diced
     Additional fresh tarragon sprigs

1. Preheat oven to 400°. Place beets in a 15x10x1-in. baking pan. Drizzle with oil; toss to coat. Roast until tender, 40-45 minutes. Cool slightly.
2. Transfer beets to a blender or food processor. Add juice and vinegar; process until smooth. Refrigerate at least 1 hour. In a small bowl, combine Greek yogurt and tarragon; refrigerate.
3. To serve, divide beet mixture among individual bowls; place a spoonful of yogurt mixture into each bowl. Top with diced peaches and additional tarragon.

⅔ cup: 159 cal., 4g fat (1g sat. fat), 3mg chol., 129mg sod., 31g carb. (26g sugars, 4g fiber), 3g pro. **Diabetic exchanges:** 2 vegetable, 1 fruit, ½ fat.

For a whole different taste sensation, simply substitute ½ tsp. chopped fresh basil, thyme or chives for the tarragon. If you prefer, the herb of your choice may be blended with the beets rather than mixed with the yogurt. For a creamier soup, add additional plain Greek yogurt to your liking.

GRANDMA'S OLD-FASHIONED STRAWBERRY SHORTCAKE

When my grandma served this shortcake, she usually topped it with homemade vanilla ice cream. What a great way to celebrate a warm summer evening!
—*Angela Lively, Conroe, TX*

Prep: 30 min. + standing
Bake: 20 min.
Makes: 8 servings

    6 cups sliced fresh strawberries
    ½ cup sugar
    1 tsp. vanilla extract
SHORTCAKE
    3 cups all-purpose flour
    5 Tbsp. sugar, divided
    3 tsp. baking powder
    1 tsp. baking soda
    ½ tsp. salt
    ¾ cup cold butter, cubed
  1¼ cups buttermilk
    2 Tbsp. heavy whipping cream
TOPPING
  1½ cups heavy whipping cream
    2 Tbsp. sugar
    ½ tsp. vanilla extract

1. Combine strawberries with sugar and vanilla; mash slightly. Let stand for at least 30 minutes, tossing occasionally.
2. Preheat oven to 400°. For shortcake, whisk together flour, 4 Tbsp. sugar, baking powder, baking soda and salt. Cut in butter until crumbly. Add buttermilk; stir just until combined (do not overmix). Drop batter by ⅓ cupfuls 2 in. apart onto an ungreased baking sheet. Brush with 2 Tbsp. heavy cream; sprinkle with remaining 1 Tbsp. sugar. Bake until golden, 18-20 minutes. Remove to wire racks to cool completely.
3. For topping, beat heavy whipping cream until it begins to thicken. Add sugar and vanilla; beat until soft peaks form. To serve, cut biscuits in half; top with strawberries and whipped cream.

1 shortcake with ½ cup strawberries and ⅓ cup whipped cream: 638 cal., 36g fat (22g sat. fat), 102mg chol., 710mg sod., 72g carb. (33g sugars, 4g fiber), 9g pro.

SECRETS TO TENDER SHORTCAKE

KEEP IT COLD
Make sure the butter is cold and cut it in until it's about pea size; as it melts during baking, small air pockets are created, giving the biscuit its flakiness.

DON'T HAVE BUTTERMILK?
Place 1 Tbsp. of white vinegar or lemon juice in a measuring cup and fill with regular milk to reach the 1 cup mark.

GOLDEN BROWN GOODNESS
Brushing the biscuit tops with cream helps the sugar stay in place as well as giving the top a rich golden brown color when it's baked.

BUMP UP THE BISCUIT
Stir grated lemon peel, orange peel or a bit of ground cardamom into the biscuit mixture. Add a pinch of cinnamon and nutmeg to the sugar on top.

WHIP SMART
It's important the heavy cream is cold when you mix it—you'll get more volume. Start out on low speed and be patient. You can make the whipped cream up to 2 hours ahead, then gently stir to reincorporate when you're ready to serve it.

SPICY PLUM SALMON

I created this grilled sweet-spicy salmon after being challenged to cook with healthy ingredients. The fresh plum sauce really complements the smoky grilled fish.
—*Cheryl Hochstettler, Richmond, TX*

Prep: 25 min.
Grill: 10 min.
Makes: 6 servings

- 5 medium plums, divided
- ½ cup water
- 2 Tbsp. ketchup
- 1 chipotle pepper in adobo sauce, finely chopped
- 1 Tbsp. sugar
- 1 Tbsp. olive oil
- 6 salmon fillets (6 oz. each)
- ¾ tsp. salt

1. Coarsely chop two plums; place in a small saucepan. Add water; bring to a boil. Reduce heat; simmer, uncovered, 10-15 minutes or until plums are softened and liquid is almost evaporated. Cool slightly. Transfer to a food processor; add ketchup, chipotle, sugar and oil. Process until pureed. Reserve ¾ cup sauce for serving.

2. Sprinkle salmon with salt; place on a greased grill rack, skin side up. Grill, covered, over medium heat until fish just begins to flake easily with a fork, about 10 minutes. Brush with the remaining sauce during last 3 minutes. Slice remaining plums. Serve salmon with plum slices and reserved sauce.

1 fillet with ½ plum and 2 Tbsp. sauce: 325 cal., 18g fat (3g sat. fat), 85mg chol., 460mg sod., 10g carb. (9g sugars, 1g fiber), 29g pro. **Diabetic exchanges:** 5 lean meat, 1 fruit, ½ fat.

GRILLED PORK TENDERLOIN WITH CHERRY SALSA MOLÈ

The combo of grilled pork and cherries is a favorite of mine. The hint of spice and chocolate in the salsa mole makes the combination even more special.
—*Roxanne Chan, Albany, CA*

Prep: 25 min.
Grill: 15 min. + standing
Makes: 6 servings

- 2 pork tenderloins (¾ lb. each)
- 1 Tbsp. canola oil
- ½ tsp. salt
- ¼ tsp. ground cumin
- ¼ tsp. chili powder
- 1 cup pitted fresh or frozen dark sweet cherries, thawed, chopped
- 1 jalapeno pepper, seeded and minced
- ½ cup finely chopped peeled jicama
- 1 oz. semisweet chocolate, grated
- 2 Tbsp. minced fresh cilantro
- 1 green onion, thinly sliced
- 1 Tbsp. lime juice
- 1 tsp. honey
  Salted pumpkin seeds or pepitas

1. Brush tenderloins with oil; sprinkle with salt, cumin and chili powder. Grill, covered, over medium heat until a thermometer reads 145°, 15-20 minutes, turning occasionally. Let stand 10-15 minutes.
2. Meanwhile, combine cherries, jalapeno, jicama, chocolate, cilantro, green onion, lime juice and honey. Slice pork; serve with cherry salsa and pumpkin seeds.

3 oz. cooked pork with ¼ cup salsa: 218 cal., 8g fat (3g sat. fat), 64mg chol., 248mg sod., 11g carb. (9g sugars, 2g fiber), 23g pro.
Diabetic exchanges: 3 lean meat, ½ starch, ½ fat.

BERRY-APPLE-RHUBARB PIE

I make this family favorite every year for a get-together at my sister's home, where the recipe is known as "Uncle Mike's Pie." I use fresh berries, apples and rhubarb that I grow myself.
—*Michael Powers, New Baltimore, VA*

Prep: 30 min. + chilling
Bake: 65 min. + cooling
Makes: 8 servings

2⅔ cups all-purpose flour
1 tsp. salt
1 cup butter-flavored shortening
6 to 8 Tbsp. cold water
FILLING
2 cups thinly sliced peeled tart apples
1 Tbsp. lemon juice
1 tsp. vanilla extract
1 cup halved fresh strawberries
1 cup fresh blueberries
1 cup fresh raspberries
1 cup fresh blackberries
1 cup sliced fresh or frozen rhubarb
⅓ cup all-purpose flour
1 tsp. ground allspice
1 tsp. ground cinnamon
1½ cups plus 1 tsp. sugar, divided
2 Tbsp. butter
1 Tbsp. 2% milk

1. In a large bowl, combine flour and salt; cut in shortening until crumbly. Gradually add water, tossing with a fork until dough forms a ball. Divide dough in half so that one portion is slightly larger than the other; wrap each in plastic wrap. Refrigerate 30 minutes or until easy to handle.
2. Preheat oven to 400°. On a lightly floured surface, roll out larger portion of dough to fit a 9-in. deep-dish pie plate or cast iron skillet. Transfer pastry to pie plate.

3. In a large bowl, toss apples with lemon juice and vanilla; add berries and rhubarb. Combine flour, allspice, cinnamon and 1½ cups sugar; add to the apple mixture and toss gently to coat. Spoon into the crust; dot with butter.
4. Roll out remaining pastry; make a lattice crust. Carefully trim, seal and flute edges. Brush milk over lattice top. Sprinkle with remaining sugar.
5. Bake 15 minutes. Reduce heat to 350°; bake 50-60 minutes longer or until crust is golden brown and filling is bubbly. Cover edges with foil during the last 15 minutes to prevent overbrowning if necessary. Cool on a wire rack.
Note: If using frozen rhubarb, measure rhubarb while still frozen, then thaw completely. Drain in a colander, but do not press liquid out.

1 slice: 615 cal., 28g fat (8g sat. fat), 8mg chol., 318mg sod., 86g carb. (46g sugars, 5g fiber), 6g pro.

Keeping the pie dough chilled helps with the pliability while weaving the lattice crust. If the dough gets too soft, place it in the freezer for a few moments to firm it up bit.

MINTED FRUIT SALAD

Filled with the season's best and freshest fruit, this salad shouts, summer. The hint of mint adds a refreshing note to the sweet combo.
—*Edie DeSpain, Logan, UT*

Prep: 20 min. + cooling
Makes: 6 servings

- 1 cup unsweetened apple juice
- 2 Tbsp. honey
- 4 tsp. finely chopped crystallized ginger
- 4 tsp. lemon juice
- 4 cups cantaloupe balls
- 1 cup sliced fresh strawberries
- 1 cup fresh blueberries
- 2 tsp. chopped fresh mint leaves

1. In a small saucepan, combine the apple juice, honey, ginger and lemon juice. Bring to a boil over medium-high heat. Cook and stir for 2 minutes or until mixture is reduced to ¾ cup. Remove from the heat. Cool.
2. In a serving bowl, combine the cantaloupe, strawberries, blueberries and mint. Drizzle with the cooled apple juice mixture; gently toss to coat.

1 cup: 113 cal., 1g fat (0 sat. fat), 0 chol., 14mg sod., 28g carb. (23g sugars, 2g fiber), 1g pro. **Diabetic exchanges:** 1 fruit, ½ starch.

JALAPENO CORNBREAD FILLED WITH BLUEBERRY QUICK JAM

Fresh jalapenos and blueberry quick jam make the perfect blend of sweet and spicy in this special cornbread. After you eat one piece, you won't be able to resist going back for second.
—*Colleen Delawder, Herndon, VA*

Prep: 20 min. + chilling
Bake: 30 min. + cooling
Makes: 12 servings

- 2 cups fresh blueberries
- 1 cup sugar
- 1 Tbsp. cider vinegar
- ¼ tsp. kosher salt

CORNBREAD

- ½ cup whole milk
- 1 Tbsp. lemon juice
- 1½ cups all-purpose flour
- ½ cup yellow cornmeal
- ½ cup sugar
- 3 tsp. baking powder
- ½ tsp. kosher salt
- 2 Tbsp. unsalted butter
- 1 Tbsp. honey
- 2 large eggs, room temperature
- ⅓ cup canola oil
- 2 jalapeno peppers, seeded and minced

1. In a large heavy saucepan, combine blueberries, sugar, vinegar and kosher salt. Bring to a boil over high heat. Cook, stirring constantly, 5 minutes. Cool completely. Refrigerate, covered, overnight.
2. For cornbread, preheat oven to 350°. Combine milk and lemon juice; let stand briefly. In another bowl, whisk the next 5 ingredients. In a small bowl, microwave butter and honey on high for 30 seconds; cool slightly. Whisk eggs and oil into milk mixture (mixture may appear curdled). Add butter mixture; whisk until well combined. Add flour mixture; whisk just until combined. Fold in jalapenos.
3. Pour 2 cups batter into a well-buttered 10-in. fluted tube pan. Spoon half to three-fourths of blueberry quick jam over batter. Cover with remaining batter. Bake until a toothpick inserted in center comes out clean, 30-35 minutes. Cool 10 minutes; invert onto a cake plate or serving platter. Drizzle with remaining blueberry quick jam.

1 slice: 289 cal., 10g fat (2g sat. fat), 37mg chol., 258mg sod., 48g carb. (30g sugars, 1g fiber), 4g pro.

For best results, always make the jam a day ahead. It needs plenty of time to cool before being added to the cornbread batter.

PERFECT PLUM & PEACH PIE

I created this recipe to fit with in-season summer fruit. The plums give the pie a splash of color and flavor, and the easy crumb topping tastes excellent.
—*Rachel Johnson, Shippensburg, PA*

Prep: 25 min.
Bake: 40 min. + cooling
Makes: 8 servings

1	sheet refrigerated pie crust

FILLING

6	medium peaches, peeled and sliced
6	medium black plums, sliced
½	cup all-purpose flour
½	cup confectioners' sugar
½	tsp. ground cinnamon
½	tsp. ground nutmeg

TOPPING

¼	cup all-purpose flour
¼	cup packed brown sugar
2	Tbsp. butter, softened
¼	tsp. ground cinnamon

1. Preheat oven to 375°. Unroll crust onto a lightly floured surface; roll to a 12-in. circle. Transfer to a 9-in. deep-dish pie plate; trim and flute edge. Refrigerate while preparing the filling.

2. Toss peaches and plums with flour, sugar and spices; transfer to crust. Using a fork, mix the topping ingredients until crumbly; sprinkle over the fruit.

3. Bake on a lower oven rack until golden brown and bubbly, 40-50 minutes. Cool on a wire rack.

1 slice: 311 cal., 10g fat (5g sat. fat), 13mg chol., 125mg sod., 53g carb. (29g sugars, 3g fiber), 4g pro.

Using a crumb topping instead of a top pastry crust is an easy way to lighten up your favorite fruit pie. Here it saves over 50 cal. and 5g fat per serving.

GRILLED HALIBUT WITH BLUEBERRY SALSA

It's a snap to give halibut a summery spin. The berry salsa may seem sophisticated, but it's really a cinch to toss together.
—*Donna Goutermont, Sequim, WA*

Takes: 30 min.
Makes: 6 servings

2 cups fresh blueberries, divided
1 small red onion, chopped
¼ cup minced fresh cilantro
1 jalapeno pepper, seeded
   and chopped
2 Tbsp. orange juice
1 Tbsp. balsamic vinegar
1 tsp. plus 2 Tbsp. olive oil, divided
⅛ tsp. plus 1 tsp. salt, divided
⅛ tsp. pepper
6 halibut fillets (5 oz. each)

1. In a small bowl, coarsely mash 1 cup blueberries. Stir in the onion, cilantro, jalapeno, orange juice, vinegar, 1 tsp. oil, ⅛ tsp. salt, pepper and remaining blueberries. Cover and chill until serving.

2. Meanwhile, drizzle fillets with remaining oil; sprinkle with remaining salt. Grill halibut, covered, over medium heat for 4-5 minutes on each side or until fish flakes easily with a fork. Serve with salsa.

1 fillet with ⅓ cup salsa: 239 cal., 9g fat (1g sat. fat), 45mg chol., 521mg sod., 9g carb. (6g sugars, 1g fiber), 30g pro. **Diabetic exchanges:** 4 lean meat, 1 fat, ½ starch.

HOMEMADE STRAWBERRY ICE CREAM

What could be better than luscious homemade ice cream made with fresh strawberries? Having an ice cream social at church with more of the same!
—*Esther Johnson, Merrill, WI*

Prep: 20 min. + cooling
Process: 20 min./batch + freezing
Makes: 12 servings (about 1½ qt.)

- 6 large egg yolks
- 2 cups whole milk
- 1 cup sugar
- ¼ tsp. salt
- 1 tsp. vanilla extract
- 2 cups heavy whipping cream
- 2 cups crushed fresh strawberries, sweetened

1. Place egg yolks and milk in the top of a double boiler; beat. Add sugar and salt. Cook over simmering water, stirring until mixture is thickened and coats a metal spoon. Cool.

2. Add the vanilla, cream and strawberries. Pour into the cylinder of an ice cream freezer and freeze according to manufacturer's directions. When ice cream is frozen, transfer to a freezer container; freeze for 2-4 hours before serving.

½ cup: 265 cal., 19g fat (11g sat. fat), 166mg chol., 88mg sod., 22g carb. (21g sugars, 1g fiber), 4g pro.

ONE-POT SALSA CHICKEN

Plump nectarines add a hint of sweetness to this Southwestern entree. It's a colorful and healthy main dish that can be on the table in just over an hour.
—*Ann Sheehy, Lawrence, MA*

Prep: 20 min.
Cook: 45 min.
Makes: 6 servings

- 2 Tbsp. canola oil
- 2 lbs. boneless skinless chicken thighs, cut into 1-in. pieces
- 1 tsp. pepper
- ½ tsp. salt
- 2 medium sweet potatoes, peeled and chopped
- 1 jar (16 oz.) medium salsa
- 2 medium nectarines, peeled and chopped
- 2 Tbsp. Tajin seasoning
- 1 cup uncooked instant brown rice
- 1 cup water
- ¼ cup minced fresh parsley
  Minced fresh chives

1. In a Dutch oven, heat oil over medium-high heat. Sprinkle chicken with pepper and salt. Brown chicken in batches; return to pan. Add the sweet potatoes, salsa, nectarines and seasoning. Bring to a boil; reduce heat. Cover and simmer until potatoes are almost tender, about 15 minutes.

2. Stir in rice and water; bring to a boil. Reduce heat. Cover and simmer until the potatoes are tender, about 10 minutes. Stir in parsley. Serve in bowls; sprinkle with chives.

1⅔ cups: 432 cal., 16g fat (3g sat. fat), 101mg chol., 1254mg sod., 39g carb. (13g sugars, 4g fiber), 31g pro.

Tajin seasoning is a unique blend of lime, chili peppers and sea salt. Look for it in the spice aisle.

QUICK WATERMELON SALSA

On hot days, this sweet combo of watermelon, pineapple and fresh cilantro is sure to satisfy. Best of all, the change-of-pace appetizer comes together in minutes.

—Betsy Hanson, Tiverton, RI

Prep: 15 min. + chilling
Makes: 3 cups

2 cups chopped seedless watermelon
1 can (8 oz.) unsweetened crushed pineapple, drained
¼ cup chopped sweet onion
¼ cup minced fresh cilantro
3 Tbsp. orange juice
⅛ tsp. hot pepper sauce
Tortilla chips

In a large bowl, combine the first six ingredients. Cover and refrigerate for at least 1 hour. Serve with tortilla chips.

¼ cup: 23 cal., 0 fat (0 sat. fat), 0 chol., 1mg sod., 5g carb. (5g sugars, 0 fiber), 0 pro.
Diabetic exchanges: ½ fruit.

5i ❄

BERRY WHITE ICE POPS

Kids and adults alike love these ice pops, speckled with colorful mixed berries for a frosty treat.
—*Sharon Guinta, Stamford, CT*

Prep: 10 min. + freezing
Makes: 10 pops

1¾	**cups whole milk, divided**
1	**to 2 Tbsp. honey**
¼	**tsp. vanilla extract**
1½	**cups fresh raspberries**
1	**cup fresh blueberries**
10	**freezer pop molds or 10 paper cups (3 oz. each) and wooden pop sticks**

1. In a microwave, warm ¼ cup milk; stir in honey until blended. Stir in remaining 1½ cups milk and vanilla.
2. Divide berries among molds; cover with milk mixture. Top molds with holders. If using cups, top with foil and insert sticks through foil. Freeze until firm.

1 pop: 51 cal., 2g fat (1g sat. fat), 4mg chol., 19mg sod., 8g carb. (6g sugars, 2g fiber), 2g pro. **Diabetic exchanges:** ½ starch.

VEGGIE DISHES

Juicy tomatoes enjoyed right off the vine, buttery corn cobs seasoned to perfection and brillant peppers that spark up any dish...it's time to sink your teeth into the colorful veggies you've been anticipating all year long.

GUIDE TO VEGETABLES

			COOKING METHOD AND TIME (IN MINUTES)		
	BLANCHING	**STEAMING**	**BOILING**	**SAUTEING/STIR-FRYING**	**ROASTING/BAKING**
BEANS GREEN OR WAX LIMA	3 1 to 3	8 to 10	COVER WITH WATER; BOIL COVERED 3 to 5, pieces 4 to 7, whole 10 to 15	4 to 5	425° 10 to 12, trimmed
BEETS			COVER WITH WATER; BOIL UNCOVERED 30 to 60, whole 20 to 25, cubed		350° COVERED 30 to 60
BOK CHOY STALKS LEAVES		5 to 6 2 to 3	3 to 4 1 to 1½	5	
BROCCOLI FLORETS SPEARS	3 5	4 to 7 5 to 8	1 IN. WATER; BOIL COVERED 3 to 5 5 to 8	5 to 7	425° 8 to 10 12 to 14
CABBAGE, GREEN **OR RED** SHREDDED WEDGES	1 1½	6 to 8 15	1 IN. WATER; SIMMER COVERED 3 to 5 6 to 8	7 to 10	
CABBAGE, NAPA				3 to 4	
CARROTS SLICES WHOLE BABY	3 5	7 to 10 12 to 15	1 IN. WATER; SIMMER COVERED 5 to 8 8 to 15		425° 10 to 14 23 to 26
CAULIFLOWER FLORETS	1 to 2	5 to 12	1 IN. WATER; SIMMER COVERED 5 to 10	BLANCH FIRST 5	425° 15 to 20
CORN ON THE COB KERNELS	6 to 10 5 to 6	4 to 5	COVER WITH WATER; COOK COVERED 5 to 10 3 to 4		450°; PREPARE AS FOR GRILLING 15 to 20
EGGPLANT CUBED	4	5 to 7	COVER WITH WATER; BOIL UNCOVERED 5 to 8	6 to 8	400° 30 to 40 FOR WHOLE, PIERCE WITH FORK; COVER
OKRA	3 to 5		1 IN. WATER; SIMMER COVERED 8 to 10		
SQUASH, **SUMMER**	1 to 2	3 to 5	½ IN. WATER; COOK COVERED 3 to 5	4 to 7	425°, UNCOVERED 15 to 20
TOMATOES	30 SECONDS				400°, UNCOVERED 10 to 15

HOW TO BUY	HOW TO STORE	HOW TO PREP
Look for green beans that are uniform in color and size, so they will cook more or less consistently. Green beans should be firm and snap in half when bent.	Store unwashed beans in an airtight container in the refrigerator for up to 1 week.	Remove both ends and wash the beans under cold running water. If you want to retain more of the sweet taste, cook washed beans whole and then trim.
Look for firm, smooth outer skin on the beet. If the greens are attached, make sure that the stalk is bright green and crisp. Choose smaller beets of similar sizes to ensure even cooking.	First, twist off the green to separate it from the stalk and the body of the beet. The stalk will last for a few days in a refrigerator if wrapped in a damp paper towel; the body, or root, should be placed in the refrigerator's crisper bin.	Wash the beet, cutting off the root tail from the body of the beet. Then remove the stalk, which can be used in other recipes. After cooking the beet and allowing it to cool slightly, put on plastic gloves and massage the skin off.
Select bunches of bok choy with firm white stalks and crisp leaves. Avoid bunches with brown spots on stalks.	Store unwashed bok choy in the crisper drawer in the refrigerator for up to 4 days.	Wash before using. Cut leaves from stalks. Slice, chop or shred stalks. The leaves can be sliced or chopped. Always start by cooking the crunchy stalk first, then add the tender leaves during the last few minutes of cooking.
Select firm but tender stalks of broccoli with compact, dark green or slightly purplish florets.	Store unwashed broccoli in an open bag in the refrigerator crisper drawer up to 4 days. If freezing, blanch 3-5 minutes before placing in freezer. Freeze for up to 1 year.	Remove larger leaves and tough ends of lower stalks; wash. If using whole spears, cut lengthwise into 1-in.-wide pieces; stalks may also be peeled for more even cooking. If using florets, cut 1/4-1/2 in. below heads; discard stalks.
Look for cabbage that has crisp leaves and a compact head. When you pick it up, it should feel heavy for its size. Check the stem to ensure it isn't cracked, and avoid choosing a cabbage with lots of discolored or wilted leaves.	Place the head in a bag in the crisper bin in the refrigerator and store for up to 2 weeks. If cabbage has been cut or shredded, wrap in plastic wrap before refrigerating, and use within several days.	Remove any wilted or browning leaves. Wash cabbage thoroughly under running water to remove any soil that may have collected between leaves. Cut in half, then into quarters. Make a V-shaped cut around the core and remove.
Select Napa cabbage heads that are compact with crisp, fresh-looking leaves.	Store unwashed Napa cabbage in an open bag in the refrigerator's crisper drawer for up to 3 days. Store away from fruits such as apples or bananas.	Napa cabbage can be used raw or cooked. Remove outer leaves or any wilted leaves. Rinse in cold water. Cut according to recipe directions.
When it comes to carrots, the darker the better, because darker carrots have more beta carotene. Look for carrots with consistent color and no gnarled ends or cracks. Also make sure they aren't shriveled, wrinkled or soft.	For carrots with tops, cut off the stalk so that only 1 in. remains above the root. Otherwise, the greens will wilt and rot. You may choose to remove the greens entirely. Store carrots in a bag in the refrigerator for up to 2 weeks.	Don't wash carrots until you're ready to eat them. Then scrub under running water to remove any dirt. No need to peel carrots unless the recipe directs to do so.
Look for cauliflower that has a creamy white color and no discoloration or blemishes. The florets should be tightly packed, and the head should feel heavy for its relative size. The leaves should be a vibrant green, with no wilting.	Place the cauliflower loosely in a bag; insert a paper towel to gather up moisture. Close the bag and refrigerate for up to 1 week.	Cut the cauliflower down the center to expose the stem, then cut away the core to leave the florets behind. Cut florets to desired size. Wash thoroughly to remove dirt; pat dry.
When buying sweet corn, look for green husks and fresh-looking silk. Pull the husk down slightly to check for firm kernels. Inspect the kernels to ensure they don't appear milky, and avoid buying corn that has uneven rows or rows with gaps.	Keep corn, with husks intact, in the refrigerator for up to 2 days.	Remove the husk and silk by grabbing both at the end of the stalk and pulling down. Then snap or cut off the stalk.
Select a firm, round or pear-shaped, heavy eggplant with a uniformly smooth color and glossy, taut skin. The eggplant should be free from blemishes and rust spots with intact green caps and mold-free stems.	Store unwashed eggplant in an open bag in the refrigerator's crisper drawer for up to 3 days.	Wash eggplant; cut off stem and peel if desired. Cut eggplant discolors quickly, so cut into slices, strips or cubes just before salting. Salt the eggplant at least 30 minutes before cooking.
Select young, tender, unblemished, bright green pods less than 4 in. long. Pods may be smooth or ridged. They should snap easily and not have any hard seeds.	Store unwashed okra in an airtight container in the refrigerator crisper drawer for up to 2 days.	Wash and remove stem ends. Leave small pods whole; cut larger pods into 1/2-in. slices.
Look for summer squash that are firm and about 6 in. long and 2 in. in diameter. The skin should be glossy and prickly.	Keep unwashed squash in a perforated bag in the refrigerator for up to 5 days.	Wash with cool water before preparing. The skin does not need to be peeled prior to eating.
Look for tomatoes with deep, consistent coloring. A tomato should feel heavier than it looks and be firm with little give.	Place tomatoes on a counter away from direct sunlight, allowing them to ripen. Do not store in refrigerator.	Tomatoes are particularly susceptible to pesticides, so if you're not going with organic, wash with soap and water.

GRILLED GREEN BEANS

I cook almost everything outdoors, including green beans. I prepare this snappy side dish while the entree is cooking. The recipe has won over my picky eaters.
—*Carol Traupman-Carr, Breinigsville, PA*

Prep: 25 min.
Grill: 10 min.
Makes: 4 servings

1	lb. fresh green beans, trimmed
2	Tbsp. butter
1	small shallot, minced
1	garlic clove, minced
½	cup grated Parmesan cheese

1. In a 6-qt. stockpot, bring 4 qt. water to a boil. Add beans; cook, uncovered, just until crisp-tender, 2-3 minutes. Remove beans and immediately drop into ice water.

2. In a small skillet, melt the butter over medium-high heat. Add shallot; cook and stir until lightly browned, 2-3 minutes. Add garlic; cook 30 seconds longer. Remove from heat. Drain beans and pat dry.

3. In a large bowl, combine beans, shallot mixture and cheese; toss to coat. Transfer to a piece of heavy-duty foil (about 18 in. square) coated with cooking spray. Fold foil around beans, sealing tightly.

4. Grill, covered, over medium heat or broil 4 in. from heat 7-9 minutes. Open the foil carefully to allow steam to escape.

1 cup: 137 cal., 9g fat (5g sat. fat), 24mg chol., 234mg sod., 12g carb. (3g sugars, 2g fiber), 5g pro.

HEIRLOOM TOMATO PIE

My green-thumb neighbors like to share produce with me. I return the delicious favor by baking tomato pies for all.
—*Angela Benedict, Dunbar, WV*

Prep: 45 min.
Bake: 35 min. + cooling
Makes: 8 servings

1¼	lbs. heirloom tomatoes (about 4 medium), cut into ¼-in. slices
¾	tsp. salt, divided
1½	cups shredded extra-sharp cheddar cheese
¾	cup all-purpose flour
¼	cup cold butter, cubed
1	to 2 Tbsp. half-and-half cream
5	bacon strips, cooked and crumbled

FILLING
1	pkg. (8 oz.) cream cheese, softened
½	cup loosely packed basil leaves, thinly sliced
2	Tbsp. minced fresh marjoram
1½	tsp. minced fresh thyme
½	tsp. garlic powder
⅛	tsp. coarsely ground pepper

1. Preheat oven to 350°. Place tomato slices in a single layer on paper towels; sprinkle with ½ tsp. salt. Let stand 45 minutes. Pat dry.

2. Meanwhile, place the cheese, flour and remaining salt in a food processor; pulse until blended. Add butter; pulse until butter is the size of peas. While pulsing, add just enough cream to form moist crumbs. Press dough onto bottom and up sides of an ungreased 9-in. fluted tart pan with removable bottom. Gently press the bacon into the dough. Bake 20-22 minutes or until light brown. Cool on a wire rack.

3. In a large bowl, beat cream cheese, herbs and garlic powder until blended. Spread over crust. Top with the tomato slices; sprinkle with pepper. Bake 35-40 minutes longer or until edges are golden brown and tomatoes are softened. Cool on a wire rack. Refrigerate any leftovers.

1 slice: 320 cal., 25g fat (14g sat. fat), 74mg chol., 603mg sod., 14g carb. (3g sugars, 1g fiber), 11g pro.

Heirloom tomatoes are valued for their vibrant colors and sometimes unconventional shapes. For best results, slice them with a serrated knife.

GRILLED VEGETABLE PLATTER

Here's the best of summer in one incredible dish! These pretty veggies are pefect for entertaining. Grilling brings out their natural sweetness, and the easy marinade really perks up the flavor.
—*Heidi Hall, North St. Paul, MN*

Prep: 20 min. + marinating
Grill: 10 min.
Makes: 6 servings

- ¼ cup olive oil
- 2 Tbsp. honey
- 4 tsp. balsamic vinegar
- 1 tsp. dried oregano
- ½ tsp. garlic powder
- ⅛ tsp. pepper
  Dash salt
- 1 lb. fresh asparagus, trimmed
- 3 small carrots, cut in half lengthwise
- 1 large sweet red pepper, cut into 1-in. strips
- 1 medium yellow summer squash, cut into ½-in. slices
- 1 medium red onion, cut into wedges

1. In a small bowl, whisk first 7 ingredients. Place 3 Tbsp. marinade in a large bowl. Add vegetables and turn to coat. Cover; marinate 1½ hours at room temperature.
2. Transfer vegetables to a grilling grid; place grid on grill rack. Grill vegetables, covered, over medium heat 8-12 minutes or until crisp-tender, turning occasionally. Place vegetables on a large serving plate. Drizzle with remaining marinade.

1 serving: 144 cal., 9g fat (1g sat. fat), 0 chol., 50mg sod., 15g carb. (11g sugars, 3g fiber), 2g pro. **Diabetic exchanges:** 2 vegetable, 2 fat.

If you do not have a grilling grid, use a disposable foil pan. Poke holes in the bottom of the pan with a meat fork to allow liquid to drain.

ZUCCHINI IN DILL CREAM SAUCE

My husband and I were dairy farmers until we retired, so I always use fresh, real dairy products in my recipes. This creamy side dish combines all of our favorite foods!
—*Josephine Vanden Heuvel, Hart, MI*

Takes: 30 min.
Makes: 8 servings

- 7 cups unpeeled zucchini, cut into ¼-in. slices
- ¼ cup finely chopped onion
- ½ cup water
- 1 tsp. salt
- 1 tsp. chicken bouillon granules or 1 chicken bouillon cube
- ½ tsp. dill weed
- 2 Tbsp. butter, melted
- 2 tsp. sugar
- 1 tsp. lemon juice
- 2 Tbsp. all-purpose flour
- ¼ cup sour cream

1. In large saucepan, combine the zucchini, onion, water, salt, bouillon and dill; bring to a boil. Add the butter, sugar and lemon juice; mix. Remove from heat; do not drain.
2. Combine flour and sour cream; stir half the mixture into hot zucchini. Return to heat; add remaining cream mixture and cook until thickened.

¾ each: 73 cal., 4g fat (0 sat. fat), 11mg chol., 419mg sod., 8g carb. (0 sugars, 0 fiber), 2g pro. **Diabetic exchanges:** 1 vegetable, 1 fat.

YELLOW SQUASH & ZUCCHINI GRATIN

My gratin is the perfect way to use up an abundance of summer squash. It's easy to prepare, takes just 10 minutes in the oven, and serves up bubbly and delicious.
—*Jonathan Lawler, Greenfield, IN*

Prep: 25 min.
Bake: 10 min.
Makes: 6 servings

- 2 Tbsp. butter
- 2 medium zucchini, cut into ¼-in. slices
- 2 medium yellow summer squash, cut into ¼-in. slices
- 2 shallots, minced
- ½ tsp. sea salt
- ¼ tsp. coarsely ground pepper
- 4 garlic cloves, minced
- ½ cup heavy whipping cream
- 1 cup panko (Japanese) bread crumbs, divided
- ½ cup grated Parmesan cheese, divided

1. Preheat oven to 450°. In a large skillet, melt butter over medium heat; add zucchini, yellow squash and shallots. Sprinkle with salt and pepper. Cook, stirring occasionally, until the zucchini and squash are crisp-tender, 4-6 minutes. Add garlic; cook 1 minute more.
2. Add heavy cream; cook until thickened, 3-5 minutes. Remove from heat; stir in ½ cup bread crumbs and ¼ cup Parmesan cheese. Spoon mixture into a greased 11x7-in. or 2-qt. baking dish. Sprinkle with remaining bread crumbs and cheese. Bake until golden brown, 8-10 minutes.

1 cup: 203 cal., 14g fat (8g sat. fat), 39mg chol., 357mg sod., 15g carb. (4g sugars, 2g fiber), 6g pro.

EGGPLANT PARMESAN

We really like eggplant and would rather have it baked than fried. This colorful dish can be served as a side or a main.
—*Donna Wardlow-Keating, Omaha, NE*

Prep: 10 min.
Bake: 45 min. + cooling
Makes: 2 servings

- 2 Tbsp. olive oil
- 1 garlic clove, minced
- 1 small eggplant, peeled and cut into ¼-in. slices
- 1 Tbsp. minced fresh basil or 1 tsp. dried basil
- 1 Tbsp. grated Parmesan cheese
- 1 medium tomato, thinly sliced
- ½ cup shredded mozzarella cheese
  Additional basil, optional

1. Combine oil and garlic; brush over both sides of eggplant slices. Place on a greased baking sheet. Bake at 425° for 15 minutes; turn. Bake until golden brown, about 5 minutes longer. Cool on a wire rack.
2. Place half of the eggplant in a greased 1-qt. baking dish. Sprinkle with half of the basil and Parmesan cheese. Arrange tomato slices over top; sprinkle with remaining basil and Parmesan. Layer with half of the mozzarella cheese and the remaining eggplant; top with remaining mozzarella. Cover and bake at 350° for 20 minutes. Uncover; bake until cheese is melted, about 5-7 minutes longer. Garnish with additional basil, if desired.

1 serving: 275 cal., 21g fat (6g sat. fat), 24mg chol., 164mg sod., 16g carb. (9g sugars, 5g fiber), 9g pro.

Young, tender eggplants do not need to be peeled before using; however, larger eggplants may be bitter and will taste better when peeled.

 5j

ASPARAGUS, SQUASH & RED PEPPER SAUTE

The flavor of this appealing vegetable trio is enhanced by a delicate wine saute.
—*Deirdre Cox, Kansas City, MO*

Takes: 30 min.
Makes: 4 servings

- 2 medium sweet red peppers, julienned
- 2 medium yellow summer squash, halved lengthwise and cut into ¼-in. slices
- 6 oz. fresh asparagus, trimmed and cut into 1½-in. pieces
- ¼ cup white wine or ¼ cup vegetable broth
- 4½ tsp. olive oil
- ¼ tsp. salt
- ¼ tsp. pepper

In a large cast-iron or other heavy skillet, saute the peppers, squash and asparagus in wine and oil until crisp-tender. Sprinkle with salt and pepper.

¾ cup: 90 cal., 5g fat (1g sat. fat), 0 chol., 163mg sod., 8g carb. (5g sugars, 3g fiber), 2g pro. **Diabetic exchanges:** 1 vegetable, 1 fat.

This recipe is adaptable, so feel free to use your favorite summer produce. Try it with zucchini, corn or even fresh green beans.

5i

MEXICAN STREET CORN BAKE

We discovered Mexican street corn at a festival. This easy one-pan version saves on prep and cleanup. Every August, I freeze a lot of our own fresh sweet corn, and I use that in this recipe, but store-bought corn works just as well.
—*Erin Wright, Wallace, KS*

Prep: 10 min.
Bake: 35 min.
Makes: 6 servings

  6 **cups frozen corn (about 30 oz.), thawed and drained**
  1 **cup mayonnaise**
  1 **tsp. ground chipotle pepper**
  ¼ **tsp. salt**
  ¼ **tsp. pepper**
  6 **Tbsp. chopped green onions, divided**
  ½ **cup grated Parmesan cheese**
     Lime wedges, optional

1. Preheat oven to 350°. Mix the first 5 ingredients and 4 Tbsp. green onions; transfer to a greased 1½-qt. baking dish. Sprinkle with cheese.
2. Bake, covered, 20 minutes. Uncover; bake until bubbly and lightly browned, 15-20 minutes. Sprinkle with remaining chopped green onions. If desired, serve with lime wedges.

⅔ cup: 391 cal., 30g fat (5g sat. fat), 8mg chol., 423mg sod., 30g carb. (4g sugars, 3g fiber), 6g pro.

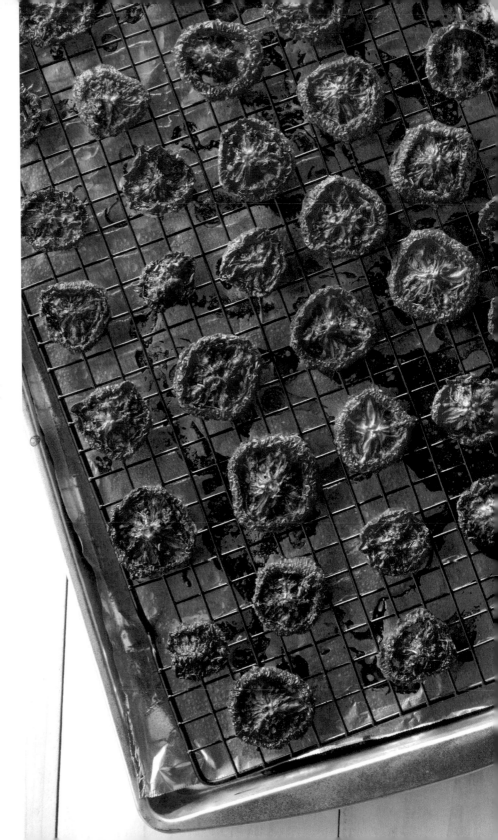

5i ❄

OVEN-ROASTED TOMATOES

I love tomatoes, as they're healthy, versatile and oh, so juicy in the summer. Use these roasted tomatoes as a side dish, serve over grilled chicken, or use them as sandwich or omelet fixings.
—*Julie Gomez, Downey, CA*

Prep: 20 min.
Bake: 3 hours + cooling
Makes: 4 cups

20	**plum tomatoes (about 5 lbs.)**
¼	**cup olive oil**
5	**tsp. Italian seasoning**
2½	**tsp. salt**

1. Cut tomatoes into ½-in. slices. Brush with oil; sprinkle with Italian seasoning and salt.
2. Place on racks coated with cooking spray in foil-lined 15x10x1-in. baking pans. Bake, uncovered, at 325° for 3-3½ hours or until tomatoes are deep brown around the edges and shriveled. Cool for 10-15 minutes. Serve warm or at room temperature.
3. Store tomatoes in an airtight container in the refrigerator for up to 1 week.
Freeze option: Place in freezer container; freeze for up to 3 months. Bring tomatoes to room temperature before using.

¼ cup: 45 cal., 4g fat (0 sat. fat), 0 chol., 373mg sod., 3g carb. (2g sugars, 1g fiber), 1g pro.

REFRIGERATOR GARDEN PICKLES

Canning isn't necessary for these crisp-tender, tangy pickles; they'll keep in the fridge for up to a month.
—*Linda Chapman, Meriden, IA*

Prep: 20 min.
Cook: 15 min. + chilling
Makes: 7 pints

    6 cups sugar
    6 cups white vinegar
    ¼ cup celery seed
    ¼ cup mustard seed
    2 Tbsp. canning salt
   10 medium carrots, halved lengthwise
       and cut into 2-in. pieces
    3 medium cucumbers, sliced
    3 medium sweet red peppers,
       cut into 1-in. pieces
    2 large onions, halved and sliced
    1 bunch green onions, cut
       into 2-in. pieces

1. In a Dutch oven, combine the first 5 ingredients; bring to a boil, stirring to dissolve sugar. Meanwhile, place the remaining ingredients in a large bowl.
2. Pour hot liquid over vegetables; cool. Transfer to jars, if desired; cover tightly. Refrigerate for 6-8 hours before serving. Store in the refrigerator for up to 1 month.

¼ cup: 55 cal., 0 fat (0 sat. fat), 0 chol., 28mg sod., 13g carb. (11g sugars, 1g fiber), 1g pro.

GARDEN POTATO PANCAKES

My family eats potato pancakes regularly. Your picky eaters will be happy to know they don't even taste like they're full of fresh veggies. We especially like them with the cheese mixed in.
—*Peggy Roos, Minneapolis, MN*

Prep: 20 min.
Cook: 5 min./batch
Makes: 12 pancakes

- 2   medium zucchini, grated
- 2   large eggs
- ¼   cup whole wheat flour
- ½   tsp. salt
- ¼   tsp. pepper
- ¼   tsp. dried basil
- 1   large onion, finely chopped
- 1   medium potato, grated
- 1   medium carrot, grated
- ⅓   cup frozen corn, thawed
- ¼   cup shredded sharp white cheddar cheese
    Oil for frying
    Coarsely ground black pepper and sour cream, optional

1. In a strainer or colander, drain zucchini, squeezing to remove excess liquid. Pat dry. In a large bowl, whisk eggs, flour, salt, pepper and basil until blended. Stir in onion, potato, carrot, corn, cheese and zucchini.

2. In an electric skillet, heat ¼ in. of oil to 375°. Working in batches, drop vegetable mixture by ⅓ cupfuls into oil; press to flatten slightly. Fry 2-3 minutes on each side or until golden brown. Drain on paper towels. If desired, sprinkle with pepper and serve with sour cream.

2 pancakes: 269 cal., 20g fat (3g sat. fat), 76mg chol., 266mg sod., 18g carb. (4g sugars, 3g fiber), 6g pro.

PERFECT POTATO PANCAKES

Liven up meals with this easy side dish. Crispy on the outside yet tender on the inside, potato pancakes are so much easier than you might think.

STEP 1
Use a large bowl to easily combine all the pancake ingredients. One bowl means less cleanup!

STEP 2
Don't have an electric skillet? Use a cast-iron or heavy skillet. Remember to press the pancakes flat early on.

GRILLED CABBAGE

I don't really like cabbage, but I fixed this recipe and couldn't believe how good it was! We threw some burgers on the grill and our dinner was complete. I never thought I'd skip dessert because I was full from eating too much cabbage!
—*Elizabeth Wheeler, Thornville, OH*

Takes: 30 min.
Makes: 8 servings

1   medium head cabbage
    (about 1½ lbs.)
⅓   cup butter, softened
¼   cup chopped onion
½   tsp. garlic salt
¼   tsp. pepper

1. Cut cabbage into 8 wedges; place on a double thickness of heavy-duty foil (about 24x12 in.). Spread cut sides with butter. Sprinkle with onion, garlic salt and pepper.
2. Fold foil around cabbage and seal tightly. Grill, covered, over medium heat until tender, about 20 minutes. Open the foil carefully to allow steam to escape.

1 wedge: 98 cal., 8g fat (5g sat. fat), 20mg chol., 188mg sod., 7g carb. (4g sugars, 3g fiber), 2g pro. **Diabetic exchanges:** 1½ fat, 1 vegetable.

GRILLED CAULIFLOWER WEDGES

This recipe is easy yet packed with flavor. It looks like a dish from a five-star restaurant. The grill leaves the cauliflower cooked but crisp, and the red pepper flakes add a spicy bite.
—Carmel Hall, San Francisco, CA

Takes: 30 min.
Makes: 8 servings

- 1 large head cauliflower
- 1 tsp. ground turmeric
- ½ tsp. crushed red pepper flakes
- 2 Tbsp. olive oil
  Lemon juice, additional olive oil and pomegranate seeds, optional

1. Remove leaves and trim stem from cauliflower. Cut cauliflower into 8 wedges. Mix turmeric and the red pepper flakes. Brush wedges with oil; sprinkle with the turmeric mixture.
2. Grill, covered, over medium-high heat or broil 4 in. from heat until cauliflower is tender, 8-10 minutes on each side. If desired, drizzle with lemon juice and additional oil and serve with pomegranate seeds.

1 wedge: 57 cal., 4g fat (1g sat. fat), 0 chol., 32mg sod., 5g carb. (2g sugars, 2g fiber), 2g pro. **Diabetic exchanges:** 1 vegetable, 1 fat.

CHERRY TOMATO MOZZARELLA SAUTE

This side dish is full of flavor, and so quick to put together. Cherry tomatoes and mozzarella make the perfect complement to almost any entree.
—Summer Jones, Pleasant Grove, UT

Takes: 25 min.
Makes: 4 servings

- 2 tsp. olive oil
- ¼ cup chopped shallots
- 1 tsp. minced fresh thyme
- 1 garlic clove, minced
- 2½ cups cherry tomatoes, halved
- ¼ tsp. salt
- ¼ tsp. pepper
- 4 oz. fresh mozzarella cheese cut into ½-in. cubes

In a large skillet, heat oil over medium-high heat; saute shallots with thyme until tender. Add garlic; cook and stir 1 minute. Stir in tomatoes, salt and pepper; heat through. Remove from heat; stir in cheese.

⅔ cup: 127 cal., 9g fat (4g sat. fat), 22mg chol., 194mg sod., 6g carb. (4g sugars, 2g fiber), 6g pro.

It's easy to mince a fresh garlic clove when you start by crushing the clove with the blade of a chef's knife. Once you crush it, peel away the skin and then use the knife to mince (or chop) the garlic.

5j

EASY GRILLED CORN WITH CHIPOTLE-LIME BUTTER

Grilling corn in the husks is so easy. There's no need to remove the silk and tie the husk closed before grilling. Just soak, grill and add your favorite flavored butter.
—Taste of Home *Test Kitchen*

Prep: 5 min. + soaking
Grill: 25 min.
Makes: 8 servings

8	large ears sweet corn in husks
½	cup butter, softened
1½	tsp. grated lime zest
1	tsp. minced fresh cilantro
½	tsp. salt
½	tsp. ground chipotle pepper
	Coarse sea salt, optional

1. In a large stockpot, cover corn with cold water. Soak 30 minutes; drain. Grill corn, covered, over medium heat until tender, turning occasionally, 25-30 minutes.
2. Meanwhile, combine the remaining ingredients. Carefully peel back husks; discard silk. Spread the butter mixture over the corn.

1 ear of corn with 2 Tbsp. butter: 225 cal., 13g fat (8g sat. fat), 31mg chol., 265mg sod., 27g carb. (9g sugars, 3g fiber), 5g pro.

🕐 5i

SPICY EGGPLANT

This grilled side goes well with pasta or grilled meats. Thanks to the Cajun seasoning, it gets more attention than an ordinary veggie.
—*Greg Fontenot, The Woodlands, TX*

Takes: 20 min.
Makes: 8 servings

- 2 **small eggplants, cut into ½-in. slices**
- ¼ **cup olive oil**
- 2 **Tbsp. lime juice**
- 3 **tsp. Cajun seasoning**

1. Brush eggplant slices with oil. Drizzle with lime juice; sprinkle with Cajun seasoning. Let stand 5 minutes.
2. Grill the eggplant slices, covered, over medium heat or broil 4 in. from heat until tender, 4-5 minutes per side.

1 serving: 88 cal., 7g fat (1g sat. fat), 0 chol., 152mg sod., 7g carb. (3g sugars, 4g fiber), 1g pro. **Diabetic exchanges:** 1½ fat, 1 vegetable.

PEPPER PARMESAN BEANS

A colorful mixture of peppers and green beans gets an Italian treatment with basil and Parmesan cheese in this delightful vegetable dish.
—*Marian Platt, Sequim, WA*

Takes: 15 min.
Makes: 8 servings

- 1 large sweet red pepper, diced
- 1 small green pepper, diced
- ¼ cup chopped onion
- 1 garlic clove, minced
- ¼ cup olive oil
- 1½ lbs. fresh green beans, cut into 2-in. pieces
- 1 Tbsp. minced fresh basil or 1 tsp. dried basil
- 1 tsp. salt
- ⅓ to ½ cup shredded Parmesan cheese

In a large skillet, saute the peppers, onion and garlic in oil until the vegetables are tender, about 3 minutes. Add the beans, basil and salt; toss to coat. Cover and cook over medium-low heat for 7-8 minutes or until beans are crisp-tender. Stir in cheese; serve immediately.

¾ cup: 107 cal., 8g fat (2g sat. fat), 2mg chol., 357mg sod., 8g carb. (3g sugars, 3g fiber), 3g pro.

GRILLED MUSHROOM KABOBS

Earthy grilled mushrooms taste like flame-kissed goodness. The balsamic vinegar adds just enough tanginess to the savory side.
—*Melissa Hoddinott, Sherwood Park, AB*

Prep: 30 min.
Cook: 10 min.
Makes: 4 servings

- 16 pearl onions
- 20 medium fresh mushrooms
- ⅓ cup balsamic vinegar
- ¼ cup butter, cubed
- 2 garlic cloves, minced
- ½ tsp. salt
- ½ tsp. pepper
  Minced fresh parsley, optional

1. In a small saucepan, bring 6 cups water to a boil. Add pearl onions; boil 5 minutes. Drain and rinse with cold water. Peel.

2. On four metal or soaked wooden skewers, alternately thread mushrooms and onions, skewering mushrooms horizontally through cap. In a microwave-safe bowl, combine balsamic vinegar, butter, garlic, salt and pepper; microwave, covered, on high until butter is melted, 30-45 seconds. Whisk to combine. Reserve half of the vinegar mixture for serving. Brush kabobs with remaining vinegar mixture.

3. Grill kabobs, covered, over medium heat or broil 4 in. from heat until vegetables are tender, 10-12 minutes, turning occasionally and basting frequently with vinegar mixture. If desired, sprinkle with parsley; serve with reserved vinegar mixture.

1 kabob: 161 cal., 12g fat (7g sat. fat), 31mg chol., 393mg sod., 13g carb. (7g sugars, 1g fiber), 3g pro.

SUMMER'S EASIEST

WEEKNIGHT ENTREES

It's easy to keep the spotlight on seasonal favorites with these no-fuss dinners. You'll keep the kitchen cool and step into summer fun fast with 30-minute dinners, main-dish salads, grilled greats and other workweek staples.

 CRAB-TOPPED FISH FILLETS

Elegant but truly no bother, this recipe is perfect for company. Toasting the almonds gives them a little more crunch, which is a delightful way to top these fast fish fillets.
—*Mary Tuthill, Fort Myers Beach, FL*

Takes: 30 min.
Makes: 4 servings

- 4 **sole or cod fillets, or fish fillets of your choice (6 oz. each)**
- 1 **can (6 oz.) crabmeat, drained and flaked, or 1 cup imitation crabmeat, chopped**
- ½ **cup grated Parmesan cheese**
- ½ **cup mayonnaise**
- 1 **tsp. lemon juice**
- ⅓ **cup slivered almonds, toasted Paprika, optional**

1. Place fillets in a greased 13x9-in. baking dish. Bake, uncovered, at 350° until fish flakes easily with a fork, 18-22 minutes. Meanwhile, in a large bowl, combine the crab, cheese, mayonnaise and lemon juice.
2. Drain cooking juices from baking dish; spoon crab mixture over fish fillets. Broil 4-5 in. from the heat until topping is lightly browned, about 5 minutes. Sprinkle with almonds and paprika if desired.

1 fillet: 429 cal., 31g fat (6g sat. fat), 128mg chol., 1063mg sod., 3g carb. (0 sugars, 1g fiber), 33g pro.

 CALIFORNIA BURGER BOWLS

Burgers are a weekly staple at our house all year round. Skip the fries, chips and bun—you won't need them with these loaded turkey patties. To spice up the mayo, stir in a little chipotle powder.
—*Courtney Stultz, Weir, KS*

Takes: 25 min.
Makes: 4 servings

- 3 **Tbsp. fat-free milk**
- 2 **Tbsp. quick-cooking oats**
- ¾ **tsp. salt**
- ½ **tsp. ground cumin**
- ½ **tsp. chili powder**
- ½ **tsp. pepper**
- 1 **lb. lean ground turkey**
- 4 **cups baby kale salad blend**
- 1½ **cups cubed fresh pineapple (½ in.)**
- 1 **medium mango, peeled and thinly sliced**
- 1 **medium ripe avocado, peeled and thinly sliced**
- 1 **medium sweet red pepper, cut into strips**
- 4 **tomatillos, husks removed, thinly sliced**
- ¼ **cup reduced-fat chipotle mayonnaise**

1. In a large bowl, mix milk, oats and seasonings. Add turkey; mix lightly but thoroughly. Shape into four ½-in.-thick patties.

2. Place the burgers on an oiled grill rack over medium heat. Grill, covered, until a thermometer reads 165°, 4-5 minutes per side. Serve over salad blend, along with remaining ingredients.

1 serving: 390 cal., 19g fat (4g sat. fat), 83mg chol., 666mg sod., 33g carb. (22g sugars, 7g fiber), 26g pro. **Diabetic exchanges:** 3 lean meat, 2 vegetable, 1 fruit, 2½ fat.

→

Save even more time when you top the burger bowls with prepared guacamole instead of the spicy chipotle mayonnaise.

LEMONY SCALLOPS WITH ANGEL HAIR PASTA

This light and lively dish tastes so bright with a touch of lemon and tender sauteed scallops. Serve with a fresh garden salad, and you have an impressive dinner that comes together in a flash.
—*Thomas Faglon, Somerset, NJ*

Takes: 25 min.
Makes: 4 servings

- 8 oz. uncooked multigrain angel hair pasta
- 3 Tbsp. olive oil, divided
- 1 lb. sea scallops, patted dry
- 2 cups sliced radishes (about 1 bunch)
- 2 garlic cloves, sliced
- ½ tsp. crushed red pepper flakes
- 6 green onions, thinly sliced
- ½ tsp. kosher salt
- 1 Tbsp. grated lemon zest
- ¼ cup lemon juice

1. In a 6-qt. stockpot, cook pasta according to package directions; drain and return to the pot.
2. Meanwhile, in a large skillet, heat 2 Tbsp. oil over medium-high heat; sear scallops in batches until opaque and edges are golden brown, about 2 minutes per side. Remove from skillet; keep warm.
3. In the same skillet, saute radishes, garlic and pepper flakes in remaining oil until radishes are tender, 2-3 minutes. Stir in green onions and salt; cook 1 minute. Add to pasta; toss to combine. Sprinkle with lemon zest and juice. Top with scallops to serve.

1½ cups: 404 cal., 13g fat (2g sat. fat), 27mg chol., 737mg sod., 48g carb. (4g sugars, 6g fiber), 25g pro.

CHICKEN ARTICHOKE SKILLET

This quick chicken entree features artichokes and olives for authentic Greek flair. Seasoned with lemon juice and oregano, the chicken always turns out flavorful and tender.
—*Carol Latimore, Arvada, CO*

Takes: 25 min.
Makes: 4 servings

- 4 **boneless skinless chicken breast halves (4 oz. each)**
- ¼ **tsp. salt**
- ¼ **tsp. pepper**
- 2 **tsp. olive oil**
- 1 **can (14 oz.) water-packed quartered artichoke hearts, rinsed and drained**
- ⅔ **cup reduced-sodium chicken broth**
- ¼ **cup halved pimiento-stuffed olives**
- ¼ **cup halved pitted Greek olives**
- 2 **Tbsp. minced fresh oregano or 2 tsp. dried oregano**
- 1 **Tbsp. lemon juice**

1. Sprinkle chicken with salt and pepper. In a large skillet, heat oil over medium-high heat; brown chicken on both sides.
2. Add the remaining ingredients; bring to a boil. Reduce heat; simmer, covered, until a thermometer inserted in chicken reads 165°, 4-5 minutes.

1 serving: 225 cal., 9g fat (1g sat. fat), 63mg chol., 864mg sod., 9g carb. (0 sugars, 0 fiber), 26g pro. **Diabetic exchanges:** 3 lean meat, 1 vegetable.

OLIVE OIL OPTIONS

With so many types of olive oil on grocery store shelves today, it can be a little tricky to decide which one makes the most sense for your meal. Olive oils are graded by their acidity and offer the following characteristics.

VIRGIN OLIVE OIL

Extra virgin olive oil comes from the first pressing of olives and has an extremely low acidity of 1%. It has a deep color and intense olive flavor. Virgin olive oil has a slightly higher acidity (2%), lighter color and less fruity flavor. Both are best used in dishes where their stronger flavors can be appreciated.

OLIVE OIL

Bottles simply labeled olive oil contain oil with 3% acidity. Sometimes called "light olive oil" or "pure olive oil," this variety has a light color and faint flavor. Use this oil for baking. You can also use olive oil for cooking when you don't want to give the dish a particularly strong flavor from the oil.

MARINATED STEAK WITH GRILLED ONIONS

This marinade is magic! It makes even economy cuts of beef tender and delicious in no time.
—*Gail Garcelon, Beaverton, OR*

Prep: 10 min. + marinating
Grill: 10 min.
Makes: 12 servings (1 cup cooked onions)

- 1¼ cups balsamic vinaigrette
- 4 tsp. ground mustard
- 2¼ tsp. Worcestershire sauce
- 2 garlic cloves, minced
- 3 beef top sirloin steaks
     (¾ in. thick and 1 lb. each)
- 5 medium onions, sliced

1. Whisk together the vinaigrette, mustard, Worcestershire sauce and garlic. Pour ¼ cup into a shallow dish. Add the beef and turn to coat. Cover and refrigerate for 6 hours or overnight. Cover and refrigerate remaining marinade.

2. Drain beef, discarding marinade from dish. Grill the steaks and onions, covered, over medium heat or broil 4 in. from the heat until meat reaches desired doneness (for medium-rare, a thermometer should read 135°; medium, 140°; medium-well, 145°) and onions are tender, 4-7 minutes per side. Drizzle reserved marinade over onions. Cut steak into thin slices; serve with onions.

3 oz. cooked beef with ⅛ cup onion slices: 209 cal., 8g fat (2g sat. fat), 46mg chol., 294mg sod., 6g carb. (3g sugars, 1g fiber), 25g pro. **Diabetic exchanges:** 3 lean meat.

AVOCADO CRAB BOATS

These boats are wonderful with tortilla chips, beans or rice. You can also cover them, pack them on ice, and take them to a picnic or potluck. Straight from the oven or cold, they're always delicious.
—*Frances Benthin, Scio, OR*

Takes: 20 min.
Makes: 8 servings

5	medium ripe avocados, peeled and halved
½	cup mayonnaise
2	Tbsp. lemon juice
2	cans (6 oz. each) lump crabmeat, drained
4	Tbsp. chopped fresh cilantro, divided
2	Tbsp. minced chives
1	serrano pepper, seeded and minced
1	Tbsp. capers, drained
¼	tsp. pepper
1	cup shredded pepper jack cheese
½	tsp. paprika
	Lemon wedges

1. Preheat broiler. Place 2 avocado halves in a large bowl; mash lightly with a fork. Add mayonnaise and lemon juice; mix until well blended. Stir in crab, 3 Tbsp. cilantro, chives, serrano pepper, capers and pepper. Spoon into remaining avocado halves.
2. Transfer avocados to a 15x10x1-in. baking pan. Sprinkle with pepper jack cheese and paprika. Broil 4-5 in. from heat until cheese is melted, 3-5 minutes. Sprinkle with the remaining cilantro; serve with lemon wedges.
Note: Wear disposable gloves when cutting hot peppers; the oils can burn skin. Avoid touching your face.

1 filled avocado half: 325 cal., 28g fat (6g sat. fat), 57mg chol., 427mg sod., 8g carb. (0 sugars, 6g fiber), 13g pro.

STEAK & FRIES SALAD

This is a very popular dish at restaurants in central Pennsylvania. Prepared sweet-and-sour dressing is good on this salad, too.
—*Nancy Collins, Clearfield, PA*

Takes: 30 min.
Makes: 2 servings

- 3 Tbsp. sugar
- 2 Tbsp. canola oil
- 1 to 2 Tbsp. malt vinegar
- 1½ tsp. water
- 1 cup frozen french-fried potatoes
- ½ lb. beef top sirloin steak
- 3 cups torn iceberg lettuce
- ⅓ cup chopped tomato
- ¼ cup chopped red onion
- ½ cup shredded part-skim mozzarella cheese

1. For dressing, whisk first 4 ingredients until sugar is dissolved. Cook potatoes according to package directions.

2. Meanwhile, place a skillet coated with cooking spray over medium heat. Add steak; cook until meat reaches desired doneness (for medium-rare, a thermometer should read 135°; medium, 140°), 5-6 minutes per side. Remove from heat; let stand 5 minutes before slicing.

3. To serve, divide lettuce, tomato and onion between 2 plates; top with potatoes, steak and cheese. Drizzle with dressing.

1 serving: 513 cal., 26g fat (7g sat. fat), 64mg chol., 429mg sod., 34g carb. (22g sugars, 2g fiber), 33g pro.

SOUTHWESTERN FISH TACOS

These bright tacos take me on an instant trip to sunny Southern California. This easy recipe has been on my family's most-requested list for years.
—*Joan Hallford, North Richland Hills, TX*

Takes: 20 min.
Makes: 2 servings

- ¼ cup mayonnaise
- ¼ cup sour cream
- 2 Tbsp. minced fresh cilantro
- 4 tsp. taco seasoning
- ½ lb. cod or haddock fillets, cut into 1-in. pieces
- 1 Tbsp. lemon juice
- 1 Tbsp. canola oil
- 4 taco shells
  Optional ingredients: Shredded lettuce, chopped tomato and lime wedges

1. For sauce, mix mayonnaise, sour cream, cilantro and 2 tsp. taco seasoning. In another bowl, toss cod with lemon juice and the remaining taco seasoning.
2. In a skillet, heat oil over medium-high heat; saute cod just until it begins to flake easily with a fork, 4-6 minutes (fish may break apart as it cooks). Spoon into taco shells; serve with sauce and the remaining ingredients as desired.

2 tacos: 506 cal., 38g fat (8g sat. fat), 52mg chol., 852mg sod., 20g carb. (1g sugars, 1g fiber), 20g pro.

BLT CHICKEN SALAD

Featuring all the fixings of a BLT chicken sandwich, this salad is quick, easy and delicious. I can prep the ingredients ahead of time and just throw it together at the last minute. Barbecue sauce in the dressing gives it unexpected zest. Even picky eaters love it!
—*Cindy Moore, Mooresville, NC*

Takes: 20 min.
Makes: 8 servings

- ½ cup mayonnaise
- 3 to 4 Tbsp. barbecue sauce
- 2 Tbsp. finely chopped onion
- 1 Tbsp. lemon juice
- ¼ tsp. pepper
- 8 cups torn salad greens
- 2 large tomatoes, chopped
- 1½ lbs. boneless skinless chicken breasts, cooked and cubed
- 10 bacon strips, cooked and crumbled
- 2 hard-boiled large eggs, sliced

In a bowl, combine the first 5 ingredients; mix well. Cover and refrigerate until serving. Place salad greens in a large bowl. Sprinkle with tomatoes, chicken and bacon; garnish with eggs. Drizzle with the dressing.

1 serving: 281 cal., 19g fat (4g sat. fat), 112mg chol., 324mg sod., 5g carb. (3g sugars, 2g fiber), 23g pro.

QUICK MOROCCAN SHRIMP SKILLET

When my niece was attending West Point, she was sent to Morocco for five months. I threw her a going-away party with Moroccan decorations, costumes and cuisine, including this saucy shrimp dish. Whenever I make it now, I think of her and I smile.
—*Barbara Lento, Houston, PA*

Takes: 25 min.
Makes: 4 servings

- 1 Tbsp. canola oil
- 1 small onion, chopped
- ¼ cup pine nuts
- 1 lb. uncooked shrimp (16-20 per lb.), peeled and deveined
- 1 cup uncooked pearl (Israeli) couscous
- 2 Tbsp. lemon juice
- 3 tsp. Moroccan seasoning (ras el hanout)
- 1 tsp. garlic salt
- 2 cups hot water
  Minced fresh parsley, optional

1. In a large skillet, heat the canola oil over medium-high heat; saute onion and pine nuts until onion is tender, 2-3 minutes. Stir in all remaining ingredients except parsley; bring just to a boil. Reduce heat; simmer, covered, until shrimp turn pink, 4-6 minutes.
2. Remove from heat; let stand 5 minutes. If desired, top with parsley.
Note: This recipe was tested with McCormick Gourmet Moroccan Seasoning (ras el hanout).

1 cup: 335 cal., 11g fat (1g sat. fat), 138mg chol., 626mg sod., 34g carb. (1g sugars, 1g fiber), 24g pro.

Letting the mixture stand before serving helps the pasta absorb more liquid. It's still a saucy dish, however, so serve it in a shallow bowl.

THAI PEANUT NAAN PIZZAS

I'm a huge fan of Thai food, but don't always have the time to make it at home. To get my fix, I top fluffy naan bread with a ginger-peanut sauce, fresh veggies, a sprinkle of cilantro and a spicy squiggle of Sriracha.
—*Rachel Bernhard Seis, Milwaukee, WI*

Takes: 25 min.
Makes: 4 servings

¼ cup creamy peanut butter
3 Tbsp. sesame ginger salad dressing
1 Tbsp. water
1 tsp. soy sauce
2 naan flatbreads
1 cup shredded part-skim mozzarella cheese
1 small sweet red pepper, julienned
½ cup julienned carrot
½ cup sliced baby portobello mushrooms
¼ cup chopped fresh cilantro
   Sriracha chili sauce, optional

1. Preheat oven to 425°. For sauce, mix first 4 ingredients until blended. Place naan on a baking sheet; spread with sauce. Top with cheese and vegetables.
2. Bake until mozzarella is melted and crust is golden brown, 8-10 minutes. Top with the chopped cilantro and, if desired, drizzle with chili sauce.

½ pizza: 316 cal., 19g fat (6g sat. fat), 21mg chol., 698mg sod., 25g carb. (8g sugars, 2g fiber), 13g pro.

To wash cilantro, dunk or soak in a deep container of water to allow any dirt or grit to settle on the bottom, changing out the water 2-3 times. Gently blot the leaves dry and proceed with recipe as directed.

CARAMELIZED PORK SLICES

This easy treatment for pork caught my eye when I was thumbing through a cookbook and saw the word *caramelized*. I like to serve it over noodles or rice, or alongside servings of mashed potatoes.
—*Elisa Lochridge, Beaverton, OR*

Takes: 25 min.
Makes: 4 servings

1	pork tenderloin (1 lb.)
2	tsp. canola oil, divided
2	garlic cloves, minced
2	Tbsp. brown sugar
1	Tbsp. orange juice
1	Tbsp. molasses
½	tsp. salt
¼	tsp. pepper

1. Cut tenderloin into 8 slices; pound each with a meat mallet to ½-in. thickness. In a nonstick skillet, heat 1 tsp. oil over medium-high heat; brown the pork on both sides. Remove from pan.
2. In same skillet, heat remaining oil over medium-high heat; saute garlic 1 minute. Stir in the remaining ingredients. Add pork, turning to coat; cook, uncovered, until a thermometer inserted in tenderloin reads 145°, 3-4 minutes. Let stand for 5 minutes before serving.

2 pork slices: 198 cal., 6g fat (2g sat. fat), 64mg chol., 344mg sod., 12g carb. (11g sugars, 0 fiber), 23g pro. **Diabetic exchanges:** 3 lean meat, ½ starch.

SOUTHWEST TORTILLA-TURKEY SKILLET

Here's a great way to spice up summer meals. I wanted to cut back on red meat, but my husband thinks ground turkey can be dry. I think the taco seasoning and jalapeno juice in this recipe give the turkey added flavor and moistness—and he agrees.
—*Lindsay Ludden, Omaha, NE*

Takes: 25 min.
Makes: 2 servings

½ lb. ground turkey
¾ cup black beans, rinsed and drained
½ cup water
⅓ cup sliced ripe olives
2 Tbsp. reduced-sodium taco seasoning
1 Tbsp. juice from pickled jalapeno slices
1 flour tortilla (10 in.), cut into 1-in. pieces
½ cup shredded reduced-fat Mexican cheese blend
2 Tbsp. pickled jalapeno slices
2 Tbsp. reduced-fat sour cream

1. In a large skillet, cook turkey over medium heat until no longer pink; drain. Stir in the beans, water, olives, taco seasoning and juice from jalapenos. Bring to a boil. Reduce heat; simmer, uncovered, for 6-7 minutes or until thickened.
2. Stir in tortilla pieces. Sprinkle with cheese and jalapeno. Remove from the heat and cover for 1-2 minutes or until cheese is melted. Serve with sour cream.

1½ cups: 496 cal., 21g fat (8g sat. fat), 91mg chol., 1502mg sod., 41g carb. (6g sugars, 6g fiber), 39g pro.

TZATZIKI CHICKEN

A refreshing cucumber-dill sauce makes this classic chicken dish a fast summer specialty. Try the sauce as a salad dressing, too!
—*Kristen Heigl, Staten Island, NY*

Takes: 30 min.
Makes: 4 servings

1½ cups finely chopped peeled English cucumber
1 cup plain Greek yogurt
2 garlic cloves, minced
1½ tsp. chopped fresh dill
1½ tsp. olive oil
⅛ tsp. salt
CHICKEN
⅔ cup all-purpose flour
1 tsp. salt
1 tsp. pepper
¼ tsp. baking powder
1 large egg
⅓ cup 2% milk
4 boneless skinless chicken breast halves (6 oz. each)

¼ cup canola oil
¼ cup crumbled feta cheese
Lemon wedges, optional

1. For sauce, mix the first 6 ingredients; refrigerate until serving.
2. In a shallow bowl, whisk together flour, salt, pepper and baking powder. In another bowl, whisk together egg and milk. Pound chicken breasts with a meat mallet to ½-in. thickness. Dip in flour mixture to coat both sides; shake off excess. Dip in egg mixture, then again in flour mixture.
3. In a large skillet, heat oil over medium heat. Cook chicken until golden brown and juices run clear, 5-7 minutes per side. Top with cheese. Serve with sauce and, if desired, lemon wedges.

1 chicken breast half with ⅓ cup sauce: 482 cal., 27g fat (7g sat. fat), 133mg chol., 737mg sod., 17g carb. (4g sugars, 1g fiber), 41g pro.

An English cucumber works well in this recipe because it's seedless and doesn't thin out the sauce. A regular cucumber can be used, too; just seed it before chopping.

ZUCCHINI BEEF SKILLET

This is a speedy summer recipe that uses up your abundant garden goodies: zucchini, tomatoes and green peppers.
—*Becky Calder, Kingston, MO*

Takes: 30 min.
Makes: 4 servings

- 1   **lb. ground beef**
- 1   **medium onion, chopped**
- 1   **small green pepper, chopped**
- 2   **tsp. chili powder**
- ¾   **tsp. salt**
- ¼   **tsp. pepper**
- 3   **medium zucchini, cut into ¾-in. cubes**
- 2   **large tomatoes, chopped**
- ¼   **cup water**
- 1   **cup uncooked instant rice**
- 1   **cup shredded cheddar cheese**

1. In a large skillet, crumble beef and cook with onion and pepper over medium-high heat until no longer pink, 5-7 minutes; drain.
2. Stir in seasonings, vegetables, water and rice; bring to a boil. Reduce heat; simmer, covered, until rice is tender, 10-15 minutes. Sprinkle with cheese. Remove from heat; let stand until cheese is melted.

2 cups: 470 cal., 24g fat (11g sat. fat), 98mg chol., 749mg sod., 33g carb. (8g sugars, 4g fiber), 32g pro.

PAN-SEARED SALMON WITH DILL SAUCE

This is one of my husband's favorite recipes. Salmon is a go-to for busy summer nights because it cooks so quickly and goes with so many different flavors. The creamy dill sauce with cucumber tastes light and fresh.
—*Angela Spengler, Niceville, FL*

Takes: 25 min.
Makes: 4 servings

- 1 **Tbsp. canola oil**
- 4 **salmon fillets (6 oz. each)**
- 1 **tsp. Italian seasoning**
- ¼ **tsp. salt**
- ½ **cup reduced-fat plain yogurt**
- ¼ **cup reduced-fat mayonnaise**
- ¼ **cup finely chopped cucumber**
- 1 **tsp. snipped fresh dill**

1. In a large skillet, heat the canola oil over medium-high heat. Sprinkle the salmon with Italian seasoning and salt. Place in skillet, skin side down. Reduce heat to medium. Cook until fish just begins to flake easily with a fork, about 5 minutes on each side.

2. Meanwhile, in a small bowl, combine yogurt, mayonnaise, cucumber and dill. Serve with salmon.

1 salmon fillet with ¼ cup sauce: 366 cal., 25g fat (4g sat. fat), 92mg chol., 349mg sod., 4g carb. (3g sugars, 0 fiber), 31g pro. **Diabetic exchanges:** 4 lean meat, 2½ fat.

Always keep an eye on salmon. If the skillet gets too hot, the outside of the salmon will get too dark before it's cooked through.

LEMON PORK WITH MUSHROOMS

This is a favorite summer dish that you wouldn't guess is good for you. A little squeeze of lemon gives these crispy, seasoned chops a bright boost.
—*Christine Datian, Las Vegas, NV*

Takes: 30 min.
Makes: 4 servings

- 1   **large egg, lightly beaten**
- 1   **cup seasoned bread crumbs**
- 8   **thin boneless pork loin chops (2 oz. each)**
- ¼   **tsp. salt**
- ⅛   **tsp. pepper**
- 1   **Tbsp. olive oil**
- 1   **Tbsp. butter**
- ½   **lb. sliced fresh mushrooms**
- 2   **garlic cloves, minced**
- 2   **tsp. grated lemon zest**
- 1   **Tbsp. lemon juice**
      Lemon wedges, optional

1. Place the beaten egg and bread crumbs in separate shallow bowls. Sprinkle pork chops with salt and pepper; dip in egg, then coat with crumbs, pressing to adhere.
2. In a large skillet, heat oil over medium heat. In batches, cook pork until golden brown, 2-3 minutes per side. Remove from pan; keep warm.

3. Wipe pan clean. In skillet, heat butter over medium heat; saute sliced mushrooms until tender, 2-3 minutes. Stir in minced garlic, lemon zest and lemon juice; cook and stir 1 minute. Serve over pork. If desired, serve with lemon wedges.

1 serving: 331 cal., 15g fat (5g sat. fat), 109mg chol., 601mg sod., 19g carb. (2g sugars, 1g fiber), 28g pro. **Diabetic exchanges:** 3 lean meat, 1½ fat, 1 starch.

Cooking the pork chops in batches keeps them from overcrowding the pan. More space means less steam and a crispier crust.

TEQUILA LIME SHRIMP ZOODLES

If you don't have a spiralizer for the zucchini noodles, thinly julienne the zucchini instead. The tangy dish is a great way to cut carbs without sacrificing flavor.
—*Brigette Schroeder, Yorkville, IL*

Takes: 30 min.
Makes: 4 servings

- 3 **Tbsp. butter, divided**
- 1 **shallot, minced**
- 2 **garlic cloves, minced**
- ¼ **cup tequila**
- 1½ **tsp. grated lime zest**
- 2 **Tbsp. lime juice**
- 1 **Tbsp. olive oil**
- 1 **lb. uncooked shrimp (31-40 per lb.), peeled and deveined**
- 2 **medium zucchini, spiralized (about 6 cups)**
- ½ **tsp. salt**
- ¼ **tsp. pepper**
- ¼ **cup minced fresh parsley Additional grated lime zest**

1. In a large skillet, heat 2 Tbsp. butter over medium heat. Add shallot and garlic; cook 1-2 minutes. Remove from heat; stir in tequila, lime zest and lime juice. Cook over medium heat until the liquid is almost evaporated, 2-3 minutes.
2. Add olive oil and remaining butter; stir in shrimp and zucchini. Sprinkle with salt and pepper. Cook and stir until the shrimp begin to turn pink and zucchini is crisp-tender, 4-5 minutes. Sprinkle with minced parsley and additional lime zest.

1¼ cups: 246 cal., 14g fat (6g sat. fat), 161mg chol., 510mg sod., 7g carb. (3g sugars, 1g fiber), 20g pro. **Diabetic exchanges:** 3 lean meat, 3 fat, 1 vegetable.

SALSA BLACK BEAN BURGERS

Meatless meals are extra tasty when these fast, hearty bean burgers are on the menu. Guacamole and sour cream make them a bit more decadent.
—*Jill Reichardt, St. Louis, MO*

Takes: 30 min.
Makes: 4 servings

- 1 can (15 oz.) black beans, rinsed and drained
- ⅔ cup dry bread crumbs
- 1 small tomato, seeded and finely chopped
- 1 jalapeno pepper, seeded and finely chopped
- 1 large egg
- 1 tsp. minced fresh cilantro
- 1 garlic clove, minced
- 1 Tbsp. olive oil
- 4 whole wheat hamburger buns, split
  Reduced-fat sour cream and guacamole, optional

1. Place black beans in a food processor; cover and process until blended. Transfer to a large bowl. Add the bread crumbs, tomato, jalapeno, egg, cilantro and garlic. Mix until combined. Shape into 4 patties.
2. In a large nonstick skillet, cook patties in oil in batches over medium heat until lightly browned, 4-6 minutes on each side. Serve on buns. If desired, top burgers with sour cream and guacamole.
Note: Wear disposable gloves when cutting hot peppers; the oils can burn skin. Avoid touching your face.

1 burger: 323 cal., 8g fat (1g sat. fat), 53mg chol., 557mg sod., 51g carb. (6g sugars, 9g fiber), 13g pro.

COUSCOUS TABBOULEH WITH FRESH MINT & FETA

Using couscous instead of bulgur for tabbouleh really speeds up the process of making this colorful salad. Other quick-cooking grains such as barley or quinoa work well, too.
—*Elodie Rosinovsky, Brighton, MA*

Takes: 20 min.
Makes: 3 servings

¾ cup water
½ cup uncooked couscous
1 can (15 oz.) garbanzo beans or chickpeas, rinsed and drained
1 large tomato, chopped
½ English cucumber, halved and thinly sliced
3 Tbsp. lemon juice
2 tsp. grated lemon zest
2 tsp. olive oil
2 tsp. minced fresh mint
2 tsp. minced fresh parsley
¼ tsp. salt
⅛ tsp. pepper
¾ cup crumbled feta cheese
Lemon wedges, optional

1. In a small saucepan, bring water to a boil. Stir in couscous. Remove from the heat; cover and let stand for 5-8 minutes or until water is absorbed. Fluff with a fork.
2. In a large bowl, combine the garbanzo beans, tomato and cucumber. In a small bowl, whisk the lemon juice, lemon zest, oil and seasonings. Drizzle over bean mixture. Add the couscous; toss to combine. Serve immediately or refrigerate until chilled. Sprinkle with cheese. If desired, serve with lemon wedges.

1⅔ cups: 362 cal., 11g fat (3g sat. fat), 15mg chol., 657mg sod., 52g carb. (7g sugars, 9g fiber), 15g pro.

Make this refreshing main dish salad gluten-free by replacing the couscous with about 1½ cups cooked quinoa.

TILAPIA WITH JASMINE RICE

This tender, full-flavored tilapia with fragrant jasmine rice is absolutely to die for. And it gets better—each serving has only 9 grams of fat!
—*Shirl Parsons, Cape Carteret, NC*

Takes: 25 min.
Makes: 2 servings

- ¾ cup water
- ½ cup uncooked jasmine rice
- 1½ tsp. butter
- ¼ tsp. ground cumin
- ¼ tsp. seafood seasoning
- ¼ tsp. pepper
- ⅛ tsp. salt
- 2 tilapia fillets (6 oz. each)
- ¼ cup Italian salad dressing

1. In a small saucepan, combine water, rice and butter; bring to a boil. Reduce heat; simmer, covered, until liquid is absorbed and rice is tender, 15-20 minutes.

2. Meanwhile, mix seasonings; sprinkle over tilapia. In a large skillet, heat salad dressing over medium heat until hot. Add fillets; cook until fish just begins to flake easily with a fork, 3-4 minutes per side. Serve with rice.

1 fillet with ¾ cup rice: 412 cal., 9g fat (3g sat. fat), 90mg chol., 615mg sod., 42g carb. (2g sugars, 1g fiber), 36g pro. **Diabetic exchanges:** 4 lean meat, 3 starch, ½ fat.

SAUSAGE COBB SALAD LETTUCE WRAPS

I substituted sausage for the bacon to make a lettuce roll-up your family and friends will adore. It's flavorful, crunchy and pretty on the plate.
—*Devon Delaney, Westport, CT*

Takes: 25 min.
Makes: 6 servings

- ¾ cup ranch salad dressing
- ⅓ cup crumbled blue cheese
- ¼ cup watercress, chopped
- 1 lb. bulk pork sausage
- 2 Tbsp. minced fresh chives
- 6 large iceberg lettuce leaves, edges trimmed
- 1 medium ripe avocado, peeled and diced
- 4 hard-cooked large eggs, chopped
- 1 medium tomato, chopped

1. Mix ranch salad dressing, blue cheese and watercress. In a large skillet, cook and crumble sausage over medium heat until no longer pink, 5-7 minutes; drain. Stir in chives.
2. To serve, spoon sausage into lettuce leaves. Top with avocado, eggs and tomato. Drizzle with dressing mixture.

1 serving: 433 cal., 38g fat (10g sat. fat), 174mg chol., 887mg sod., 7g carb. (3g sugars, 3g fiber), 15g pro.

EASY STUFFED POBLANOS

My partner adores these saucy stuffed peppers—and I love how quickly they come together. Top with low-fat sour cream and your favorite salsa.
—*Jean Erhardt, Portland, OR*

Takes: 25 min.
Makes: 4 servings

- ½ **lb. Italian turkey sausage links, casings removed**
- ½ **lb. lean ground beef (90% lean)**
- 1 **pkg. (8.8 oz.) ready-to-serve Spanish rice**
- 4 **large poblano peppers**
- 1 **cup enchilada sauce**
- ½ **cup shredded Mexican cheese blend**
  Minced fresh cilantro, optional

1. Preheat broiler. In a large skillet, cook turkey sausage and beef over medium heat until no longer pink, 5-7 minutes, breaking into crumbles; drain. Prepare rice according to package directions. Add rice to meat mixture.
2. Cut peppers lengthwise in half; remove seeds. Place on a foil-lined 15x10x1-in. baking pan, cut side down. Broil 4 in. from heat until skins blister, about 5 minutes. With tongs, turn peppers.
3. Fill peppers with turkey mixture; top with enchilada sauce and sprinkle with cheese. Broil until the cheese is melted, 1-2 minutes longer. If desired, top with cilantro.

2 stuffed pepper halves: 312 cal., 13g fat (4g sat. fat), 63mg chol., 1039mg sod., 27g carb. (5g sugars, 2g fiber), 22g pro.

BLACK BEAN BULGUR SALAD

The only cooking in this easy bulgur salad is heating the broth in the microwave. You can adapt the recipe to your preference; if you want to add chopped, cooked chicken, use chicken broth in place of vegetable broth.
—*Carole Resnick, Cleveland, OH*

Takes: 30 min.
Makes: 4 servings

- 1 **cup bulgur**
- 2 **cups vegetable broth**
- ¼ **cup orange juice**
- ¼ **cup lime juice**
- 1 **jalapeno pepper, seeded and minced**
- 2 **Tbsp. olive oil**
- ¼ **tsp. ground cumin**
- 1 **cup shredded carrots**
- 3 **Tbsp. minced fresh cilantro**
- 1 **can (15 oz.) black beans, rinsed and drained**
- 1 **cup frozen corn, thawed**
- ¾ **cup shredded Monterey Jack cheese**
  Sliced jalapeno pepper, optional

1. Place bulgur and vegetable broth in a small saucepan; bring to a boil. Reduce the heat; simmer, covered, until tender, 12-15 minutes. Transfer to a large bowl; cool slightly.
2. For dressing, whisk together citrus juices, minced jalapeno, olive oil and cumin. Add ⅓ cup of the dressing to bulgur; stir in the carrots and cilantro.
3. To serve, divide bulgur mixture among 4 bowls. Top with beans, corn, cheese and, if desired, sliced jalapeno. Drizzle with the remaining dressing.

1 serving: 402 cal., 14g fat (5g sat. fat), 19mg chol., 688mg sod., 56g carb. (6g sugars, 10g fiber), 16g pro.

Bulgur is sometimes called cracked wheat. It's a whole grain that's been boiled, dried and ground. Since it's been precooked, it cooks up a bit faster than other whole grains.

SUMMER'S BEST

INSTANT POT®
& AIR-FRYER
RECIPES

Take advantage of your Instant Pot and air fryer to serve classic summer dishes with ease. These popular devices get you out of the kitchen and into summertime fun while cooking up the mouthwatering specialties everyone craves.

PRESSURE-COOKER TIPS

Using a multipurpose cooker requires some reading and practice, so be patient. It will definitely be worth it in the end. Keep these hints in mind when using your cooker.

- Read the instruction manual that came with your electric pressure cooker before you make anything. Not all brands and models are the same, so get to know your pot!

- For food safety and efficiency, the total amount of food and liquid should never exceed the maximum level indicated in the pot.

- Make sure the pressure-release valve is closed before you start cooking. Even the pros at the *Taste of Home* Test Kitchen have forgotten to close the valve and returned to see the pot venting instead of building pressure.

- The pressure-release valve should feel loose to the touch. The valve may release a little bit of steam while the food cooks.

- The power cord on some models is removable, which makes the appliance easier to store. If you plug it in and the light doesn't go on, check the cord. Is it attached securely? When the cooker isn't in use, consider storing the cord in the inner pot.

- After each use, remove and clean the sealing ring, pressure-release valve and anti-block shield.

- If your pot smells like food even after cleaning, put the sealing ring through the dishwasher. If that doesn't work, try steam-cleaning: Pour 2 cups water and 1 tablespoon lemon zest into the inner pot. Place the lid on and run the steam program for 2 minutes. Carefully remove the sealing ring and let it air dry.

HERE'S HOW TO ADAPT YOUR OWN RECIPES:

Recipes written specifically for an Instant Pot will help you get the hang of using a multipurpose cooker. Once you are comfortable with the process, you may want to convert some of your other recipes. Making the favorites you've always enjoyed, but getting out of the kitchen faster—that's a win-win! These tips will help.

PASTA.
For al dente pasta, cook for half the boiling time recommended on the package.

RICE
To substitute brown rice for white rice, increase the liquid by ¼ cup and increase the cook time by 5 minutes.

GRAVY
Increase the amount of cornstarch or flour a bit, because liquid won't evaporate in the cooker as with traditional cooking methods.

PRESSURE COOKER PARTS
A. Appliance exterior
B. Inner pot
C. Lid
D. Sealing ring
E. Anti-block shield
F. Condensation cup
G. Trivet

AIR-FRYER TIPS

Serve up crispy fries and onion rings alongside your grilled hamburgers this summer without the unpleasant mess or excess fat of deep-frying! Here's how to get started with an air fryer.

An air fryer is basically a countertop convection oven. Because of its small size, this appliance heats up fast, helping get you out of the kitchen quick.

The main unit holds a heating coil and fan, and you put food in the removable fryer basket below. Hot air rushes down and around the food in the basket. This rapid circulation makes the food crisp much like deep-frying, but with little or no added cooking oil. Keep these points in mind when learning to cook with an air fryer.

- Some air fryers have digital screens with the setting options; others have simple timer and temperature dials. Choose the style you are most comfortable using.

- Some models can perform functions besides air-frying. These are often more expensive and can be larger; choose the model that best suits your needs.

- Many models are sized to cook for one or two people. Some have a larger capacity, allowing you to cook for up to four people. Purchase the model that works best for your household.

- With a smaller appliance, you may have to cook in batches, so be sure to account for that in your planning.

- Read the instruction manual before getting started.

- Ensure all packing material, tape, etc., has been removed from both outside and inside the appliance.

- Look up into the heating element to make sure no stray material is in the coil or fan, which could cause the appliance to smoke.

- Thoroughly wipe down the heating coil before the first use to remove any residue.

AIR-FRYER TEMPERATURE

The *Taste of Home* Test Kitchen tested recipes using six different air-fryer models. Testing revealed that cook times can vary dramatically across different brands. To accommodate this variance, the recipes in this chapter have a wider than normal range of suggested cook times. Check the food at the first time listed in the recipe and adjust as needed. Follow these tips for doneness when using your air fryer:

- Verify the temperature, as it will vary among models, just as it does with ovens. Test your air fryer before using to see if it runs above or below the selected temperature setting.

- Do not overcrowd food in the basket. Cook food in a single layer, with room for air to circulate. Don't forget to flip, rotate or shake the basket's contents halfway through cooking.

- Use a thermometer when cooking meat. Air-fried meats brown nicely and may look done before reaching an appropriate temperature on the inside.

AIR-FRYER PARTS

A. Heating coil (inside unit)
B. Fan (inside unit)
C. Basket
D. Maximum fill line
E. Temperature setting
F. Time setting
G. Power
H. Basket release

PRESSURE-COOKER CINNAMON BLUEBERRY FRENCH TOAST

Fresh blueberries make this sunny breakfast starter healthy and hearty, and the all-in-one cooker makes it a snap! That's the best way to describe this satisfying breakfast. It's one dish worth jumping out of bed for.
—*Angela Lively, Conroe, TX*

Prep: 15 min. + standing
Cook: 20 min. + releasing
Makes: 4 servings

  2 **large eggs**
1⅓ **cups 2% milk**
  3 **Tbsp. sugar**
  1 **tsp. ground cinnamon**
  1 **tsp. vanilla extract**
  ¼ **tsp. salt**
  6 **cups cubed French bread (about 6 oz.)**
  ¾ **cup fresh or frozen blueberries**
     Maple syrup

1. Whisk together the first 6 ingredients. Arrange half the bread in a greased 1½-qt. baking dish. Top with half the blueberries and half the milk mixture. Repeat layers.

2. Place trivet insert and 1 cup water in a 6-qt. electric pressure cooker. Cover baking dish with foil. Fold an 18x12-in. piece of foil lengthwise into thirds, making a sling. Use the sling to lower the dish onto the trivet.

3. Lock lid; close pressure-release valve. Adjust to pressure-cook on high for 20 minutes. Let pressure release naturally for 10 minutes; quick-release any remaining pressure. Using foil sling, carefully remove baking dish. Let stand 10 minutes. Serve with maple syrup.

1 serving: 273 cal., 6g fat (2g sat. fat), 100mg chol., 479mg sod., 44g carb. (19g sugars, 1g fiber), 11g pro.

AIR-FRYER NASHVILLE HOT CHICKEN

I live in Tennessee and absolutely love our famous Nashville hot chicken. To make cooking it easier, I thought I'd try air-frying. I'm so glad I did—this is almost better than the original.
—*April Lane, Greeneville, TN*

Prep: 30 min.
Cook: 10 min./batch
Makes: 6 servings

  2 **Tbsp. dill pickle juice, divided**
  2 **Tbsp. hot pepper sauce, divided**
  2 **lbs. chicken tenderloins**
  1 **cup all-purpose flour**
  1 **tsp. salt, divided**
  ½ **tsp. pepper**
  1 **large egg**
  ½ **cup buttermilk**
  ½ **cup olive oil**
  2 **Tbsp. cayenne pepper**
  2 **Tbsp. dark brown sugar**
  1 **tsp. paprika**
  1 **tsp. chili powder**
  ½ **tsp. garlic powder**
     Cooking spray
     Dill pickle slices

1. In a bowl or shallow dish, combine 1 Tbsp. pickle juice, 1 Tbsp. hot sauce and ½ tsp. salt. Add chicken and turn to coat. Refrigerate, covered, at least 1 hour. Drain, discarding any marinade.

2. Preheat air fryer to 375°. In a shallow bowl, mix flour, ½ tsp. salt and pepper. In another shallow bowl, whisk the egg, buttermilk, remaining 1 Tbsp. pickle juice and 1 Tbsp. hot sauce. Dip chicken in flour to coat both sides; shake off excess. Dip in egg mixture, then again in flour mixture.

3. In batches, arrange chicken in a single layer in generously greased air-fryer basket; spritz chicken with cooking spray. Cook until golden brown, 5-6 minutes. Turn and spritz with cooking spray. Cook until golden brown, 5-6 minutes longer.

4. Whisk together remaining ingredients; pour over hot chicken. Serve with pickles.

5 oz. cooked chicken: 413 cal., 21g fat (3g sat. fat), 96mg chol., 170mg sod., 20g carb. (5g sugars, 1g fiber), 39g pro.

PRESSURE-COOKER PORK TACOS WITH MANGO SALSA

To me, warm pork wrapped in a tortilla is a combination born in culinary heaven.
—*Amber Massey, Argyle, TX*

Prep: 25 min.
Cook: 5 min.
Makes: 12 servings

- 2 Tbsp. white vinegar
- 2 Tbsp. lime juice
- 3 cups cubed fresh pineapple
- 1 small red onion, coarsely chopped
- 3 Tbsp. chili powder
- 2 chipotle peppers in adobo sauce
- 2 tsp. ground cumin
- 1½ tsp. salt
- ½ tsp. pepper
- 1 bottle (12 oz.) dark Mexican beer
- 3 lbs. pork tenderloin, cut into 1-in. cubes
- ¼ cup chopped fresh cilantro
- 1 jar (16 oz.) mango salsa
- 24 corn tortillas (6 in.), warmed
Optional toppings: Cubed fresh pineapple, cubed avocado and queso fresco

1. Puree the first 9 ingredients in blender; stir in beer. In a 6-qt. electric pressure cooker, combine pork and pineapple mixture. Lock lid; close pressure-release valve. Adjust to pressure-cook on high for 3 minutes. Quick-release pressure. A thermometer inserted into pork should read at least 145°. Stir to break up pork.
2. Stir cilantro into salsa. Using a slotted spoon, serve pork mixture in tortillas; add salsa and toppings as desired.
Freeze option: Freeze cooled meat mixture and cooking juices in freezer containers. To use, partially thaw in refrigerator overnight. Heat through in a saucepan, stirring occasionally.

2 tacos: 284 cal., 6g fat (2g sat. fat), 64mg chol., 678mg sod., 30g carb. (5g sugars, 3g fiber), 26g pro.

PRESSURE-COOKER CAJUN-STYLE BEANS & SAUSAGE

Beans and rice make the perfect meal because they're well-balanced, an excellent source of protein and easy to prepare. They also make a worthy side dish with grilled entrees. Sausage adds full flavor to the recipe, and traditional pork sausage lovers won't even notice the switch to chicken sausage.
—*Robin Haas, Cranston, RI*

Prep: 25 min.
Cook: 5 min. + releasing
Makes: 8 servings

1 pkg. (12 oz.) fully cooked spicy chicken sausage links, halved lengthwise and cut into ½-in. slices
¾ cup reduced-sodium chicken broth
2 cans (16 oz. each) red beans, rinsed and drained
2 cans (14½ oz. each) diced tomatoes, undrained
3 medium carrots, chopped
1 large onion, chopped
1 large green pepper, chopped
½ cup chopped roasted sweet red peppers
3 garlic cloves, minced
1 tsp. Cajun seasoning
1 tsp. dried oregano
½ tsp. dried thyme
½ tsp. pepper
5⅓ cups cooked brown rice

1. Select saute or browning setting on a 6-qt. electric pressure cooker. Adjust for medium heat; brown sausage. Add broth and cook for 1 minute, stirring to loosen the browned bits. Press cancel. Stir in beans, tomatoes, vegetables, garlic and seasonings.
2. Lock lid; close pressure-release valve. Adjust to pressure-cook for 5 minutes on high. Let pressure release naturally for 10 minutes and quick-release any remaining pressure. Serve with rice.

Freeze option: Freeze the cooled sausage mixture in freezer containers. To use, partially thaw in refrigerator overnight. Microwave, covered, on high in a microwave-safe dish until heated through, stirring gently and adding a little water if necessary.

1 cup sausage and bean mixture with ⅔ cup rice: 377 cal., 5g fat (1g sat. fat), 33mg chol., 826mg sod., 63g carb. (7g sugars, 10g fiber), 18g pro.

The sealing ring on your cooker can absorb food odors, so you'll want to clean it after every use. Wash in the dishwasher or by hand. Ensure it's completely dry before placing in the lid.

PRESSURE-COOKER SPICY SAUSAGE & BLUE CHEESE PEPPERS

I had an old pressure cooker I inherited from my aunt before I was married many years ago. This was a recipe I had back then and adapted it to my Instant Pot® with a few changes. A quick and easy as well as delicious meal.
—*Joan Hallford, North Richland Hills, TX*

Prep: 35 min.
Cook: 10 min.
Makes: 4 servings

- 4 large sweet bell peppers
- 1 lb. bulk spicy pork sausage
- 4 green onions, sliced
- 1 garlic clove, minced
- 1 cup cooked brown rice
- ⅓ cup pasta sauce
- 1 tsp. dried oregano
- ¼ tsp. salt
- ¼ tsp. pepper
- 1 cup crumbled blue cheese
- 1 cup beef broth

1. Cut tops from peppers and remove seeds. Finely chop enough tops to measure ¼ cup for filling.

2. Select saute or browning setting on a 6-qt. electric pressure cooker; adjust for medium heat. Cook sausage, green onions, chopped peppers and garlic until sausage is no longer pink and vegetables are tender, 6-8 minutes, breaking up sausage into crumbles; drain. Press cancel.

3. Return to pressure cooker. Stir in rice, pasta sauce, oregano, salt and pepper. Stir in blue cheese. Fill peppers with sausage mixture. Wipe the pressure cooker clean.

4. Place trivet insert and broth in pressure cooker; place peppers on trivet. Lock lid; close pressure-release valve. Adjust to pressure-cook on high for 7 minutes. Quick-release pressure.

1 stuffed pepper: 509 cal., 35g fat (14g sat. fat), 87mg chol., 1,336mg sod., 27g carb. (6g sugars, 5g fiber), 23g pro.

PRESSURE-COOKER PORK CHOPS

Everyone will enjoy these fork-tender pork chops with a light gravy. Serve with a green vegetable or garden-fresh salad.
—*Sue Bingham, Madisonville, TN*

Prep: 15 min.
Cook: 5 min.
Makes: 4 servings

- ½ cup all-purpose flour, divided
- ½ tsp. ground mustard
- ½ tsp. garlic pepper blend
- ¼ tsp. seasoned salt
- 4 boneless pork loin chops (4 oz. each)
- 2 Tbsp. canola oil
- 1 can (14½ oz.) chicken broth, divided

1. In a shallow bowl, mix ¼ cup flour, mustard, garlic pepper and seasoned salt. Add pork chops, 1 at a time, and toss to coat; shake off excess.
2. Select saute or browning setting on a 6-qt. electric pressure cooker. Adjust for medium heat; add oil. When oil is hot, brown pork in batches. Add 1½ cups broth to pressure cooker. Cook for 30 seconds, stirring to loosen browned bits from pan. Press cancel. Return all to pressure cooker.
3. Lock the lid and close pressure-release valve. Adjust to pressure-cook on high for 3 minutes. Quick-release pressure. A thermometer inserted in pork should read at least 145°. Remove pork chops to a serving plate and keep warm.
4. In a small bowl, mix the remaining ¼ cup flour and ¼ cup broth until smooth; stir into pressure cooker. Select saute setting and adjust for low heat. Simmer, stirring constantly, until thickened, 1-2 minutes. Serve with pork.

1 pork chop with ⅓ cup gravy: 257 cal., 14g fat (3g sat. fat), 57mg chol., 606mg sod., 8g carb. (0g sugars, 0g fiber), 23g pro. **Diabetic exchanges:** 3 lean meat, 1.5 fat.

PRESSURE-COOKED MESQUITE RIBS

When we don't feel like heating up the grill, these tangy ribs give us that same smoky barbecue taste we love. They're so simple, and fall-off-the-bone delicious, too!
—*Sue Evans, Marquette, MI*

Prep: 10 min. + broiling
Cook: 35 min. + releasing
Makes: 8 servings

1   cup water
2   Tbsp. cider vinegar
1   Tbsp. soy sauce
4   lbs. pork baby back ribs, cut into serving-size portions
2   Tbsp. mesquite seasoning
¾   cup barbecue sauce, divided

1. Combine water, vinegar and soy sauce in a 6-qt. electric pressure cooker. Rub ribs with mesquite seasoning; add to pressure cooker. Lock lid; close pressure-release valve. Adjust to pressure-cook on high for 35 minutes. Let pressure release naturally for 10 minutes, then quick-release any remaining pressure.
2. Remove ribs to a foil-lined baking sheet. Preheat broiler. Brush the ribs with half the barbecue sauce. Broil 4-6 in. from heat until glazed. Brush with the remaining sauce.

1 serving: 329 cal., 21g fat (8g sat. fat), 81mg chol., 678mg sod., 10g carb. (8g sugars, 0 fiber), 23g pro.

AIR-FRYER GREEN TOMATO BLT

I have used this frying method with eggplant slices for years and decided to try it for my green tomatoes. It worked! Now my family loves these crispy-juicy slices in BLTs.
—*Jolene Martinelli, Fremont, NH*

Prep: 20 min.
Cook: 10 min./batch
Makes: 4 servings

    Cooking spray
2   medium green tomatoes (about 10 oz.)
½   tsp. salt
¼   tsp. pepper
1   large egg, beaten
¼   cup all-purpose flour
1   cup panko bread crumbs
½   cup reduced-fat mayonnaise
2   green onions, finely chopped
1   tsp. snipped fresh dill or ¼ tsp. dill weed
8   slices whole wheat bread, toasted
8   cooked center-cut bacon strips
4   Bibb or Boston lettuce leaves

1. Preheat air fryer to 350°. Spritz basket with cooking spray. Cut tomato into 8 slices, each about ¼ in. thick. Sprinkle the tomato slices with salt and pepper. Place egg, flour and bread crumbs in separate shallow bowls. Dip tomato slices in flour, shaking off excess, then dip into egg, and finally into bread crumb mixture, patting to help adhere.
2. Working in batches as needed, place tomato slices in air-fryer basket in a single layer; spritz with cooking spray. Cook until golden brown, 8-12 minutes, turning halfway and spritzing with additional cooking spray. Remove and keep warm; repeat with the remaining tomato slices.

3. Meanwhile, mix mayonnaise, green onions and dill. Layer each of 4 slices of bread with 2 bacon strips, 1 lettuce leaf and 2 tomato slices. Spread mayonnaise mixture over remaining slices of bread; place over top. Serve immediately.

1 sandwich: 390 cal., 17g fat (3g sat. fat), 45mg chol., 1006mg sod., 45g carb. (7g sugars, 5g fiber), 16g pro.

PRESSURE-COOKER CILANTRO-LIME CHICKEN WITH SCOOPS

I came up with this recipe when I was preparing for a large party and wanted a healthy Tex-Mex appetizer. The dish can be made ahead of time, and leftovers make for a tasty next-day burrito filling.
—Lori Terry, Chicago, IL

Prep: 15 min.
Cook: 10 min.
Makes: 16 servings

- 1 lb. boneless skinless chicken breasts
- ½ cup reduced-sodium chicken broth
- 2 Tbsp. lime juice
- 2 tsp. chili powder
- 1½ cups frozen petite corn (about 5 oz.), thawed
- 1½ cups chunky salsa
- 1½ cups finely shredded cheddar cheese
- 1 medium sweet red pepper, finely chopped
- 4 green onions, thinly sliced
  Baked tortilla chip scoops
  Minced fresh cilantro

1. Place chicken in a 6-qt. electric pressure cooker; add the broth, lime juice and chili powder. Lock lid; close pressure-release valve. Adjust to pressure-cook on high for 7 minutes, then quick-release pressure. A thermometer inserted in chicken should read at least 165°.
2. Remove chicken; discard cooking juices. Shred chicken with 2 forks and return to pressure cooker. Select saute setting and adjust for low heat. Add corn and salsa; cook and stir until heated through, about 5 minutes.
3. Transfer to a large bowl; stir in cheese, red pepper and green onions. Serve with tortilla scoops; sprinkle with cilantro.

¼ cup chicken mixture: 97 cal., 4g fat (2g sat. fat), 26mg chol., 202mg sod., 6g carb. (2g sugars, 1g fiber), 9g pro.
Diabetic exchanges: 1 medium-fat meat.

AIR-FRYER HERB & CHEESE-STUFFED BURGERS

Tired of the same old ground beef burgers? These quick air fryer hamburgers, with their creamy cheese filling, will wake up your taste buds on busy summer nights.
—*Sherri Cox, Lucasville, OH*

Prep: 20 min.
Cook: 15 min./batch
Makes: 4 servings

2	green onions, thinly sliced
2	Tbsp. minced fresh parsley
4	tsp. Dijon mustard, divided
3	Tbsp. dry bread crumbs
2	Tbsp. ketchup
½	tsp. salt
½	tsp. dried rosemary, crushed
¼	tsp. dried sage leaves
1	lb. lean ground beef (90% lean)
2	oz. cheddar cheese, sliced
4	hamburger buns, split
	Optional toppings: Lettuce leaves, tomato slices and mayonnaise

1. Preheat air fryer to 375°. In a small bowl, combine green onions, parsley and 2 tsp. mustard. In another bowl, mix bread crumbs, ketchup, seasonings and remaining 2 tsp. mustard. Add beef to bread crumb mixture; mix lightly but thoroughly.

2. Shape mixture into 8 thin patties. Place sliced cheese in center of 4 patties; spoon green onion mixture over cheese. Top with remaining patties, pressing edges together firmly, taking care to seal completely.

3. Place burgers in a single layer in air-fryer basket. Working in batches as needed, air-fry for 8 minutes; flip and continue cooking until a thermometer reads 160°, 6-8 minutes longer. Serve burgers on buns, with toppings if desired.

1 burger: 369 cal., 14g fat (6g sat. fat), 79mg chol., 850mg sod., 29g carb. (6g sugars, 1g fiber), 29g pro.

AIR-FRYER FISH & FRIES

Looking for easy air-fryer recipes? Try these simple fish and chips. The fish fillets have a fuss-free coating that's healthier but just as crunchy and golden as the deep-fried kind. Simply seasoned, the crispy fries are perfect on the side.

—*Janice Mitchell, Aurora, CO*

Prep: 15 min.
Cook: 25 min.
Makes: 4 servings

- 1 lb. potatoes (about 2 medium)
- 2 Tbsp. olive oil
- ¼ tsp. pepper
- ¼ tsp. salt

FISH
- ⅓ cup all-purpose flour
- ¼ tsp. pepper
- 1 large egg
- 2 Tbsp. water
- ⅔ cup crushed cornflakes
- 1 Tbsp. grated Parmesan cheese
- ⅛ tsp. cayenne pepper
- ¼ tsp. salt
- 1 lb. haddock or cod fillets
    Tartar sauce, optional

1. Preheat air fryer to 400°. Peel and cut potatoes lengthwise into ½-in.-thick slices; cut slices into ½-in.-thick sticks.

2. In a large bowl, toss potatoes with oil, pepper and salt. Working in batches as needed, place potatoes in a single layer in air-fryer basket; cook until just tender, 5-10 minutes Toss potatoes in basket to redistribute; continue to cook until lightly browned and crisp, 5-10 minutes longer.

3. Meanwhile, in a shallow bowl, mix flour and pepper. In another shallow bowl, whisk egg with water. In a third bowl, toss crushed cornflakes with cheese and cayenne. Sprinkle fish with salt; dip into flour mixture to coat both sides; shake off excess. Dip in egg mixture, then in cornflake mixture, patting to help coating adhere.

4. Remove fries from basket; keep warm. Place fish in a single layer in air-fryer basket. Cook until fish is lightly browned and just beginning to flake easily with a fork, turning halfway through cooking, 8-10 minutes. Do not overcook. Return fries to basket to heat through. Serve immediately. If desired, serve with tartar sauce.

1 serving: 312 cal., 9g fat (2g sat. fat), 85mg chol., 503mg sod., 35g carb. (3g sugars, 1g fiber), 23g pro. **Diabetic exchanges:** 3 lean meat, 2 starch, 2 fat.

PRESSURE-COOKER CAROLINA-STYLE VINEGAR BBQ CHICKEN

I live in Georgia but I appreciate the tangy, sweet and slightly spicy taste of Carolina vinegar chicken.
—Ramona Parris, Canton, GA

Takes: 25 min.
Makes: 6 servings

- 2 cups water
- 1 cup white vinegar
- ¼ cup sugar
- 1 Tbsp. reduced-sodium chicken base
- 1 tsp. crushed red pepper flakes
- ¾ tsp. salt
- 1½ lbs. boneless skinless chicken breasts
- 6 whole wheat hamburger buns, split, optional

1. In a 6-qt. electric pressure cooker, mix the first 6 ingredients; add chicken. Lock lid; close pressure-release valve. Adjust to pressure-cook on high for 5 minutes.
2. Allow pressure to naturally release for 8 minutes. Quick-release remaining pressure.
3. Remove chicken; cool slightly. Reserve 1 cup cooking juices and discard remaining juices. Shred chicken with 2 forks. Combine with reserved juices. If desired, serve chicken mixture on buns.

½ cup: 135 cal., 3g fat (1g sat. fat), 63mg chol., 228mg sod., 3g carb. (3g sugars, 0 fiber), 23g pro. **Diabetic exchanges:** 3 lean meat.

PRESSURE-COOKER SUMMER SQUASH

We love squash, but I got tired of fixing plain old squash and cheese. I decided to jazz it up a bit. This was a huge hit with the family.
—*Joan Hallford, North Richland Hills, TX*

Prep: 20 min.
Cook: 5 min.
Makes: 8 servings

  1 **lb. medium yellow summer squash**
  1 **lb. medium zucchini**
  2 **medium tomatoes, chopped**
  1 **cup vegetable broth**
  ¼ **cup thinly sliced green onions**
  ½ **tsp. salt**
  ¼ **tsp. pepper**
 1½ **cups Caesar salad croutons, coarsely crushed**
  ½ **cup shredded cheddar cheese**
  4 **bacon strips, cooked and crumbled**

1. Cut squash into ¼-in.-thick slices; place in a 6-qt. electric pressure cooker. Add tomatoes, broth, green onions, salt and pepper. Lock lid; close pressure-release valve. Adjust to pressure-cook on high for 1 minute. Quick-release pressure. Remove squash with a slotted spoon.
2. To serve, top with crushed croutons, cheese and bacon.

¾ cup: 111 cal., 6g fat (2g sat. fat), 12mg chol., 442mg sod., 10g carb. (4g sugars, 1g fiber), 6g pro. **Diabetic exchanges:** 1 vegetable, 1 fat.

PRESSURE-COOKER CUBAN PULLED PORK SANDWICHES

I lived in Florida for a while and loved the pork served there, so I went about making it for myself! The flavorful meat makes amazing Cuban sandwiches, but you can use it in traditional pulled pork sandwiches and tacos, too.
—*Lacie Griffin, Austin, TX*

Prep: 20 min.
Cook: 25 min. + releasing
Makes: 16 servings

  1 **boneless pork shoulder butt roast (4 to 5 lbs.)**
  2 **tsp. salt**
  2 **tsp. pepper**
  1 **Tbsp. olive oil**
  1 **cup orange juice**
  ½ **cup lime juice**
 12 **garlic cloves, minced**
  2 **Tbsp. spiced rum, optional**
  2 **Tbsp. ground coriander**
  2 **tsp. white pepper**
  1 **tsp. cayenne pepper**

SANDWICHES
  2 **loaves (1 lb. each) French bread**
    Yellow mustard, optional
 16 **dill pickle slices**
 1½ **lbs. thinly sliced deli ham**
 1½ **lbs. Swiss cheese, sliced**

1. Cut pork into 2-in.-thick pieces; season with salt and pepper. Select saute setting on a 6-qt. electric pressure cooker; adjust for medium heat. Add olive oil; working in batches, brown pork on all sides. Remove from cooker.
2. Add orange and lime juices, stirring to scrape browned bits from bottom of cooker. Add garlic, rum if desired, coriander, white pepper and cayenne pepper. Return pork and any collected juices to cooker. Lock lid; close pressure-release valve. Adjust to pressure-cook on high for 25 minutes.

3. Naturally release pressure for 10 minutes, then quick-release any remaining pressure. Remove roast; when cool enough to handle, shred with 2 forks. Remove 1 cup cooking liquid from pressure cooker; add to pork and toss together.
4. Cut each loaf of bread in half lengthwise. If desired, spread mustard over cut sides of bread. Layer bottom halves of bread with pickles, pork, ham and cheese. Replace tops. Cut each loaf into 8 slices.

1 sandwich: 573 cal., 28g fat (12g sat. fat), 126mg chol., 1240mg sod., 35g carb. (5g sugars, 2g fiber), 45g pro.

Make Cuban wraps by wrapping meat and toppings in a tortilla.

PRESSURE-COOKER COLA BBQ CHICKEN

This recipe is rich with sweet smoky deliciousness. The meat is juicy and tender, and I like to add a few tasty toppings—sliced dill pickles and a slice of pepper jack cheese—for a boost of flavor. This can be cooked in the slow cooker on low for 8 hours.
—*Ashley Lecker, Green Bay, WI*

Prep: 10 min.
Cook: 10 min.
Makes: 14 servings

- 1   bottle (18 oz.) barbecue sauce
- 1   cup cola
- 2   Tbsp. cider vinegar
- 1   tsp. garlic powder
- 1   tsp. onion powder
- 1   tsp. salt
- ½   tsp. pepper
- 2½ lbs. boneless skinless chicken breasts
- 14 hamburger buns, split
- 14 slices pepper jack cheese
- 1   cup sliced sweet pickles

1. Place the first 7 ingredients in a 6-qt. electric pressure cooker; add the chicken. Lock the lid and close pressure-release valve. Adjust to pressure-cook on high for 7 minutes. Quick-release pressure. Press cancel.

2. Remove chicken; cool slightly. Reserve 2 cups cooking juices; discard remaining juices. Shred chicken with 2 forks. Combine with reserved juices. Serve on buns with cheese and pickles.

Freeze option: Freeze cooled meat mixture in freezer containers. To use, partially thaw in refrigerator overnight. Heat through in a saucepan, stirring occasionally and adding a little water if necessary.

1 sandwich: 367 cal., 10g fat (5g sat. fat), 66mg chol., 971mg sod., 41g carb. (18g sugars, 1g fiber), 26g pro.

PRESSURE-COOKER BEEF BURRITOS WITH GREEN CHILES

Here's a favorite that gets mouths watering with its aroma! Hearty and flavorful, it's quick comfort food when I want to get out of the kitchen and enjoy summer.
—*Sally Pahler, Palisade, CO*

Prep: 20 min.
Cook: 1 hour 20 min. + releasing
Makes: 14 servings

  4 cans (7 oz. each) whole
      green chiles, undrained
  1 can (28 oz.) diced
      tomatoes, undrained
  1 large onion, diced
  1 boneless beef chuck roast (4 lbs.)
  2 garlic cloves, minced
  1 tsp. salt
  2 tsp. ground cumin
  1 tsp. cayenne pepper
 14 whole wheat tortillas
      (8 in.), warmed
      Optional toppings: Shredded
      cheddar cheese, salsa, sour cream,
      sliced ripe olives

1. Drain chiles, reserving liquid. Coarsely chop chiles; place in a 6-qt. electric pressure cooker. Add tomatoes, onion and reserved drained liquid. Cut roast in half. Combine garlic, salt, cumin and cayenne; rub over roast. Place in pressure cooker. Lock lid; close pressure-release valve. Adjust to pressure-cook on high for 80 minutes. Let pressure release naturally for 10 minutes; quick-release any remaining pressure. A thermometer inserted in beef should read at least 165°.
2. Remove roast; shred with 2 forks. Return to pressure cooker; heat through. Using a slotted spoon, serve in tortillas with toppings if desired.

1 burrito: 355 cal., 13g fat (5g sat. fat), 84mg chol., 499mg sod., 28g carb. (4g sugars, 4g fiber), 30g pro. **Diabetic exchanges:** 1 starch, 4 lean meat.

133

PRESSURE-COOKER TEQUILA POACHED PEARS

Tequila may seem an unusual ingredient in this dessert, but give it a try! The fresh pears and mint make this deliciously refreshing. Bring out this creative sweet when you want to impress your guests
—*Nancy Heishman, Las Vegas, NV*

Prep: 20 min. + simmering
Cook: 5 min.
Makes: 8 servings

- 2 cups water
- 1 can (11.3 oz.) pear nectar
- 1 cup tequila
- ½ cup sugar
- 2 Tbsp. lime juice
- 2 tsp. grated lime zest
- 1 cinnamon stick (3 in.)
- ¼ tsp. ground nutmeg
- 8 whole Anjou pears, peeled
      Sweetened whipped cream, optional
      Fresh mint leaves

1. Select saute setting on a 6-qt. pressure cooker and adjust for low heat. Add the first 8 ingredients; cook and stir until sugar is dissolved, about 3 minutes. Press cancel. Add pears. Lock lid; close pressure-release valve. Adjust to pressure-cook on high for 3 minutes. Quick-release pressure. Remove pears and keep warm.
2. Reserve 3 cups cooking juices; discard remaining juices and cinnamon stick. Return the reserved juices to the pressure cooker. Select saute setting and adjust for medium heat. Simmer, uncovered, until the liquid is reduced to 1 cup, about 30 minutes, stirring occasionally.
3. Halve pears lengthwise and core. Serve with sauce, whipped cream if desired, and mint leaves.

1 pear with 2 tablespoons sauce: 155 cal., 0g fat (0g sat. fat), 0mg chol., 3mg sod., 40g carb. (30g sugars, 6g fiber), 1g pro.

AIR-FRYER SOUTHERN-STYLE CHICKEN

I call this "America's Best-Loved Air-Fryer Chicken." The secret is in the breading, which makes the chicken super moist, flavorful and golden brown.
—*Elaina Morgan, Rickman, TN*

Prep: 15 min.
Cook: 20 min./batch
Makes: 6 servings

Cooking spray
2 cups crushed Ritz crackers (about 50)
1 Tbsp. minced fresh parsley
1 tsp. garlic salt
1 tsp. paprika
½ tsp. pepper
¼ tsp. ground cumin
¼ tsp. rubbed sage
1 large egg, beaten
1 broiler/fryer chicken (3 to 4 lbs.), cut up

1. Preheat air fryer to 375°. Spritz air-fryer basket with cooking spray.
2. In a bowl, mix the next 7 ingredients. Place egg in a separate shallow bowl. Dip chicken in egg, then in cracker mixture, patting to help coating adhere. Place a few pieces of chicken in a single layer in the prepared basket, spritz with additional cooking spray.
3. Cook 10 minutes. Turn the chicken and spritz with additional cooking spray; cook until chicken is golden brown and juices run clear, 10-20 minutes longer. Repeat with the remaining chicken.

5 oz. cooked chicken: 410 cal., 23g fat (6g sat. fat), 135mg chol., 460mg sod., 13g carb. (2g sugars, 1g fiber), 36g pro.

AIR-FRYER SHRIMP PO'BOYS

My husband loves crispy coconut shrimp and po'boys, so I combined them with a spicy remoulade and voila! This air-fryer shrimp is a big hit with family and friends and is frequently requested. For catfish po'boys, substitute cornmeal for the coconut and add a few minutes to the cooking time.
—*Marla Clark, Albuquerque, NM*

Prep: 35 min.
Cook: 10 min./batch
Makes: 4 servings

- ½ cup mayonnaise
- 1 Tbsp. Creole mustard
- 1 Tbsp. chopped cornichons or dill pickles
- 1 Tbsp. minced shallot
- 1½ tsp. lemon juice
- ⅛ tsp. cayenne pepper
- COCONUT SHRIMP
- 1 cup all-purpose flour
- 1 tsp. herbes de Provence
- ½ tsp. sea salt
- ½ tsp. garlic powder
- ½ tsp. pepper
- ¼ tsp. cayenne pepper
- 1 large egg
- ½ cup 2% milk
- 1 tsp. hot pepper sauce
- 2 cups sweetened shredded coconut
- 1 lb. uncooked shrimp (26-30 per lb.), peeled and deveined
- Cooking spray
- 4 hoagie buns, split
- 2 cups shredded lettuce
- 1 medium tomato, thinly sliced

1. For remoulade, in a small bowl, combine the first 6 ingredients. Refrigerate, covered, until serving.

2. Preheat air fryer to 375°. In a shallow bowl, mix flour, herbes de Provence, sea salt, garlic powder, pepper and cayenne. In a separate shallow bowl, whisk egg, milk and hot pepper sauce. Place coconut in a third shallow bowl. Dip shrimp in flour to coat both sides; shake off excess. Dip in egg mixture and then in coconut, patting to help adhere.

3. In batches, arrange shrimp in a single layer in greased air-fryer basket and spritz with cooking spray. Cook until coconut is lightly browned and shrimp turn pink, 3-4 minutes on each side.

4. Spread cut side of buns with remoulade. Top with shrimp, lettuce and tomato.

1 sandwich: 716 cal., 40g fat (16g sat. fat), 173mg chol., 944mg sod., 60g carb. (23g sugars, 4g fiber), 31g pro.

Want to liven up your fish and seafood entrees this summer? Whip up this no-fuss remoulade instead of reaching for the same-old bottle of tartar sauce.

PRESSSURE-COOKED TENDER BBQ CHICKEN

When we can't barbecue on the grill, I bring out my pressure cooker for this fall-off-the-bone chicken. My jazzed-up sauce always adds a burst of tangy flavor.
—*Diane Hixon, Niceville, FL*

Prep: 20 min.
Cook: 10 min. + cooling
Makes: 4 servings

- 1 broiler/fryer chicken (3 to 4 lbs.), cut up
- 2 Tbsp. canola oil
- 2 cups barbecue sauce
- 1½ cups coarsely chopped onions
- 1 large green pepper, chopped

1. Select saute or browning setting on a 6-qt. electric pressure cooker. Adjust for medium heat; add oil. When oil is hot, brown chicken in batches. Press cancel. Return all to pressure cooker. Combine remaining ingredients. Pour over chicken.
2. Lock lid and close pressure-release valve. Adjust to pressure-cook on high for 10 minutes. Let pressure release naturally. A thermometer inserted in chicken should read at least 170°. If desired, thicken the cooking juices.

1 serving: 423 cal., 18g fat (4g sat. fat), 110mg chol., 1114mg sod., 24g carb. (19g sugars, 3g fiber), 40g pro.

To prepare this on the stovetop: In a pressure cooker, brown chicken in oil in batches over medium heat. Remove chicken and keep warm. Combine remaining ingredients in pressure cooker. Return chicken to the pan; stir to coat.

137

SUMMER'S ALL-TIME

GRILLED GREATS

You can't mention summer without thinking about the charbroiled favorites everyone craves. From sizzling steaks and juicy burgers to flame-kissed pizzas and seasonal sides, the 22 fiery dishes found here take dining al fresco to new heights.

LEARN HOW TO GRILL (ALMOST) EVERYTHING

Savoring food prepared over an open flame is tough to beat! While grilling is simple, there are a few pitfalls to be mindful of, so follow these quick and easy tips and you'll grill like a pro in no time! This summer, make the most of your grill when you master these basics.

HOW TO GRILL CHICKEN THIGHS, WINGS & DRUMSTICKS

Typically sold bone-in, these parts will take longer to grill. Keep them away from direct heat to avoid the meat drying out, and cook over medium heat.

Poultry is especially tasty if you slather it with a sauce as you grill. Leave the basting until the last 15 minutes of grilling. If you start adding the sauce too soon, you could burn the chicken. Don't baste if the chicken still looks raw, since doing so creates the risk of transferring bacteria from uncooked to cooked chicken.

WINGS: Grill 20 to 30 minutes, covered, over indirect heat.

THIGHS AND DRUMSTICKS: Grill for 40 to 50 minutes, covered, over indirect heat. Flip periodically to ensure even cooking.

TEMPERATURE WHEN DONE: 170° to 175° (Make sure to take the temperature in the thickest part of the bird, near the bone.)

HOW TO GRILL CHICKEN BREASTS

Buying bone-in or boneless poultry will affect the grilling method. That said, most poultry grills well over medium heat. If using a charcoal grill, you can gauge the temperature by holding your hand 5 inches above the cooking grate. If you can keep it there comfortably for 4 to 6 seconds, it's at medium heat.

BONELESS: Grill 5 to 6 minutes per side. Go ahead and grill over direct heat to get the best sear. Since the boneless breasts will cook nice and quickly, they won't dry out unless you overcook them (so keep a close eye, and take the temperature frequently).

BONE-IN: Grill 40 to 50 minutes, covered, over indirect heat, so the meat doesn't dry out over the long cooking time. Flip periodically to ensure even cooking.

TEMPERATURE WHEN DONE: 165°

HOW TO GRILL STEAK

A perfectly grilled steak is a thing of beauty: charred to a delicious crust outside, juicy and tender inside. Start by choosing the right cut. Ribeye, porterhouse, T-bone and sirloin are great for grilling. Flank and hanger steaks are tasty as well. Be careful with filet mignon, as it's easy to overcook.

Let the steak's surface dry as much as possible before grilling. Let it sit uncovered on a rack in the fridge for a day or pat it dry with a paper towel before cooking. This will help create a wonderful crust.

Begin grilling slow and finish hot. Start cooking on the indirect side of the grill, which allows the steak to cook a bit before it starts seriously browning. Near the end of cooking, move it to direct heat, ensuring that the exterior gets crisp and browned.

½-TO-1-INCH-THICK STEAK: Grill roughly 4 to 6 minutes per side.

1-TO-1½-INCH-THICK STEAK: Grill 4 to 5 minutes per side over direct heat, then 4 to 10 minutes longer over indirect heat.

TEMPERATURE WHEN DONE: 135° for medium-rare, 140° for medium and 145° for medium-well.

HOW TO GRILL BURGERS

Prepare with beef patties, about ½-inch thick, with a light hand; overhandling burger patties makes the meat tough. Cook them over medium heat, and do not press down on the patties with a spatula, which presses out all of the juices.

½-INCH BEEF BURGER PATTIES: Grill for 5 to 7 minutes per side over medium heat.

TEMPERATURE WHEN DONE: 160°

HOW TO GRILL BRATWURST

If you haven't tried grilled brats, get on it! They're a quintessential midwestern food that has the country buzzing.

Precook brats in a saucepan filled with simmering beer or water for 10 to 15 minutes. When ready to grill, arrange brats so they're indirectly over the heat. If you're using a round grill, for example, place them in a circle around the edge of the grate. Putting the brats directly over the flames causes them to heat too quickly and burst, ultimately leading to dry brats.

BRATS: Grill for 10 to 20 minutes, depending on how long you have precooked them in simmering beer or water.

TEMPERATURE WHEN DONE: 160°

HOW TO GRILL RIBS

Barbecued ribs are a summertime essential. Because they cook low and slow, they have a wider window of perfection than, for instance, a T-bone steak that relies on a savvy sense of timing and temperature. If you take some time to prep ribs correctly and learn where to cook them on the grill, they're easy enough for beginners.

Baby back ribs are the most common and the easiest to find. They are smaller, meatier and leaner than other types. Spareribs are larger with flat bones. They have more connective tissues, so after a long cooking time, they'll become very tender. St. Louis-style ribs are spareribs with the rib tips removed. They have a more uniform, rectangular shape than the other types. They are slightly trickier to prepare, so you might want to start experimenting with baby backs or spareribs first.

To test for doneness, twist a rib bone just a little bit; you should feel it give easily but not fall apart from the meat. If the meat falls off the bone, the ribs are overcooked.

BABY BACK (ABOUT 4½ POUNDS): Grill ribs, covered, on an oiled rack over indirect medium heat 1½ to 2 hours, turning every 30 minutes.

TEMPERATURE WHEN DONE: 145°

HOW TO GRILL FISH, SHRIMP & SCALLOPS

Fish is a healthy alternative to grilled meats. Best of all, this tender choice grills quickly for busy nights.

1-INCH-THICK FISH FILLET: Grill 3 to 5 minutes per side, turning carefully.

TEMPERATURE WHEN DONE: The fish should turn opaque, and it should flake when you scrape a fork over the top.

SHRIMP AND SCALLOPS: Grill 1 to 2 minutes per side.

TEMPERATURE WHEN DONE: Shrimp is safe to eat when the flesh turns pink. Scallops should turn from translucent to opaque, white and firm.

HOW TO GRILL PORK CHOPS

When you're tired of chicken, pork chops are a versatile alternative. Look for thicker chops to stand up to the higher heat of the grill without drying out.

When it's done cooking, take pork off the grill, and let it stand for 5 minutes. As it sits, the pork chop's internal temperature will continue to rise (from 140° to 145°), leaving you with a tender, perfectly cooked chop.

¾-TO-1-INCH-THICK CHOPS: Grill for 5 to 7 minutes per side.

TEMPERATURE WHEN DONE: 145°

GRILLED PINEAPPLE WITH LIME DIP

Serve this dish as an appetizer or dessert—the choice is yours! If desired, the pineapple wedges can be rolled in flaked coconut before grilling.
—Taste of Home *Test Kitchen*

Prep: 20 min. + marinating
Grill: 10 min.
Makes: 8 servings

- 1   fresh pineapple
- ¼   cup packed brown sugar
- 3   Tbsp. honey
- 2   Tbsp. lime juice

LIME DIP

- 3   oz. cream cheese, softened
- ¼   cup plain yogurt
- 2   Tbsp. honey
- 1   Tbsp. brown sugar
- 1   Tbsp. lime juice
- 1   tsp. grated lime zest

1. Peel and core the pineapple; cut vertically into 8 wedges. Cut each wedge horizontally into 2 spears. In a bowl or shallow dish, combine the brown sugar, honey and lime juice; add pineapple and turn to coat. Cover and refrigerate for 1 hour.

2. In a small bowl, beat cream cheese until smooth. Beat in the yogurt, honey, brown sugar, lime juice and lime zest. Cover and refrigerate until serving.

3. Coat grill rack with cooking spray before starting the grill. Drain pineapple, discarding marinade. Grill pineapple spears, covered, over medium heat for 3-4 minutes on each side or until golden brown. Serve with the lime dip.

2 spears with 2 Tbsp. dip: 160 cal., 4g fat (2g sat. fat), 12mg chol., 41mg sod., 32g carb. (28g sugars, 2g fiber), 2g pro.

GRILLED CHICKEN RANCH BURGERS

This is one of the most fantastic, flavorful burgers I've ever made. Ranch is a favorite in dips and dressings, and, believe me, it doesn't disappoint in these burgers, either!
—*Kari Shifflett, Lake Mills, IA*

Prep: 15 min. + chilling
Grill: 10 min.
Makes: 16 servings

- ¾   cup ranch salad dressing
- ¾   cup panko bread crumbs
- ¾   cup grated Parmesan cheese
- 3   Tbsp. Worcestershire sauce
- 3   garlic cloves, minced
- 3   tsp. pepper
- 4   lbs. ground chicken
- 3   Tbsp. olive oil
- 16   hamburger buns, split
     Optional toppings: Tomato slices, lettuce leaves, sliced red onion, sliced avocado and ranch dip

1. In a large bowl, mix the first 6 ingredients. Add chicken; mix lightly but thoroughly. Shape mixture into sixteen ½-in.-thick patties. Brush both sides with oil; refrigerate, covered, 15 minutes to allow patties to firm up.

2. Grill burgers, covered, over medium heat or broil 3-4 in. from heat 5-6 minutes on each side or until a thermometer reads 165°. Serve on buns with desired toppings.

1 burger: 371 cal., 19g fat (5g sat. fat), 79mg chol., 498mg sod., 26g carb. (4g sugars, 1g fiber), 24g pro.

GINGERED HONEY SALMON

Ginger, garlic powder and green onion blend nicely in an easy marinade that gives a big flavor boost to salmon. We also like to use this versatile mixture when grilling chicken.
—*Dan Strumberger, Farmington, MN*

Prep: 10 min. + marinating
Grill: 15 min.
Makes: 6 servings

- ⅓ cup orange juice
- ⅓ cup reduced-sodium soy sauce
- ¼ cup honey
- 1 green onion, chopped
- 1 tsp. ground ginger
- 1 tsp. garlic powder
- 1 salmon fillet (1½ lbs. and ¾ in. thick)

1. For marinade, mix first 6 ingredients. In a shallow bowl, combine salmon and ⅔ cup marinade; refrigerate 30 minutes, turning occasionally. Reserve remaining marinade for basting.

2. Place salmon on an oiled grill rack over medium heat, skin side down; discard marinade remaining in bowl. Grill salmon, covered, until fish just begins to flake easily with a fork, 15-18 minutes, basting with reserved marinade during the last 5 minutes.

3 oz. cooked fish: 237 cal., 10g fat (2g sat. fat), 57mg chol., 569mg sod., 15g carb. (13g sugars, 0 fiber), 20g pro. **Diabetic exchanges:** 3 lean meat, 1 starch.

Everyone thinks of omega-3s when it comes to salmon, but the fish is also a good source of most B vitamins, which are important to boost energy.

RHUBARB-APRICOT BARBECUED CHICKEN

Spring and summer bring back memories of rhubarb that grew in the yard of my childhood home. When I found ruby red stalks in the store, I created this recipe for them. My family gives this a big thumbs-up.

—*Laurie Hudson, Westville, FL*

Prep: 30 min.
Grill: 30 min.
Makes: 6 servings

- 1 Tbsp. olive oil
- 1 cup finely chopped sweet onion
- 1 garlic clove, minced
- 2 cups chopped fresh or frozen rhubarb
- ¾ cup ketchup
- ⅔ cup water
- ⅓ cup apricot preserves
- ¼ cup cider vinegar
- ¼ cup molasses
- 1 Tbsp. honey Dijon mustard
- 2 tsp. finely chopped chipotle pepper in adobo sauce
- 5 tsp. barbecue seasoning, divided
- 1¼ tsp. salt, divided
- ¾ tsp. pepper, divided
- 12 chicken drumsticks (about 4 lbs.)

1. In a large saucepan, heat oil over medium heat. Add onion; cook and stir until tender, 4-6 minutes. Add garlic; cook 1 minute longer. Stir in rhubarb, ketchup, water, preserves, vinegar, molasses, mustard, chipotle pepper, 1 tsp. barbecue seasoning, ¼ tsp. salt and ¼ tsp. pepper. Bring to a boil. Reduce heat; simmer, uncovered, until rhubarb is tender, 8-10 minutes. Puree rhubarb mixture using an immersion blender, or cool slightly and puree in a blender. Reserve 2 cups sauce for serving.

2. Meanwhile, in a small bowl, mix the remaining barbecue seasoning, salt and pepper; sprinkle over chicken. On a lightly oiled grill rack, grill chicken, covered, over indirect medium heat 15 minutes. Turn; grill until a thermometer reads 170°-175°, 15-20 minutes longer, brushing occasionally with the remaining sauce. Serve with reserved sauce.

2 chicken drumsticks with ⅓ cup sauce: 469 cal., 19g fat (5g sat. fat), 126mg chol., 1801mg sod., 35g carb. (28g sugars, 1g fiber), 39g pro.

ALL-AMERICAN HAMBURGERS

We do a lot of camping and outdoor cooking. I must admit that hamburgers are on our menu more than any other food. These classics are a favorite.
—*Diane Hixon, Niceville, FL*

Takes: 20 min.
Makes: 4 servings

- 1 lb. ground beef
- 2 Tbsp. finely chopped onion
- 2 Tbsp. chili sauce
- 2 tsp. Worcestershire sauce
- 2 tsp. prepared mustard
- 4 slices process American cheese or cheddar cheese, halved diagonally
- 2 slices Swiss cheese, halved diagonally
- 4 hamburger buns, split and toasted
   Lettuce leaves, sliced tomato and onion, cooked bacon strips, ketchup and mustard, optional

1. Combine first 5 ingredients, mixing lightly but thoroughly. Shape into 4 patties. Grill burgers, covered, on a greased rack over medium direct heat until a thermometer reads 160° and juices run clear, about 6 minutes on each side.

2. During the last minute of cooking, top each patty with 2 triangles of American cheese and 1 triangle of Swiss cheese. Serve on buns; top as desired with lettuce, tomato, onion, bacon, ketchup and mustard.

1 hamburger: 432 cal., 21g fat (9g sat. fat), 80mg chol., 681mg sod., 26g carb. (6g sugars, 1g fiber), 30g pro.

GRILLED SWEET POTATOES WITH GORGONZOLA SPREAD

My husband originally tried this recipe with plain potatoes. They were yummy, so we experimented with sweet potatoes. Dipped in Gorgonzola spread, they're irresistible.
—*Kristen Minello, Macomb, MI*

Prep: 25 min.
Grill: 10 min.
Makes: 8 servings

- 4 large sweet potatoes
- 1 cup (4 oz.) crumbled Gorgonzola cheese
- ½ cup mayonnaise
- 1 to 2 Tbsp. lemon juice
- 3 Tbsp. olive oil
- ½ tsp. salt
- ¼ tsp. pepper
  Minced chives, optional

1. Scrub and pierce sweet potatoes with a fork; place on a microwave-safe plate. Microwave, uncovered, on high just until tender, turning once, 6-8 minutes.
2. Meanwhile, in a small bowl, combine cheese, mayonnaise and lemon juice. Refrigerate until serving.
3. Slice potatoes into ½-in.-thick rounds; brush both sides with oil. Sprinkle with salt and pepper. Grill, covered, over medium heat or broil 4 in. from heat on each side until browned, 4-5 minutes. Serve with spread. If desired, sprinkle with chives.

1 serving with 3 Tbsp. spread: 362 cal., 19g fat (5g sat. fat), 14mg chol., 425mg sod., 42g carb. (17g sugars, 6g fiber), 6g pro.

QUICK BARBECUED BEANS
This may be a simple, classic recipe, but cooking it on the grill introduces a subtle flavor. The dish features a nice blend of beans, and preparation time is minimal.
—*Millie Vickery, Lena, IL*

Takes: 25 min.
Makes: 5 servings

- 1 can (16 oz.) **kidney beans, rinsed and drained**
- 1 can (15½ oz.) **great northern beans, rinsed and drained**
- 1 can (15 oz.) **pork and beans**
- ½ cup **barbecue sauce**
- 2 Tbsp. **brown sugar**
- 2 tsp. **prepared mustard**

1. In an ungreased 8-in. square disposable foil pan, combine all ingredients.
2. Grill, covered, over medium heat until heated through, 15-20 minutes, stirring occasionally.

¾ cup: 264 cal., 2g fat (0 sat. fat), 0 chol., 877mg sod., 51g carb. (15g sugars, 13g fiber), 14g pro.

SWEET GINGER RIBS
People ask what's in the marinade of my glazed ribs with ginger, garlic and peach preserves. Now you know! Guess what? It works on steaks and chicken, too!
—*Grace McKeone, Schenectady, NY*

Prep: 15 min. + marinating
Grill: 1½ hours
Makes: 8 servings

- ½ cup **soy sauce**
- ½ cup **red wine vinegar**
- ½ cup **ketchup**
- ½ cup **peach preserves**
- ⅓ cup **minced fresh gingerroot**
- 2 Tbsp. **stone-ground mustard**
- 2 Tbsp. **brown sugar**
- 6 **garlic cloves, minced**
- ½ tsp. **crushed red pepper flakes**
- ½ tsp. **coarsely ground pepper**
- 4 lbs. **pork baby back ribs**

1. In a small bowl, whisk the first 10 ingredients until blended. In a small container, reserve 1 cup marinade for basting. Divide ribs and remaining marinade between 2 large resealable containers; seal containers and turn to coat. Refrigerate ribs and reserved marinade in containers overnight.
2. Remove ribs, discarding marinade in large containers. Grill ribs, covered, over indirect medium heat for 1½-2 hours or until tender, basting occasionally with reserved marinade during the last half hour.

1 serving: 338 cal., 21g fat (8g sat. fat), 81mg chol., 721mg sod., 13g carb. (10g sugars, 0 fiber), 24g pro.

Baby back ribs come from the blade and center section of the pork loin. They are called "baby back" ribs because they are smaller than spareribs.

GRILLED CHICKEN, MANGO & BLUE CHEESE TORTILLAS

Tortillas packed with chicken, mango and blue cheese make a fantastic appetizer to welcome summer. We double or triple the ingredients when we host parties.
—*Josee Lanzi, New Port Richey, FL*

Takes: 30 min.
Makes: 16 appetizers

- 1   **boneless skinless chicken breast (8 oz.)**
- 1   **tsp. blackened seasoning**
- ¾   **cup plain yogurt**
- 1½   **tsp. grated lime zest**
- 2   **Tbsp. lime juice**
- ¼   **tsp. salt**
- ⅛   **tsp. pepper**
- 1   **cup finely chopped peeled mango**
- ⅓   **cup finely chopped red onion**
- 4   **flour tortillas (8 in.)**
- ½   **cup crumbled blue cheese**
- 2   **Tbsp. minced fresh cilantro**

1. Sprinkle chicken with blackened seasoning. On a lightly oiled grill rack, grill chicken, covered, over medium heat for 6-8 minutes on each side or until a thermometer reads 165°.

2. Meanwhile, in a small bowl, mix yogurt, lime zest, lime juice, salt and pepper. Cool chicken slightly; finely chop and transfer to a small bowl. Stir in mango and onion.

3. Grill tortillas, uncovered, over medium heat 2-3 minutes or until puffed. Turn; top with chicken mixture and blue cheese. Grill, covered, 2-3 minutes longer or until bottoms of tortillas are lightly browned. Drizzle with yogurt mixture; sprinkle with cilantro. Cut each tortilla into 4 wedges.

1 wedge: 85 cal., 3g fat (1g sat. fat), 12mg chol., 165mg sod., 10g carb. (2g sugars, 1g fiber), 5g pro. **Diabetic exchanges:** 1 lean meat, ½ starch.

Serve these open-faced bites as a colorful lunch or light dinner alongside a green salad and white rice.

SWEET SRIRACHA WINGS

Serve these hot wings on game day or anytime friends and family gather. If you don't like a lot of sweetness, add the honey to taste.
—*Logan Holser, Clarkston, MI*

Prep: 20 min. + marinating
Grill: 15 min.
Makes: 1 dozen

12	chicken wings (about 3 lbs.)
1	Tbsp. canola oil
2	tsp. ground coriander
½	tsp. garlic salt
¼	tsp. pepper

SAUCE

¼	cup butter, cubed
½	cup orange juice
⅓	cup Sriracha chili sauce
3	Tbsp. honey
2	Tbsp. lime juice
¼	cup chopped fresh cilantro

1. Place chicken wings in a large bowl. Mix oil, coriander, garlic salt and pepper; add to wings and toss to coat. Refrigerate, covered, 2 hours or overnight.
2. For sauce, in a small saucepan, melt butter. Stir in orange juice, chili sauce, honey and lime juice until blended.
3. Grill wings, covered, over medium heat 15-18 minutes or until juices run clear, turning occasionally; brush with some of the sauce during the last 5 minutes of grilling.
4. Transfer chicken to a large bowl; add remaining sauce and toss to coat. Sprinkle with cilantro.

1 chicken wing: 201 cal., 13g fat (5g sat. fat), 46mg chol., 321mg sod., 8g carb. (7g sugars, 0 fiber), 12g pro.

BRUSCHETTA STEAK

My husband and I love bruschetta, especially in the summertime with fresh tomatoes and herbs from our garden. Here, the flavors of that favorite appetizer are turned into a quick yet impressive main course.
—*Kristy Still, Broken Arrow, OK*

Takes: 25 min.
Makes: 4 servings

- 3   medium tomatoes, chopped
- 3   Tbsp. minced fresh basil
- 3   Tbsp. chopped fresh parsley
- 2   Tbsp. olive oil
- 1   tsp. minced fresh oregano or ½ tsp. dried oregano
- 1   garlic clove, minced
- ¾   tsp. salt, divided
- 1   beef flat iron or top sirloin steak (1 lb.), cut into 4 portions
- ¼   tsp. pepper
     Grated Parmesan cheese, optional

1. Combine the first 6 ingredients; stir in ¼ tsp. salt.
2. Sprinkle beef with pepper and remaining salt. Grill, covered, over medium heat or broil 4 in. from heat until meat reaches desired doneness (for medium-rare, thermometer should read 135°; medium, 140°), 4-6 minutes per side. Top with tomato mixture. If desired, sprinkle with cheese.

1 steak with ½ cup tomato mixture:
280 cal., 19g fat (6g sat. fat), 73mg chol., 519mg sod., 4g carb. (2g sugars, 1g fiber), 23g pro. **Diabetic exchanges:** 3 lean meat, 1½ fat, 1 vegetable.

STRAWBERRY MINT CHICKEN

I hand-pick wild strawberries for this saucy chicken dish. We love it with fresh spring greens and a sweet white wine.
—*Alicia Duerst, River Falls, WI*

Takes: 30 min.
Makes: 4 servings

- 1 **Tbsp. cornstarch**
- 1 **Tbsp. sugar**
- ⅛ **tsp. ground nutmeg**
- ⅛ **tsp. pepper**
- ½ **cup water**
- 1 **cup fresh strawberries, coarsely chopped**
- ½ **cup white wine or white grape juice**
- 2 **tsp. minced fresh mint**

CHICKEN
- 4 **boneless skinless chicken breast halves (6 oz. each)**
- ½ **tsp. salt**
- ¼ **tsp. pepper**
   Sliced green onion

1. In a small saucepan, mix first 5 ingredients until smooth; stir in strawberries and wine. Bring to a boil. Reduce heat; simmer, uncovered, 3-5 minutes or until thickened and strawberries are softened, stirring occasionally. Remove from heat; stir in mint.
2. Sprinkle chicken with salt and pepper. On a lightly oiled grill rack, grill chicken, covered, over medium heat 5-7 minutes on each side or until a thermometer reads 165°; brush occasionally with ¼ cup sauce during the last 4 minutes. Serve with the remaining sauce. Sprinkle with green onion.

1 chicken breast half with ¼ cup sauce:
224 cal., 4g fat (1g sat. fat), 94mg chol., 378mg sod., 8g carb. (5g sugars, 1g fiber), 35g pro.

STEAK WITH CHIPOTLE-LIME CHIMICHURRI

Steak gets a flavor kick from chimichurri. This piquant, all-purpose herb sauce is so versatile, it complements almost any grilled meat, poultry or fish.
—*Laureen Pittman, Riverside, CA*

Takes: 30 min.
Makes: 8 servings

- 2 **cups fresh parsley leaves**
- 1½ **cups fresh cilantro leaves**
- ½ **medium red onion, coarsely chopped**
- 1 **to 2 chipotle peppers in adobo sauce**
- 5 **garlic cloves, sliced**
- ½ **cup olive oil**
- ¼ **cup white wine vinegar**
- 1 **tsp. grated lime zest**
- ¼ **cup lime juice**
- 3 **tsp. dried oregano**
- 1¼ **tsp. salt, divided**
- ¾ **tsp. pepper, divided**
- 2 **lbs. beef flat iron steaks or 2 beef top sirloin steaks (1 lb. each)**

1. For chimichurri, place first 5 ingredients in a food processor; pulse until finely chopped. Add oil, vinegar, lime zest, lime juice, oregano, ½ tsp. salt and ¼ tsp. pepper; process until blended. Transfer to a bowl; refrigerate, covered, until serving.

2. Sprinkle steaks with remaining salt and pepper. Grill, covered, over medium heat 5-8 minutes on each side or until meat reaches desired doneness (for medium-rare, a thermometer should read 135°; medium, 140°; medium-well, 145°). Let stand for 5 minutes before slicing. Serve with the chimichurri.

3 oz. cooked steak with 3 Tbsp. sauce: 336 cal., 26g fat (7g sat. fat), 73mg chol., 462mg sod., 4g carb. (1g sugars, 1g fiber), 22g pro.

CAJUN GRILLED SHRIMP

The kicked-up marinade on these shrimp makes this a flavor-packed favorite. Serve over rice, and make sure to squeeze those charred lemons over the top. That punches up the flavor even more.
—*Sharon Delaney-Chronis,*
South Milwaukee, WI

Takes: 30 min.
Makes: 6 servings

- 3   green onions, finely chopped
- 2   Tbsp. lemon juice
- 1   Tbsp. olive oil
- 3   garlic cloves, minced
- 2   tsp. paprika
- 1   tsp. salt
- ¼   tsp. pepper
- ¼   tsp. cayenne pepper
- 2   lbs. uncooked medium shrimp, peeled and deveined with tails on
- 4   medium lemons, each cut into 8 wedges

1. In a large resealable container, combine the first 8 ingredients. Add shrimp; seal container and turn to coat. Refrigerate for 15 minutes.
2. Drain shrimp, discarding marinade. On each of 12 metal or soaked wooden skewers, thread shrimp and lemon wedges.
3. Grill, covered, over medium heat or broil 4 in. from the heat until shrimp turn pink, turning once, 6-8 minutes.

2 skewers: 168 cal., 5g fat (1g sat. fat), 184mg chol., 575mg sod., 7g carb. (1g sugars, 2g fiber), 25g pro. **Diabetic exchanges:** 3 lean meat, ½ fruit, ½ fat.

SPICED GRILLED CORN

The wonderful spice mixture doesn't add heat, only great flavor. This might just be the best corn you've ever had!
—Taste of Home *Test Kitchen*

Takes: 20 min.
Makes: 8 servings

2	tsp. ground cumin
2	tsp. ground coriander
1	tsp. salt
1	tsp. dried oregano
½	tsp. ground ginger
¼	tsp. ground cinnamon
¼	tsp. pepper
⅛	tsp. ground cloves
2	Tbsp. olive oil
8	medium ears sweet corn, husked

1. In a small bowl, combine the first 8 ingredients. Brush oil over corn; sprinkle with spice mixture. Place each on a rectangle of heavy-duty foil (about 14x12 in.). Fold foil over corn, sealing tightly.
2. Grill corn, covered, over medium heat 10-12 minutes or until tender, turning occasionally. Open foil carefully to allow steam to escape.

1 ear of corn: 113 cal., 5g fat (1g sat. fat), 0 chol., 310mg sod., 18g carb. (3g sugars, 3g fiber), 3g pro. **Diabetic exchanges:** 1 starch, ½ fat.

GRILLED MARINATED RIBEYES

These juicy steaks are a favorite meal when we go camping. Let them sit in tangy, barbecue-inspired marinade overnight and you'll have a rich and hearty dinner ready to grill the next day.
—*Louise Graybiel, Toronto, ON*

Prep: 10 min. + marinating
Grill: 10 min.
Makes: 4 servings

½	cup barbecue sauce
3	Tbsp. Worcestershire sauce
3	Tbsp. olive oil
2	Tbsp. steak sauce
1	Tbsp. red wine vinegar
1	Tbsp. reduced-sodium soy sauce
2	tsp. steak seasoning
1	tsp. hot pepper sauce
1	garlic clove, minced
4	beef ribeye steaks (8 oz. each)

1. In a large resealable container, mix first 9 ingredients. Add steaks; seal container, and turn to coat. Refrigerate for 4 hours or overnight.
2. Drain steaks, discarding the marinade. Grill steaks, covered, over medium heat until meat reaches desired doneness (for medium-rare, a thermometer should read 135°; medium, 140°), 4-6 minutes per side.
Freeze option: Freeze steaks with marinade in a resealable container. To use, thaw in the refrigerator overnight. Drain beef, discarding marinade. Grill as directed.

1 steak: 570 cal., 40g fat (15g sat. fat), 134mg chol., 592mg sod., 8g carb. (6g sugars, 0 fiber), 40g pro.

Ribeyes are a favorite choice for grilling, but leaner cuts work with this marinade, too. Think top sirloin, top loin (aka strip), flank and top blade (aka flat iron) steaks.

SAUSAGE SQUASH KABOBS

Expect a crowd to gather around the grill when these flavorful kabobs are cooking. The zesty honey-mustard glaze gives a lovely sheen to the sausage and veggies.
—*Lisa Malynn-Kent, North Richland Hills, TX*

Takes: 20 min.
Makes: 4 servings

1   lb. small red potatoes,
    halved or quartered if desired
1   Tbsp. water
½   cup honey
¼   cup Dijon mustard
½   tsp. grated orange zest
1   lb. smoked turkey kielbasa,
    sliced ½ in. thick
2   small yellow summer
    squash, sliced ½ in. thick
2   small zucchini, sliced ½ in. thick

1. In a large microwave-safe bowl, combine potatoes and water. Cover and microwave on high until tender, 6-8 minutes; drain and set aside. For glaze, combine the honey, mustard and orange zest in a small bowl.
2. On 8 metal or soaked wooden skewers, alternately thread the sausage, potatoes, yellow squash and zucchini; brush with half of the glaze.
3. On a lightly oiled grill rack, grill kabobs, uncovered, over medium heat or broil 4 in. from heat until the vegetables are tender and sausage is heated through, 10-16 minutes, basting frequently with glaze.

2 kabobs: 385 cal., 7g fat (2g sat. fat), 71mg chol., 1491mg sod., 58g carb. (40g sugars, 3g fiber), 22g pro.

GINGER POUND CAKE S'MORES

Kids and adults won't be able to resist this fun spin on campfire s'mores. Pound cake replaces the traditional graham crackers, while crystallized ginger adds a flavor twist.
—*Peter Halferty, Corpus Christi, TX*

Takes: 20 min.
Makes: 8 servings

- 8 **large marshmallows**
- 5 **oz. bittersweet chocolate candy bars, broken into 8 pieces**
- 8 **tsp. crystallized ginger**
- 16 **slices pound cake (¼ in. thick)**
- 3 **Tbsp. butter, softened**

1. Cut each marshmallow lengthwise into 4 slices. Place a chocolate piece, 4 marshmallow slices and 1 tsp. ginger on each of 8 cake slices; top with the remaining cake. Spread outsides of cake slices with butter.
2. Grill, covered, over medium heat until toasted, 1-2 minutes on each side.

1 s'more: 382 cal., 24g fat (13g sat. fat), 144mg chol., 272mg sod., 44g carb. (10g sugars, 2g fiber), 5g pro.

GRILLED POTATO FANS WITH ONIONS

These seasoned potato fans are filled with tender onions, roasted garlic cloves and savory Parmesan cheese. They're my idea of the ultimate grilled potato.
—*Sharon Crabtree, Graham, WA*

Prep: 20 min.
Grill: 35 min.
Makes: 6 servings

- 6   medium potatoes
- 2   small onions, halved and thinly sliced
- 6   Tbsp. butter, diced
- 2   garlic cloves, minced
- 6   Tbsp. grated Parmesan cheese
- 1   Tbsp. minced chives
- ½   tsp. crushed red pepper flakes
      Dash salt

1. Prepare grill for indirect heat. With a sharp knife, cut each potato into ½-in. slices, leaving slices attached at the bottom. Fan potatoes slightly. Place each on a 12-in. square of heavy-duty foil.
2. Insert the onions, butter and garlic between potato slices. Combine the cheese, chives, pepper flakes and salt; sprinkle between slices. Fold foil around potatoes and seal tightly.
3. Grill, covered, over indirect medium heat for 35-45 minutes or until tender. Open foil carefully to allow steam to escape.

1 potato: 302 cal., 13g fat (8g sat. fat), 35mg chol., 195mg sod., 41g carb. (4g sugars, 4g fiber), 7g pro.

GRILLED APPLE TOSSED SALAD

The grilled apples in this salad combine so well with the blue cheese, walnuts and balsamic dressing. I like to serve it on pink Depression glass dessert plates from my great-grandmother.
—*Paul Soska, Toledo, OH*

Prep: 15 min. + marinating
Grill: 10 min.
Makes: 6 servings

- 6 **Tbsp. olive oil**
- ¼ **cup minced fresh cilantro**
- ¼ **cup orange juice**
- ¼ **cup white or regular balsamic vinegar**
- 2 **Tbsp. honey**
- 1 **garlic clove, minced**
- ½ **tsp. salt**
- ½ **tsp. Sriracha chili sauce**
- 2 **large apples, cut into ½-in. wedges**
- 1 **pkg. (5 oz.) spring mix salad greens**
- 1 **cup walnut halves, toasted**
- ½ **cup crumbled blue cheese**

1. For dressing, whisk together the first 8 ingredients. In a bowl, toss apples with ¼ cup dressing. Let stand 10 minutes.
2. Place apple slices on a grill rack over medium heat; reserve marinade left in bowl. Grill apples, covered, until tender and lightly browned, 3-4 minutes per side, brushing with reserved marinade.
3. To serve, toss greens with remaining dressing. Top with grilled apples, walnuts and cheese.

1 serving: 341 cal., 28g fat (5g sat. fat), 8mg chol., 360mg sod., 22g carb. (16g sugars, 3g fiber), 6g pro.

HONEY-MUSTARD BRATS

A honey-mustard glaze gives every bite of these brats a sweet and punchy flavor. Everyone who tries them agrees they're delicious.
—*Lily Julow, Lawrenceville, GA*

Takes: 25 min.
Makes: 4 servings

¼ cup Dijon mustard
¼ cup honey
2 Tbsp. mayonnaise
1 tsp. steak sauce
4 uncooked bratwurst links
4 brat buns, split

1. In a small bowl, mix mustard, honey, mayonnaise and steak sauce.

2. Grill bratwurst, covered, over medium heat 15-20 minutes or until a thermometer reads 160°, turning occasionally; brush frequently with mustard mixture during the last 5 minutes. Serve on buns.

1 serving: 624 cal., 35g fat (10g sat. fat), 65mg chol., 1531mg sod., 58g carb. (23g sugars, 1g fiber), 20g pro.

GRILLED ZUCCHINI & PESTO PIZZA

In the great outdoors, we surprise fellow campers who don't think it's possible to have standout pizza in the backwoods. This one with zucchini proves our point!
—*Jesse Arriaga, Reno, NV*

Takes: 20 min.
Makes: 6 servings

4 naan flatbreads
½ cup prepared pesto
2 cups shredded part-skim mozzarella cheese
1 medium zucchini, thinly sliced
1 small red onion, thinly sliced
¼ lb. thinly sliced hard salami, chopped
½ cup fresh basil leaves, thinly sliced
¼ cup grated Romano cheese

1. Over each naan, spread 2 Tbsp. pesto; top with ½ cup mozzarella and one-fourth of the zucchini, onion and salami.
2. Grill, covered, over medium-low heat until mozzarella has melted and vegetables are tender, 4-6 minutes. Rotate naan halfway through grilling for evenly browned crust.
3. Remove from heat. Top each naan with basil and Romano; cut into thirds.

2 pieces: 391 cal., 24g fat (9g sat. fat), 51mg chol., 1276mg sod., 25g carb. (4g sugars, 1g fiber), 20g pro.

Homemade pesto works well for this recipe, too. Check out the recipe for Basil & Parsley Pesto on page 265, and give it a try this summer.

SUMMER'S HOTTEST

CELEBRATIONS

Friends, family, fresh air and fantastic foods are what summer is all about. Whether you celebrate the season with backyard barbecues, casual tailgates or campfire feasts, the 11 menus that follow make summer entertaining deliciously easy.

BACKYARD
BBQ BASH

Serve a roundup of barbecue classics in all their finger-licking glory. Dig in to pulled pork, potato salad and more with this fun-loving menu that makes your backyard the neighborhood hot spot.

 LEMONY PINEAPPLE ICED TEA

I like to garnish glasses of this iced tea with some of our sweet Hawaiian pineapple.
—*Beverly Toomey, Honolulu, HI*

Prep: 20 min. + chilling
Cook: 10 min.
Makes: 20 servings

16 cups water
24 tea bags
6 fresh mint sprigs
3⅓ cups sugar
3 cups unsweetened pineapple juice
1 cup lemon juice

1. In a stockpot, bring water to boil; remove from heat. Add tea bags; steep, covered, 10 minutes. Discard tea bags. Add mint sprigs; steep for 5 minutes; discard mint. Add remaining ingredients, stirring to dissolve sugar.
2. Transfer to pitchers or a large covered container. Refrigerate, covered, until cold. If desired, serve with ice.

1 cup: 154 cal., 0 fat (0 sat. fat), 0 chol., 7mg sod., 40g carb. (38g sugars, 0 fiber), 0 pro.

CLEO'S POTATO SALAD

My mom, Cleo Lightfoot, loved cooking all kinds of different recipes, but her favorite meal was the one she made when hosting backyard barbecues in summer. She would make her famous ribs, baked beans and this delicious potato salad.
—*Joan Hallford, North Richland Hills, TX*

Prep: 25 min.
Cook: 20 min.
Makes: 12 servings

3½ lbs. red potatoes (about 12 medium), cut into 1-in. cubes
6 bacon strips, chopped
¼ cup sugar
1 Tbsp. all-purpose flour
½ cup water
1 large egg, lightly beaten
3 Tbsp. cider vinegar
1 Tbsp. grated onion
1 tsp. celery seed
1 tsp. salt
½ tsp. pepper
1 cup heavy whipping cream, whipped
4 hard-boiled large eggs, chopped
2 medium celery ribs, chopped

1. Place potatoes in a large saucepan; cover with water. Bring to a boil. Reduce heat; cook, uncovered, until tender, 10-15 minutes. Drain; cool completely.
2. Meanwhile, in a saucepan, cook bacon over medium heat until crisp. Remove with a slotted spoon; drain on paper towels. Remove all but 1 Tbsp. drippings from pan.
3. Stir sugar and flour into drippings until smooth. Gradually stir in water; cook and stir over medium-high heat until thickened and bubbly. Remove from heat. Stir a small amount of hot mixture into beaten egg; return all to pan, stirring constantly. Slowly bring to a boil, stirring constantly; remove from heat. Transfer to a large bowl; cool completely.

4. Gently stir in vinegar, onion and seasonings. Fold in whipped cream. Stir in eggs, celery, potatoes and bacon. Refrigerate, covered, until serving.

¾ cup: 211 cal., 11g fat (5g sat. fat), 90mg chol., 272mg sod., 23g carb. (5g sugars, 2g fiber), 6g pro.

Red potatoes are perfect for potato salads because they hold their shape so well when boiled.

MELON-BERRY SALAD

I think the best way to cool down on a warm day is with a chilled fruit salad. Here, yogurt and coconut milk make a creamy dressing for a decadent treat.
—*Carrie Hirsch, Hilton Head Island, SC*

Takes: 20 min.
Makes: 12 servings

- 1 cup fat-free vanilla Greek yogurt
- ½ cup coconut milk
- ½ cup orange juice
- 4 cups cubed cantaloupe (½ in.)
- 4 cups cubed watermelon (½ in.)
- 2 medium navel oranges, sectioned
- 1 cup fresh raspberries
- 1 cup fresh blueberries
- ½ cup sweetened shredded coconut, toasted

1. For dressing, whisk together yogurt, coconut milk and orange juice. Refrigerate until serving.
2. To serve, place fruit in a large bowl; toss gently with dressing. Sprinkle with coconut.
Note: To toast coconut, bake in a shallow pan in a 350° oven for 5-10 minutes or cook in a skillet over low heat until golden brown, stirring occasionally.

¾ cup: 105 cal., 3g fat (3g sat. fat), 0 chol., 30mg sod., 19g carb. (16g sugars, 2g fiber), 3g pro. **Diabetic exchanges:** 1 fruit, ½ fat.

SHRIMP TOSTADAS WITH LIME-CILANTRO SAUCE

I love shrimp and veggies marinated in citrus juice, also known as ceviche. This recipe starts with cooked shrimp and those same fresh ceviche flavors. Enjoy these tostadas as a make-ahead appetizer or casual entree.
—*Leslie Kelley, Dorris, CA*

Prep: 35 min. + standing
Makes: 10 servings

1½ lbs. peeled and deveined cooked shrimp (26-30 per lb.), coarsely chopped
1½ cups chopped, peeled English cucumber
8 radishes, thinly sliced
4 plum tomatoes, chopped
4 green onions, chopped
2 jalapeno peppers, seeded and minced
2 Tbsp. minced fresh cilantro
2 Tbsp. lime juice
3 garlic cloves, minced
1 tsp. salt
¼ tsp. pepper
1 medium ripe avocado, peeled and cubed

SAUCE
1 cup sour cream
2 Tbsp. minced fresh cilantro
1 tsp. grated lime zest
1 Tbsp. lime juice
¼ tsp. salt
¼ tsp. ground cumin
⅛ tsp. pepper

ASSEMBLY
10 tostada shells

1. Place first 11 ingredients in a large bowl; toss to combine. Gently stir in avocado; let stand 15 minutes.
2. In a small bowl, mix sauce ingredients. To serve, spread tostada shells with sauce. Top with shrimp mixture.

1 tostada: 209 cal., 12g fat (4g sat. fat), 109mg chol., 448mg sod., 12g carb. (3g sugars, 2g fiber), 16g pro.

SPICED PULLED PORK SANDWICHES

(PICTURED ON P. 166)

This pulled pork is tender and has a fabulous spice rub on it. It's my sweetie's favorite meal, and I love that it is so easy. You may add more or less salt to taste.

—Katie Citrowske, Bozeman, MT

Prep: 30 min.
Cook: 6 hours
Makes: 10 servings

- 1½ tsp. salt
- 1½ tsp. garlic powder
- 1½ tsp. ground cumin
- 1½ tsp. ground cinnamon
- 1½ tsp. chili powder
- 1½ tsp. coarsely ground pepper
- 1 boneless pork shoulder butt roast (3 to 4 lbs.), halved
- 2 Tbsp. olive oil
- 2 medium onions, halved and sliced
- 8 garlic cloves, coarsely chopped
- 1½ cups water
- 1 Tbsp. liquid smoke, optional
- 10 hamburger buns, split and toasted
  Barbecue sauce
  Sliced jalapeno pepper, optional

1. Mix seasonings; rub over pork. In large skillet, heat oil over medium heat. Brown pork on all sides. Transfer to a 5- or 6-qt. slow cooker.

2. In same pan, cook and stir sliced onions over medium heat until lightly browned, 4-5 minutes. Add chopped garlic; cook and stir 1 minute. Add water; bring to a boil, stirring to loosen browned bits from pan. If desired, stir in liquid smoke. Add to pork.

3. Cook, covered, on low until meat is tender, 6-8 hours. Remove roast; discard onion mixture. Shred the pork with 2 forks; return to slow cooker and heat through. Serve on buns with barbecue sauce and, if desired, jalapeno slices.

1 sandwich: 386 cal., 18g fat (6g sat. fat), 81mg chol., 669mg sod., 26g carb. (4g sugars, 2g fiber), 28g pro.

NUTELLA BANANA CREAM PIE

Here's a banana cream pie with a little Italian flair. The chocolate and hazelnut go well with the banana, and the homemade chocolate pie crust makes it extra special. If you don't have time to melt and pipe the chocolate stars, just sprinkle the top of the pie with grated chocolate or cocoa powder instead.
—*Crystal Schlueter, Babbitt, MN*

Prep: 45 min. + chilling
Bake: 20 min. + cooling
Makes: 10 servings

1¼ cups all-purpose flour
2 Tbsp. baking cocoa
1 Tbsp. sugar
½ cup cold butter, cubed
3 to 4 Tbsp. cold brewed coffee
DECORATIONS
¼ cup semisweet chocolate chips
¼ tsp. shortening
FILLING
1 carton (8 oz.) mascarpone cheese
¾ cup Nutella
2 medium bananas, thinly sliced
2 cups heavy whipping cream
3 Tbsp. instant banana cream pudding mix
2 Tbsp. chopped hazelnuts, toasted

1. In a small bowl, mix flour, cocoa and sugar; cut in butter until crumbly. Gradually add cold coffee, tossing with a fork until dough holds together when pressed. Shape into a disk; wrap in plastic. Refrigerate for 1 hour or overnight.
2. On a lightly floured surface, roll dough to a ⅛-in.-thick circle; transfer to a 9-in. pie plate. Trim crust to ½ in. beyond rim of plate; flute edge. Refrigerate 30 minutes. Preheat oven to 425°.

3. Line the crust with a double thickness of foil. Fill with pie weights, dried beans or uncooked rice. Bake on a lower oven rack until set, 15-20 minutes. Remove foil and weights; bake until edges are browned, about 5 minutes. Cool completely on a wire rack.
4. For decorations, in a microwave, melt chocolate chips and shortening; stir until smooth. Transfer to a pastry bag with a small round tip. Pipe designs over a waxed paper-lined baking sheet. Freeze until set, about 5 minutes.
5. For filling, mix mascarpone cheese and Nutella until blended; spread into crust. Top with bananas.
6. In another bowl, beat cream until it begins to thicken. Add pudding mix; beat until stiff peaks form. Spread or pipe with a large star tip over bananas. Sprinkle with hazelnuts. Top with chocolate decorations.

1 slice: 578 cal., 46g fat (24g sat. fat), 107mg chol., 147mg sod., 39g carb. (22g sugars, 2g fiber), 7g pro.

Let pie weights cool before storing. Beans and rice may be reused for pie weights, but not for cooking.

WARM-WEATHER BRUNCH

Rise and shine! It's so easy to bring summer flavors to the table any time of day, partucularly when you host an eye-opening brunch. Invite friends and family for sunny entrees, sweet-tart desserts and other bites bursting with seasonal flair.

CHAMPAGNE SIPPER

This is a terrific cocktail for a sunny celebration. And because you make it by the pitcher, you can mingle with your guests instead of tending bar.
—*Moffat Frazier, New York, NY*

Takes: 10 min.
Makes: 12 servings

- 1½ cups sugar
- 1 cup lemon juice
- 3 cups cold water
- 1½ cups sweet white wine, chilled
- 1 bottle (750 ml) champagne, chilled
  Sliced fresh strawberries, optional

In a 3-qt. pitcher, dissolve sugar in lemon juice. Add cold water and wine. Stir in champagne. If desired, serve with sliced fresh strawberries.

¾ cup: 162 cal., 11g fat (5g sat. fat), 49mg chol., 323mg sod., 1g carb. (0 sugars, 0 fiber), 13g pro.

ARTICHOKE & ONION FRITTATA

Fresh flavors make this pretty egg bake a great entree for a special occasion brunch or light luncheon. Just add homemade sausage patties and strawberry-topped bruschetta to make it a complete meal.
—*Joyce Moynihan, Lakeville, MN*

Prep: 15 min.
Bake: 35 min.
Makes: 8 servings

- 1 pkg. (8 oz.) frozen artichoke hearts
- 1 Tbsp. butter
- 1 Tbsp. olive oil
- 1 medium onion, chopped
- 1 garlic clove, minced
- ¼ tsp. dried oregano
- ¾ cup shredded Parmesan cheese, divided
- 6 large eggs
- ½ cup 2% milk
- ¼ tsp. salt
- ⅛ tsp. white pepper
- ⅛ tsp. ground nutmeg
- 1 cup shredded Monterey Jack cheese
  Minced chives, optional

1. Cook artichokes according to package directions; drain. Cool slightly; coarsely chop. Preheat oven to 350°.
2. In a large skillet, heat butter and oil over medium-high heat. Add chopped onion; cook and stir until tender. Add minced garlic; cook 1 minute longer. Stir in oregano and artichokes; remove from heat.
3. Sprinkle ¼ cup pf the Parmesan cheese in a greased 11x7-in. baking dish. Top with artichoke mixture.
4. In a large bowl, whisk eggs, milk, salt, pepper and nutmeg. Stir in Monterey Jack cheese and ¼ cup Parmesan cheese. Pour over artichoke mixture.

5. Bake, uncovered, 30 minutes. Sprinkle with remaining Parmesan cheese. Bake until a knife inserted in center comes out clean, 6-8 minutes longer. If desired, sprinkle with minced chives.

1 serving: 192 cal., 13g fat (7g sat. fat), 163mg chol., 373mg sod., 5g carb. (2 sugars, 2g fiber), 13g pro.

STRAWBERRY & CREAM BRUSCHETTA

This is a dessert take on bruschetta. Sweet, cinnamony toast slices are topped with a cream cheese mixture, strawberries and toasted almonds. They are like miniature cheesecakes and so yummy!

—*Christi Meixner, Aurora, IL*

Takes: 25 min.
Makes: 2 dozen

1	French bread baguette (8 oz.), cut into 24 slices
¼	cup butter, melted
3	Tbsp. sugar
½	tsp. ground cinnamon
1	pkg. (8 oz.) cream cheese, softened
¼	cup confectioners' sugar
2	tsp. lemon juice
1	tsp. grated lemon zest
2½	cups fresh strawberries, chopped
⅓	cup slivered almonds, toasted

1. Preheat oven to 375°. Place bread on an ungreased baking sheet; brush with butter. Combine sugar and cinnamon; sprinkle over bread. Bake 4-5 minutes on each side or until lightly crisp.

2. In a small bowl, beat cream cheese, confectioners' sugar, lemon juice and zest until blended; spread over toast. Top with strawberries; sprinkle with almonds.

1 appetizer: 94 cal., 6g fat (3g sat. fat), 15mg chol., 70mg sod., 8g carb. (4g sugars, 1g fiber), 2g pro.

HOMEMADE SAGE SAUSAGE PATTIES

Oregano, garlic and sage add savory flavor to these easy ground pork patties. I've had this Pennsylvania Dutch recipe for years, and it always brings compliments.
—*Diane Hixon, Niceville, FL*

Prep: 10 min. + chilling
Cook: 15 min.
Makes: 8 servings

- 1 lb. ground pork
- ¾ cup shredded cheddar cheese
- ¼ cup buttermilk
- 1 Tbsp. finely chopped onion
- 2 tsp. rubbed sage
- ¾ tsp. salt
- ¾ tsp. pepper
- ⅛ tsp. garlic powder
- ⅛ tsp. dried oregano

1. In a bowl, combine all the ingredients, mixing lightly but thoroughly. Shape into eight ½-in.-thick patties. Refrigerate 1 hour.
2. In a large cast-iron or other heavy skillet, cook patties over medium heat until a thermometer reads 160°, 6-8 minutes on each side.

1 patty: 162 cal., 11g fat (5g sat. fat), 49mg chol., 323mg sod., 1g carb. (0 sugars, 0 fiber), 13g pro.

Wrap cooked and cooled patties in foil and store then all in a freezer storage bag. This makes it a snap to grab one or two to heat up on busy mornings.

CRAB CAKE LETTUCE WRAPS

I love dishes you can put together and eat with your hands. These little crab cakes are healthy, fast and flavorful.
—*Joyce Huang, New York, NY*

Takes: 10 min.
Makes: 1 dozen

- 2 cans (6 oz. each) lump crabmeat, drained
- ¼ cup finely chopped celery
- ¼ cup seasoned stuffing cubes, coarsely crushed
- ¼ cup plain Greek yogurt
- ⅛ tsp. salt
- ⅛ tsp. pepper
- 12 Bibb or Boston lettuce leaves
     Finely chopped tomatoes, optional

In a large bowl, mix crab, celery, stuffing cubes, yogurt, salt and pepper. To serve, spoon 2 Tbsp. crab mixture into each lettuce leaf. If desired, sprinkle with tomatoes. Fold lettuce over filling.

1 filled lettuce wrap: 37 cal., 0 fat (0 sat. fat), 25mg chol., 139mg sod., 1g carb. (0 sugars, 0 fiber), 7g pro.

LIME-RASPBERRY PIE WITH COCONUT CREAM

In my many family trips to Florida, I've had Key lime pie from many restaurants, and each one is different. I wanted to create my own spin on the pie to make it my signature dessert. Whipped egg whites in the filling make it light and mousselike, sweet raspberries balance the tart filling, and coconut and cashews amp up the tropical flavor. Garnish with fresh raspberries and toasted shredded coconut if you like.
—*Elise Easterling, Chapel Hill, NC*

Prep: 50 min.
Bake: 25 min. + chilling
Makes: 12 servings

- 3 large egg whites
- 18 whole graham crackers, crushed (about 2½ cups)
- ½ cup packed brown sugar
- ½ cup unsalted cashews, finely chopped
- ¾ cup butter, melted
- 2 cans (14 oz. each) sweetened condensed milk
- ¾ cup Key lime juice
- 6 large egg yolks
- ¼ cup sugar

TOPPINGS
- 1 can (13.66 oz.) coconut milk
- 1 cup heavy whipping cream
- ½ cup confectioners' sugar
- ½ cup seedless raspberry jam
     Fresh raspberries and toasted flaked coconut, optional

1. Place egg whites in a small bowl; let stand at room temperature 30 minutes. Preheat oven to 350°.
2. In a large bowl, mix crushed crackers, brown sugar and cashews; stir in melted butter. Press onto bottom and 2 in. up sides of a greased 9-in. springform pan.
3. In a large bowl, mix condensed milk, lime juice and egg yolks until blended. With clean beaters, beat egg whites on medium speed until soft peaks form. Gradually add sugar, 1 Tbsp. at a time, beating on high after each addition until sugar is dissolved. Continue beating until stiff peaks form. Fold into milk mixture; pour into crust.
4. Bake 25-30 minutes or until filling is set. Cool 4 hours on a wire rack. Refrigerate 6 hours or overnight, covering when cold.
5. Spoon cream layer from top of coconut milk into a large bowl (discard remaining liquid). Add the whipping cream and the confectioners' sugar to bowl; beat until stiff peaks form.

6. Spread jam over pie. Dollop coconut cream over pie or serve on the side. If desired, top with raspberries and coconut.
Note: To toast coconut, bake in a shallow pan in a 350° oven for 5-10 minutes or cook in a skillet over low heat until golden brown, stirring occasionally. Light coconut milk is not recommended for this recipe.

1 slice: 678 cal., 34g fat (20g sat. fat), 168mg chol., 349mg sod., 86g carb. (69 sugars, 1g fiber), 11g pro.

SUMMER SOLSTICE

BLOCK PARTY

The June solstice marks the official start of summer. Why not salute the longest day of the year with a memorable outdoor bash? After all, few things are better than a great time with friends on a warm summer's eve—so let's get this party started!

HONEYDEW & PROSCIUTTO SALAD

For parties, I turn melon and prosciutto into an easy salad with a honey mustard dressing. To add zip, stir in fresh basil and mint.
—*Julie Merriman, Seattle, WA*

Takes: 30 min.
Makes: 12 servings

⅓ cup olive oil
½ tsp. grated lime zest
2 Tbsp. lime juice
2 Tbsp. white wine vinegar
2 Tbsp. honey
1 tsp. Dijon mustard
¼ tsp. salt
¾ cup fresh cilantro leaves
SALAD
8 cups fresh arugula or baby spinach (about 5 oz.)
½ medium red onion, thinly sliced
¼ cup thinly sliced fresh mint leaves
¼ cup thinly sliced fresh basil leaves
8 cups diced honeydew melon

1 pkg. (8 oz.) fresh mozzarella cheese pearls
¼ lb. thinly sliced prosciutto, cut into wide strips

Place first 8 ingredients in a blender; cover and process until smooth. Place arugula, onion and herbs in a large bowl. Drizzle with ⅓ cup vinaigrette and toss lightly to coat. In large serving bowl layer with a quarter of the arugula mixture, honeydew, mozzarella cheese and prosciutto. Repeat layers 3 times. Serve with remaining vinaigrette.

1 serving: 186 cal., 12g fat (4g sat. fat), 23mg chol., 294mg sod., 15g carb. (13g sugars, 1g fiber), 7g pro. **Diabetic exchanges:** 1 medium-fat meat, 1 vegetable, 1 fruit, 1 fat.

GRILLED PIZZA WITH GREENS & TOMATOES

This smoky grilled pizza scores big with me for two reasons—it encourages my family to eat greens, and it showcases fresh produce.
—*Sarah Gray, Erie, CO*

Prep: 15 min. + rising
Grill: 10 min.
Makes: 2 pizzas (4 slices each)

1½ cups all-purpose flour
1½ cups whole wheat flour
2 tsp. kosher salt
1 tsp. active dry yeast
3 Tbsp. olive oil, divided
1¼ to 1½ cups warm water (120° to 130°)
TOPPING
2 Tbsp. olive oil
10 cups beet greens, coarsely chopped
4 garlic cloves, minced
2 Tbsp. balsamic vinegar
¾ cup prepared pesto
¾ cup shredded Italian cheese blend
½ cup crumbled feta cheese

2 medium heirloom tomatoes, thinly sliced
¼ cup fresh basil leaves, chopped

1. Place the flours, salt and yeast in a food processor; pulse until blended. While processing, add 2 Tbsp. oil and enough water in a steady stream until dough forms a ball. Turn dough onto a floured surface; knead until smooth and elastic, 6-8 minutes.
2. Place in a greased bowl, turning once to grease the top. Cover and let rise in a warm place until almost doubled, about 1½ hours.
3. Punch down dough. On a lightly floured surface, divide dough into 2 portions. Press or roll each portion into a 10-in. circle; place each on a piece of greased foil (about 12 in. square). Brush tops with remaining oil; cover and let rest 10 minutes.

4. For topping, in a 6-qt. stockpot, heat oil over medium-high heat. Add beet greens; cook and stir 3-5 minutes or until tender. Add garlic; cook 30 seconds longer. Remove from heat; stir in vinegar.
5. Carefully invert pizza crusts onto lightly oiled grill rack; remove foil. Grill, covered, over medium heat 3-5 minutes or until bottoms are lightly browned. Turn; grill 1-2 minutes or until second side begins to brown.
6. Remove from grill. Spread with pesto; top with beet greens, cheeses and tomatoes. Return pizzas to grill. Cook, covered, over medium heat 2-4 minutes or until cheese is melted. Sprinkle with basil.

1 slice: 398 cal., 21g fat (5g sat. fat), 11mg chol., 1007mg sod., 42g carb. (3g sugars, 6g fiber), 12g pro.

TRIPLE BERRY SHORTCAKE

My great-great-grandmother handed down her shortcake recipe. I'm sharing it because it's way too fabulous to keep it a secret!
—*Sara Kingsmore, Vadnais Heights, MN*

Prep: 25 min.
Bake: 25 min. + cooling
Makes: 15 servings

- 1   cup butter, softened
- 2   cups sugar
- 4   large eggs, room temperature
- 2   Tbsp. vanilla extract
- 3   cups all-purpose flour
- 1   tsp. baking powder
- ½   tsp. baking soda
- ½   tsp. salt
- 1   cup buttermilk

TOPPING
- 1½ cups fresh blueberries
- 1½ cups sliced fresh strawberries
- 1½ cups fresh raspberries
- 2   Tbsp. sugar
     Sweetened whipped cream, optional

1. Preheat oven to 350°. In a large bowl, cream butter and sugar until light and fluffy. Add 1 egg at a time, beating well after each addition. Beat in vanilla. In another bowl, whisk flour, baking powder, baking soda and salt; add to creamed mixture alternately with buttermilk, beating well after each addition.

2. Transfer batter to a greased 13x9-in. pan. Bake until a toothpick inserted in center comes out clean, 25-30 minutes. Cool completely in pan on a wire rack.

3. For topping, in a large bowl, combine the berries; add sugar and toss gently to coat. Serve with cake; top with whipped cream if desired.

1 serving: 361 cal., 14g fat (8g sat. fat), 83mg chol., 301mg sod., 54g carb. (32g sugars, 2g fiber), 5g pro.

AVOCADO ENDIVE CUPS WITH SALSA

I jazz up guacamole by serving it over endive leaves. Add a brilliant red pepper salsa, and you've got a standout appetizer for summer.
—*Gilda Lester, Millsboro, DE*

Prep: 45 min.
Makes: 2½ dozen

- 1 jar (12 oz.) roasted sweet red peppers, drained and finely chopped
- 1 cup finely chopped fennel bulb
- ¼ cup sliced ripe olives, finely chopped
- 2 Tbsp. olive oil
- 1 Tbsp. minced fresh cilantro
- ½ tsp. salt, divided
- ½ tsp. pepper, divided
- 2 medium ripe avocados, peeled and pitted
- 3 Tbsp. lime juice
- 2 Tbsp. diced jalapeno pepper
- 1 green onion, finely chopped
- 1 garlic clove, minced
- ½ tsp. ground cumin
- ¼ tsp. hot pepper sauce
- 2 plum tomatoes, choppped
- 30 endive leaves
  Chopped fennel fronds

1. In a small bowl, combine red peppers, fennel, olives, oil and cilantro; stir in ¼ tsp. each salt and pepper.
2. In another bowl, mash avocados with a fork. Stir in lime juice, diced jalapeno, green onion, garlic, cumin, pepper sauce and the remaining salt and pepper. Stir in tomatoes.
3. Spoon about 1 Tbsp. avocado mixture onto each endive leaf; top each with about 1 Tbsp. pepper mixture. Sprinkle with the chopped fennel fronds.

1 appetizer: 43 cal., 3g fat (0 sat. fat), 0 chol., 109mg sod., 4g carb. (1g sugars, 3g fiber), 1g pro. **Diabetic exchanges:** 1 vegetable, ½ fat.

5i

GRILLED LIME-BALSAMIC SWEET POTATOES

For me, tailgating is about camaraderie and preparing food that's good to grill. One of my favorites is sweet potato wedges. Yum!
—*Raquel Perazzo, West New York, NJ*

Prep: 15 min.
Grill: 10 min./batch
Makes: 8 servings

- 5 medium sweet potatoes (about 3 lbs.)
- 2 Tbsp. olive oil
- 1 tsp. salt
- ¼ tsp. pepper
- ¼ cup chopped fresh cilantro
- ¼ cup packed brown sugar
- ¼ cup lime juice
- 3 Tbsp. white or regular balsamic glaze

1. Peel and cut each sweet potato lengthwise into 8 wedges; place in a large bowl. Toss with oil, salt and pepper.
2. In batches, cook potatoes on a greased grill rack, covered, over medium heat until tender, turning occasionally, 8-10 minutes.
3. In a large bowl, mix remaining ingredients; add potatoes and toss to coat.

5 potato wedges: 197 cal., 4g fat (1g sat. fat), 0 chol., 309mg sod., 41g carb. (23g sugars, 4g fiber), 2g pro.

GRILLED CHIPOTLE SALMON TACOS

Take your taco Tuesdays to new heights! When fresh fish is available, I pull out this salmon taco recipe and fire up the grill.
—*Brenda Washnock, Negaunee, MI*

Prep: 20 min. + marinating
Grill: 10 min.
Makes: 12 servings

- ¼ cup olive oil
- ¼ cup lemon juice
- 2 Tbsp. lime juice
- 3 chipotle peppers plus 2 tsp. adobo sauce
- 3 Tbsp. reduced-sodium soy sauce
- 2 garlic cloves, minced
- ½ tsp. dried oregano
- 3 lbs. salmon fillets (about 1 in. thick)
SLAW
- ½ cup cider vinegar
- ¼ cup olive oil
- 3 Tbsp. sugar
- ½ tsp. salt
- ¼ tsp. pepper
- 2 cups shredded red cabbage
- 2 cups shredded green cabbage
- ½ medium red onion, thinly sliced
- ¼ cup fresh cilantro leaves, chopped

ASSEMBLY
- 12 corn tortillas (6 in.), warmed

1. Place oil, citrus juices, chipotle peppers, adobo sauce, soy sauce, garlic and oregano in a blender; cover and process until blended. Pour half of the marinade into a 13x9-in. dish. Add salmon, skin side down. Turn the fillets to coat both sides; refrigerate, covered, for 30 minutes. Reserve remaining marinade for basting fish.
2. For slaw, in a large bowl, whisk vinegar, oil, sugar, salt and pepper until blended. Add cabbages, onion and cilantro; toss to coat. Refrigerate until serving.
3. Remove salmon from marinade; discard any remaining marinade in dish.

4. Place salmon on a lightly oiled grill rack, skin side down. Grill, covered, over medium heat 5 minutes. Spoon some of the reserved marinade over fish. Grill 4-6 minutes longer or until the salmon just begins to flake easily with a fork, basting occasionally with the remaining marinade.
5. Break fish into bite-sized pieces, removing skin if desired. Serve in tortillas with slaw.

1 taco: 326 cal., 19g fat (3g sat. fat), 57mg chol., 297mg sod, 17g carb. (5g sugars, 2g fiber), 21g pro. **Diabetic exchanges:** 3 lean meat, 1 starch, ½ fat.

Don't have any salmon? Try these tacos with mahi mahi or whitefish instead.

SUNSET ROOFTOP BASH

Are you ready for a bang-up summer bash? No need to apply sunscreen—this party is an evening affair. Complete with a rooftop view and an appetizer buffet, it's sure to be one of your most memorable parties of the season.

FRESH HERB VEGETABLE DIP

I entertain a lot and am always looking for an easy crowd-pleaser. If it's one where I use fresh ingredients from my herb and vegetable garden, it's even better! I serve this dip in individual servings for large parties so each person has their own cup.
—*Isabel Minunni, Poughkeepsie, NY*

Takes: 15 min.
Makes: 3 cups

- ¼ cup olive oil
- 3 Tbsp. lemon juice
- 1½ cups fat-free sour cream
- 2 medium ripe avocados, peeled and cubed
- 2 Tbsp. chopped chives
- 2 Tbsp. chopped fresh parsley
- 2 Tbsp. chopped fresh basil
- 1 Tbsp. chopped fresh tarragon
- 1 Tbsp. chopped fresh thyme
- 1 garlic clove, halved
- ½ tsp. salt
- ¼ tsp. pepper
  Assorted fresh vegetables

Place the first 12 ingredients in a food processor; process until smooth. Refrigerate until serving. Serve with vegetables.

¼ cup dip: 110 cal., 8g fat (1g sat. fat), 1mg chol., 126mg sod., 4g carb. (2g sugars, 2g fiber), 3g pro. **Diabetic exchanges:** 1½ fat.

GRILLED TOMATO-PEACH PIZZA

This delicious pizza is unique, healthy and easy. The fresh flavors make it a perfect appetizer for any summer bash.
—*Scarlett Elrod, Newnan, GA*

Prep: 20 min. + standing
Grill: 5 min.
Makes: 16 pieces

- 4 medium tomatoes, thinly sliced
- ¼ tsp. salt
- 2 medium peaches, halved
  Cooking spray
- 1 Tbsp. cornmeal
- 1 tube (13½ oz.) refrigerated pizza crust
- 4 oz. fresh mozzarella cheese, sliced
- 6 fresh basil leaves, thinly sliced
- ⅛ tsp. coarsely ground pepper

1. Sprinkle tomatoes with salt; let stand for 15 minutes. Drain tomatoes on paper towels and pat dry,

2. Coat grill rack lightly with cooking oil. Grill peaches, covered, over medium heat or broil 4 in. from heat until peaches have grill marks and are tender, 2-3 minutes on each side, turning once. Remove peaches; cool slightly. Cut into slices.

3. Coat a 15x10x1-in. baking pan with cooking spray; sprinkle with cornmeal. Unroll crust into pan, pressing into a 12x10-in. rectangle. Spritz with cooking spray. Invert dough onto grill. Grill, covered, over medium heat until bottom is lightly browned, 2-3 minutes. Remove from grill, inverting onto baking pan.

4. Layer grilled side of pizza with tomatoes, peaches and cheese. Return pizza to grill. Cook, covered, until crust is lightly browned and cheese is melted, 3-4 minutes, rotating halfway through cooking to ensure an evenly browned crust. Sprinkle pizza with fresh basil and pepper.

1 piece: 98 cal., 3g fat (1g sat. fat), 6mg chol., 208mg sod., 15g carb. (3g sugars, 1g fiber), 4g pro. **Diabetic exchanges:** 1 starch.

Consider jazzing up this pizza with purple tomatoes, chopped chives or even some diced mango.

SOUTH-OF-THE-BORDER BRUSCHETTA

I like to get creative in the kitchen, and this is one of the first dishes I threw together without using a recipe. It offers a zesty Mexican flavor everyone is sure to love.
—*Rebecca Spoolstra, Pilot Point, TX*

Prep: 20 min. + chilling
Broil: 5 min.
Makes: 12 servings

2 medium ripe avocados, peeled and finely chopped
3 Tbsp. minced fresh cilantro
1 to 2 red chili peppers, finely chopped
¼ tsp. salt
2 small limes
12 slices French bread baguette (½ in. thick)
    Crumbled Cotija cheese, optional

1. In a small bowl, mix avocados, cilantro, chili peppers and salt. Finely grate lime peels. Cut limes crosswise in half; squeeze juice from limes. Stir lime zest and juice into avocado mixture. Refrigerate 30 minutes.

2. Preheat broiler. Place bread slices on an ungreased baking sheet. Broil 3-4 in. from heat 1-2 minutes on each side or until golden brown. Top with avocado mixture. If desired, sprinkle with cheese.

1 appetizer: 62 cal., 4g fat (0 sat. fat), 0 chol., 100mg sod., 7g carb. (0 sugars, 2g fiber), 2g pro.

WATERMELON MARGARITAS

Summer's best flavors get frosty in the cocktail we serve at all our backyard parties. We mix watermelon and our favorite tequila with just the right amount of ice for a thick and boozy sipper that's perfect when we're grilling and chilling.
—*Alicia Cummings, Marshalltown, IA*

Takes: 20 min.
Makes: 12 servings

- 2 **medium limes**
- ⅓ **cup sugar**
- 8 **cups cubed seedless watermelon (1 in.)**
- 2 **cups ice cubes**
- 2 **cups tequila**
- 1 **cup Triple Sec**
- ¼ **cup lime juice**
  Sugar, optional

1. Cut 1 lime into 12 wedges; reserve for garnishes. Cut remaining lime into wedges. Using these wedges, moisten the rims of 12 margarita or cocktail glasses. Sprinkle sugar on a plate; hold each glass upside down and dip rim into sugar. Discard remaining sugar.
2. Place half of the watermelon in a blender; cover and process until pureed (this should yield 3 cups). Add half of each of the following: ice cubes, tequila, Triple Sec and lime juice. If desired, add sugar to taste. Cover and process until blended.
3. Serve in prepared glasses. Repeat with remaining ingredients. Garnish with reserved lime wedges.

¾ **cup:** 188 cal., 0 fat (0 sat. fat), 0 chol., 5mg sod., 19g carb. (17g sugars, 1g fiber), 0 pro.

EASY STRAWBERRY SALSA

My salsa is sweet and colorful, with just a little bit of a bite from jalapeno peppers. I use fresh strawberries and my own home-grown vegetables, but you can also use produce that's available year round. It's delicious with chips or even as a topping for grilled chicken or pork.
—*Dianna Wara, Washington, IL*

Prep: 20 min. + chilling
Makes: 16 servings

- 3 cups chopped seeded tomatoes (about 4 large)
- 1⅓ cups chopped fresh strawberries
- ½ cup finely chopped onion (about 1 small)
- ½ cup minced fresh cilantro
- 1 to 2 jalapeno peppers, seeded and finely chopped
- ⅓ cup chopped sweet yellow or orange pepper
- ¼ cup lime juice
- ¼ cup honey
- 4 garlic cloves, minced
- 1 tsp. chili powder
  Baked tortilla chip scoops

In a large bowl, combine first 10 ingredients. Refrigerate, covered, at least 2 hours. Serve with chips.

Note: Wear disposable gloves when cutting hot peppers; the oils can burn skin. Avoid touching your face.

¼ cup: 33 cal., 0 fat (0 sat. fat), 0 chol., 4mg sod., 8g carb. (6g sugars, 1g fiber), 1g pro. **Diabetic exchanges:** ½ starch.

TURKEY SLIDERS WITH SESAME SLAW

I'm a fan of sliders, especially if they are Asian inspired. Sweet Hawaiian rolls make them especially tasty.
—*Gloria Bradley, Naperville, IL*

Takes: 30 min.
Makes: 12 servings

- ⅔ cup mayonnaise
- 2 Tbsp. hoisin sauce
- 2 tsp. Sriracha chili sauce
- 1½ lbs. ground turkey
- ½ cup panko (Japanese) bread crumbs
- 2 green onions, finely chopped
- 2 Tbsp. reduced-sodium soy sauce, divided
- 2 tsp. minced fresh gingerroot
- 2 Tbsp. rice vinegar
- 2 tsp. sugar
- 2 tsp. sesame oil
- 6 small carrots, grated (about 1½ cups)
- ⅓ cup thinly sliced red onion
- 3 Tbsp. chopped fresh cilantro
- 1 tsp. sesame seeds, toasted
- 12 slider buns or dinner rolls, split and toasted

1. In a small bowl, mix mayonnaise, hoisin sauce and chili sauce. Refrigerate until serving.
2. In a large bowl, combine turkey, bread crumbs, green onions, 1 Tbsp. soy sauce and ginger, mixing lightly but thoroughly. Shape into twelve ½-in.-thick patties.
3. In a small bowl, whisk vinegar, sugar, oil and remaining soy sauce. Add carrots, onion, cilantro and sesame seeds; toss to combine.

4. Grill sliders, covered, on a greased rack over medium heat or broil 4 in. from heat until a thermometer reads 165°, about 3 minutes on each side. Spread cut sides of buns with mayonnaise mixture. Layer each bottom with a burger and 2 Tbsp. slaw. Replace tops.

1 burger with 2 Tbsp. slaw: 314 cal., 16g fat (3g sat. fat), 56mg chol., 522mg sod., 26g carb. (6g sugars, 2g fiber), 15g pro.

LET'S HAVE
A PICNIC

Hit the park, kick off your shoes and get ready to relish every ounce of fun that summer has to offer. It's picnic time, so enjoy these no-fuss favorites. Each item travels well and makes dining al fresco a snap.

BLT MACARONI SALAD

A friend served this salad, and I just had to get the recipe. My husband loves BLT sandwiches, so this has become a favorite of his. It's nice to serve on hot and humid days, which we frequently get during summer here in Virginia.
—*Mrs. Hamilton Myers Jr., Charlottesville, VA*

Takes: 30 min.
Makes: 6 servings

½ cup mayonnaise
3 Tbsp. chili sauce
2 Tbsp. lemon juice
1 tsp. sugar
3 cups cooked elbow macaroni
½ cup chopped seeded tomato
2 Tbsp. chopped green onions
3 cups shredded lettuce
4 bacon strips, cooked and crumbled

In a large bowl, combine first 4 ingredients. Add the macaroni, chopped tomatoes and onions; toss to coat. Cover and refrigerate. Just before serving, add lettuce and bacon; toss to coat.

¾ cup: 259 cal., 17g fat (3g sat. fat), 10mg chol., 287mg sod., 21g carb. (4g sugars, 2g fiber), 5g pro.

Calling all bacon fanatics! Use thick-cut bacon or add 2 extra strips to pump up the flavor.

LAYERED PICNIC LOAVES

This big sandwich is inspired by one I fell in love with at a New York deli. It's easy to make ahead of time and cart to any party, potluck, block party or family reunion. Kids and adults alike say it's super!
—*Marion Lowery, Medford, OR*

Prep: 20 min. + chilling
Makes: 2 loaves (12 servings each)

2 unsliced loaves (1 lb. each) Italian bread
¼ cup olive oil
3 garlic cloves, minced
2 tsp. Italian seasoning, divided
½ lb. deli roast beef
12 slices part-skim mozzarella cheese (1 oz. each)
16 fresh basil leaves
3 medium tomatoes, thinly sliced
¼ lb. thinly sliced salami

1 jar (6½ oz.) marinated artichoke hearts, drained and sliced
1 pkg. (10 oz.) ready-to-serve salad greens
8 oz. thinly sliced deli chicken
1 medium onion, thinly sliced
¼ tsp. salt
⅛ tsp. pepper

1. Cut loaves in half horizontally; hollow out tops and bottoms, leaving ½-in. shells (discard the removed bread or save it for another use).

2. Combine oil and garlic; brush inside bread shells. Sprinkle with 1 tsp. Italian seasoning. Layer bottom of each loaf with a fourth of each: roast beef, mozzarella, basil, tomatoes, salami, artichokes, salad greens, chicken and onion. Repeat layers. Season with salt, pepper and remaining Italian seasoning.
3. Drizzle with the remaining oil mixture if desired. Replace bread tops; wrap tightly. Refrigerate at least 1 hour before slicing.

1 slice: 341 cal., 18g fat (7g sat. fat), 47mg chol., 991mg sod., 26g carb. (3g sugars, 2g fiber), 19g pro.

CRUNCHY COOL COLESLAW

I love the peanut slaw at Lucille's Smokehouse Bar-B-Que, a popular restaurant chain in California. This recipe is my version. I think it's a pretty close match!
—*Elaine Hoffmann, Santa Ana, CA*

Takes: 30 min.
Makes: 16 servings

2 pkg. (16 oz. each) coleslaw mix
2 medium Honeycrisp apples, julienned
1 large carrot, shredded
¾ cup chopped red onion
½ cup chopped green pepper
½ cup cider vinegar
⅓ cup canola oil
1½ tsp. sugar
½ tsp. celery seed
½ tsp. salt
½ cup coarsely chopped dry-roasted peanuts or cashews

1. In a bowl, combine first 5 ingredients. In another bowl, whisk the vinegar, oil, sugar, celery seed and salt.

2. Just before serving, pour dressing over salad; toss to coat. Sprinkle with peanuts.

1 cup: 100 cal., 7g fat (1g sat. fat), 0 chol., 128mg sod., 9g carb. (5g sugars, 2g fiber), 2g pro. **Diabetic exchanges:** 1 vegetable, 1½ fat.

FRUITY PEANUT BUTTER PITAS

My kids ask for these all the time. The sandwiches not only taste good, they're healthy, too!

—*Kim Holmes, Emerald Park, SK*

Takes: 5 min.
Makes: 2 servings

- ¼ cup peanut butter
- ⅛ tsp. each ground allspice, cinnamon and nutmeg
- 2 whole wheat pita pocket halves
- ½ medium apple, thinly sliced
- ½ medium firm banana, sliced

In a small bowl, blend the peanut butter, allspice, cinnamon and nutmeg. Spread inside pita bread halves; fill with apple and banana slices.

1 pita half: 324 cal., 17g fat (4g sat. fat), 0 chol., 320mg sod., 36g carb. (13g sugars, 6g fiber), 12g pro. **Diabetic exchanges:** 3 fat, 1 starch, 1 lean meat, 1 fruit.

If your bananas are too green, place them in a paper bag until ripe. Add an apple to the bag to help speed up the process.

GIANT LEMON SUGAR COOKIES

My wonderfully chewy cookies have a light lemon flavor from both the juice and zest. The coarse sugar adds sparkle and crunch.
—*Michael Vyskocil, Glen Rock, PA*

Prep: 25 min.
Bake: 15 min./batch
Makes: 14 cookies

1 cup unsalted butter, softened
1½ cups sugar
½ cup packed brown sugar
2 large eggs, room temperature
1½ tsp. grated lemon zest
2 Tbsp. lemon juice
3 cups all-purpose flour
1 tsp. baking soda
¼ tsp. salt
¼ tsp. cream of tartar
4 tsp. coarse sugar

1. Preheat oven to 350°. In a large bowl, cream butter and sugars until light and fluffy. Beat in eggs. Beat in lemon zest and juice. In another bowl, whisk flour, baking soda, salt and cream of tartar; gradually beat into the creamed mixture.
2. Shape ¼ cupfuls of dough into balls. Place 6 in. apart on greased baking sheets. Flatten to ¾-in. thickness with the bottom of a measuring cup. Lightly brush tops with water; sprinkle with coarse sugar.
3. Bake until light brown, 12-15 minutes. Remove from pans to wire racks to cool completely. Store in airtight containers.

1 cookie: 340 cal., 14g fat (8g sat. fat), 65mg chol., 147mg sod., 51g carb. (31g sugars, 1g fiber), 4g pro.

GRILLED LEMON CHICKEN

My chicken gets its subtle bit of pucker from lemonade concentrate. So simple, so sweet!
—*Linda Nilsen, Anoka, MN*

Prep: 5 min.
Grill: 40 min.
Makes: 12 servings

¾ cup thawed lemonade concentrate
⅓ cup soy sauce
1 garlic clove, minced
1 tsp. seasoned salt
½ tsp. celery salt
⅛ tsp. garlic powder
2 broiler/fryer chickens (3 to 3½ lbs. each), cut up

1. In a bowl, whisk the first 6 ingredients until combined. Pour half into a shallow glass dish. Cover and refrigerate remaining sauce.
2. Dip chicken into sauce, turning to coat; discard sauce. Grill chicken, covered, over medium heat for 30 minutes, turning occasionally. Brush with reserved sauce. Grill 10-20 minutes longer, brushing frequently with sauce, until a thermometer reads 165°.

5 oz. cooked chicken: 320 cal., 17g fat (5g sat. fat), 104mg chol., 504mg sod., 6g carb. (5g sugars, 0 fiber), 34g pro.

PICNIC POINTERS
Keep these ideas in mind before filling up your picnic basket and heading outisde.

KEEP IT SIMPLE
Choose recipes that make your picnic a snap to toss together. Start with pasta salads, sandwiches and potato chips, and go from there.

PACK IT UP
Pack your basket in reverse order to easily grab the items you instantly need. Consider packing two containers, one for food and one for nonperishables.

STAY COOL
Cold foods should be kept at 40° or cooler. Coolers should be about 25% ice and 75% food. Large chunks of ice melt slower than ice cubes. Remember that a full cooler will stay colder longer that one that's partially full.

CAMPFIRE CLASSICS

The easiest way to camp? Just set up a tent in your own backyard! Not only do you have all the comforts of home nearby, you can also enjoy the comforts of homemade food. Sleeping under the stars has never been so awesome.

ZUCCHINI & SUMMER SQUASH SALAD

I came up with this colorful and tasty slaw years ago for a recipe contest and was delighted when I won honorable mention! The recipe easily doubles and is the perfect dish to take to potlucks or family gatherings.
—*Paula Wharton, El Paso, TX*

Prep: 25 min. + chilling
Makes: 12 servings

- 4 medium zucchini
- 2 yellow summer squash
- 1 medium sweet red pepper
- 1 medium red onion
- 1 cup fresh sugar snap peas, trimmed and halved
- ⅓ cup olive oil
- ¼ cup balsamic vinegar
- 2 Tbsp. reduced-fat mayonnaise
- 4 tsp. fresh sage or 1 tsp. dried sage leaves
- 2 tsp. honey
- 1 tsp. garlic powder
- 1 tsp. celery seed
- 1 tsp. dill weed
- ½ tsp. salt
- ½ tsp. pepper

Thinly slice zucchini, squash, red pepper and onion; place in a large bowl. Add snap peas. In a small bowl, whisk remaining ingredients until blended. Pour over vegetables; toss to coat. Refrigerate, covered, at least 3 hours.

¾ cup: 101 cal., 7g fat (1g sat. fat), 1mg chol., 124mg sod., 8g carb. (6g sugars, 2g fiber), 2g pro.

SAUSAGE & POTATO CAMPFIRE PACKETS

My family enjoys camping and cooking over a fire. These hearty packets turn out beautifully over a campfire, on the grill or in the oven at home. We sometimes leave out the sausage and serve the potatoes as a side dish. Either way, it's so easy, and the spuds can be served right from the foil pouch for easy cleanup.
—*Julie Koets, Elkhart, IN*

Prep: 20 min.
Cook: 30 min.
Makes: 8 servings

- 3 lbs. red potatoes, cut into ½-in. cubes
- 2 pkg. (12 oz. each) smoked sausage links, cut into ½-in. slices
- 4 bacon strips, cooked and crumbled
- 1 medium onion, chopped
- 2 Tbsp. chopped fresh parsley
- ¼ tsp. salt
- ¼ tsp. garlic salt
- ¼ tsp. pepper
  Additional chopped fresh parsley, optional

1. Prepare campfire or grill for medium heat. In a large bowl, toss potatoes with sausage, bacon, onion, parsley, salts and pepper.
2. Divide mixture among eight 18x12-in. pieces of heavy-duty nonstick foil, placing food on dull side of foil. Fold foil around potato mixture, sealing tightly.
3. Place packets over campfire or grill; cook 15 minutes on each side or until potatoes are tender. Open packets carefully to allow steam to escape. If desired, sprinkle with additional parsley.

1 packet: 414 cal., 25g fat (10g sat. fat), 61mg chol., 1,181mg sod., 31g carb. (4g sugars, 3g fiber), 17g pro.

PINEAPPLE UPSIDE-DOWN CAMPFIRE CAKE

We make this fun dessert while camping or in the backyard around a fire. It's very yummy, but the sandwich iron should be opened only by adults to avoid burns.
—*Cheryl Grimes, Whiteland, IN*

Prep: 10 min.
Cook: 5 min./cake
Makes: 6 servings

6	tsp. butter
6	Tbsp. brown sugar
6	canned pineapple slices
6	maraschino cherries
6	individual round sponge cakes

1. Place 1 tsp. butter in 1 side of sandwich iron. Hold over fire to melt; remove from fire. Carefully sprinkle 1 Tbsp. brown sugar over melted butter. Top with pineapple ring; add cherry to center of pineapple. Top with cake (flat side up); close iron.

2. Cook pineapple side down over a hot campfire until brown sugar is melted and cake is heated through, 5-8 minutes. Invert iron to open, and serve the cake on an individual plate.

1 cake: 211 cal., 6g fat (3g sat. fat), 38mg chol., 214mg sod., 39g carb. (32g sugars, 1g fiber), 2g pro.

SOURDOUGH BREAD BOWL SANDWICH

I created this for when my husband and I go to the lake. I don't like to spend a lot of time hovering over a stove or grill, especially in the hot Oklahoma summer months, and this filling sandwich is ready in minutes. For extra flavor, brush melted garlic and herb butter over the top prior to cooking.
—Shawna Welsh-Garrison, Owasso, OK

Prep: 15 min.
Cook: 25 min. + standing
Makes: 8 servings

- 1 round loaf sourdough bread (1½ lbs.)
- ½ cup honey mustard salad dressing
- 4 slices sharp cheddar cheese
- ⅓ lb. thinly sliced deli ham
- 4 slices smoked provolone cheese
- ⅓ lb. thinly sliced deli smoked turkey
- 1 Tbsp. butter, melted

1. Prepare campfire or grill for low heat. Cut a thin slice off top of bread loaf. Hollow out bottom of loaf, leaving a ½-in.-thick shell (save removed bread for another use). Spread dressing on inside of hollowed loaf and under the top of the bread. Layer with cheddar, ham, provolone and turkey. Replace top. Place on a piece of heavy-duty foil (about 24x18 in.). Brush loaf with butter. Fold foil edges over top, crimping to seal.
2. Cook loaf over campfire or grill until heated through, 25-30 minutes. Let stand for 15 minutes before removing foil. Cut into wedges.

1 piece: 346 cal., 17g fat (6g sat. fat), 46mg chol., 865mg sod., 30g carb. (5g sugars, 1g fiber), 19g pro.

CAMPFIRE DESSERT CONES

Kids love to make these hand-held snacks! Set out the ingredients so they can mix and match their own creations.
—*Bonnie Hawkins, Elkhorn, WI*

Takes: 20 min.
Makes: 8 servings

- 8 ice cream sugar cones
- ½ cup milk chocolate M&M's
- ½ cup miniature marshmallows
- ½ cup salted peanuts
- ½ cup white baking chips

1. Prepare campfire or grill for medium heat. Fill cones with M&M's, marshmallows, peanuts and white chips. Fully wrap each cone with foil, sealing tightly.
2. Place packets over campfire or grill; cook until heated through, 7-10 minutes. Open the foil carefully.

1 cone: 217 cal., 11g fat (5g sat. fat), 4mg chol., 78mg sod., 26g carb. (18g sugars, 1g fiber), 5g pro.

BONFIRE COOKIES

These treats are a perfect way to celebrate having a bonfire! The cookies are great on their own but extra sweet after they're decorated.
Callic Washer, Conifer, CO

Prep: 45 min.
Bake: 10 min./batch + cooling
Makes: 2 dozen

- 1 cup butter, softened
- 1½ cups sugar
- 2 large eggs, room temperature
- 1 tsp. vanilla extract
- 3 cups all-purpose flour
- 1½ tsp. baking powder
- ¼ tsp. salt
- ¼ tsp. ground nutmeg
- 10 cherry Jolly Rancher hard candies, crushed
- 1 pouch (7 oz.) green decorating icing
- ½ cup chocolate wafer crumbs
- 36 pretzel sticks

1. Preheat oven to 350°. In a large bowl, cream butter and sugar until light and fluffy. Beat in eggs and vanilla. In another bowl, whisk flour, baking powder, salt and nutmeg; gradually beat into creamed mixture.
2. Shape level tablespoons of dough into balls; place 2 in. apart on ungreased baking sheets. Flatten slightly with the bottom of a glass. Bake until the edges are light brown, 8-10 minutes. Cool on pans 2 minutes before removing to wire racks to cool completely.
3. Meanwhile, spread crushed candies onto a parchment-lined baking sheet. Bake until candy is melted, 5-7 minutes. Cool completely on pan on a wire rack. Break into pieces.

4. Spread icing over cookies; sprinkle with wafer crumbs. Arrange broken candies to make campfire flames. For logs, break pretzel sticks in half. Place 3 halves, broken edge down, in the wet icing. Hold in place until set.

1 cookie: 238 cal., 10g fat (6g sat. fat), 36mg chol., 166mg sod., 35g carb. (20g sugars, 1g fiber), 2g pro.

If the bottom of the glass sticks to the dough, dip it in flour before flattening the balls into cookie shapes.

FOURTH OF JULY FAMILY REUNION

A great American summer deserves a great American party. This year, welcome family members from near and far with a star-spangled feast. There's no better way to celebrate life, liberty and the pursuit of happiness than with some finger-licking foods.

HONEY-MELON SALAD WITH BASIL

Put the taste of summer in your salad! Loaded with juicy cantaloupe and honeydew, and glazed with a sweet honey dressing, this will be gone in minutes. Watermelon is a tasty addition, too.
—*Khurshid Shaik, Omaha, NE*

Prep/Total: 20 min.
Makes: 12 servings

- 6 **cups cubed cantaloupe (about 1 medium)**
- 6 **cups cubed honeydew melon (about 1 medium)**
- ¼ **cup honey**
- 3 **Tbsp. lemon juice**
- ½ **tsp. paprika**
- ¼ **tsp. salt**
- ¼ **tsp. coarsely ground pepper**
- ¼ **cup minced fresh basil or mint**
  Dried cranberries, optional

In a large bowl, combine the cantaloupe and honeydew. Refrigerate, covered, until serving. In a small bowl, whisk honey, lemon juice, paprika, salt and pepper. Pour over melon cubes just before serving; toss to coat. Stir in the basil and, if desired, dried cranberries. Serve with a slotted spoon.

1 cup: 68 cal., 0 fat (0 sat. fat), 0 chol., 72mg sod., 17g carb. (16g sugars, 1g fiber), 1g pro.
Diabetic exchanges: 1 fruit.

SWEET & TANGY BARBECUED CHICKEN

My family loves to grill in the summer, and this has become our hands-down favorite to share with friends. Every bite is full of flavor and the chicken is always tender and juicy.
—*Joy Yurk, Grafton, WI*

Prep: 15 min. + marinating
Grill: 30 min.
Makes: 8 servings

- 2½ **cups white wine**
- 2 **medium onions, finely chopped (1½ cups)**
- ½ **cup lemon juice**
- 10 **garlic cloves, minced**
- 16 **chicken drumsticks**
- 3 **bay leaves**
- 1 **can (15 oz.) tomato puree**
- ¼ **cup honey**
- 1 **Tbsp. molasses**
- 1 **tsp. salt**
- ½ **tsp. dried thyme**
- ¼ **tsp. cayenne pepper**
- ¼ **tsp. pepper**
- 2 **Tbsp. white vinegar**

1. For marinade, in a large bowl, combine wine, onions, lemon juice and garlic. Pour 2 cups marinade into a large shallow dish. Add the chicken; turn to coat. Cover and refrigerate for 4 hours to overnight. Add bay leaves to the remaining marinade; cover and refrigerate.

2. Meanwhile, in a large saucepan, combine tomato puree, honey, molasses, salt, thyme, cayenne, pepper and remaining marinade. Bring to a boil. Reduce the heat; simmer, uncovered, 35-40 minutes or until liquid is reduced by half. Remove from heat. Remove bay leaves; stir in vinegar. Reserve 1 cup sauce for serving; keep warm.

3. Drain chicken, discarding marinade in bag. Grill chicken, covered, on an oiled rack over indirect medium heat 15 minutes. Turn; grill 15-20 minutes longer or until a thermometer reads 170°-175°, brushing occasionally with remaining sauce. Serve the chicken with reserved sauce.

2 drumsticks with 2 Tbsp. sauce: 334 cal., 12g fat (3g sat. fat), 95mg chol., 398mg sod., 18g carb. (13g sugars, 1g fiber), 30g pro.

PATRIOTIC COOKIE & CREAM CUPCAKES

Bring on the red, white and blue with these creative cupcakes, perfect for the Fourth of July, Memorial Day or any other warm-weather occasion. With careful arrangement, your sweet display will be a patriotic nod to the flag.
—*Rebecca Wetherbee, Marion, OH*

Prep: 40 min.
Bake: 20 min. + cooling
Makes: 2 dozen

½ cup butter, softened
1⅔ cups sugar
3 large egg whites, room temperature
2 tsp. vanilla extract
2¼ cups all-purpose flour
3 tsp. baking powder
½ tsp. salt
1 cup 2% milk
1 cup Oreo cookie crumbs
FROSTING
¾ cup butter, softened
6 cups confectioners' sugar
½ tsp. clear or regular vanilla extract
3 to 4 Tbsp. 2% milk
Blue and red paste food coloring
Star sprinkles

1. Preheat oven to 350°. Line 24 muffin cups with paper or foil liners.
2. In a large bowl, cream butter and sugar until crumbly. Add 1 egg white at a time, beating well after each addition. Beat in vanilla. In another bowl, whisk flour, baking powder and salt; add to creamed mixture alternately with milk, beating well after each addition. Fold in cookie crumbs.

3. Fill prepared cups two-thirds full. Bake 20-24 minutes or until a toothpick inserted in center comes out clean. Cool in pans for 10 minutes before removing to wire racks to cool completely.
4. In a large bowl, combine the butter, confectioners' sugar and vanilla; beat until smooth. Add enough milk to make a stiff frosting. Remove 1 cup frosting to a small bowl; tint with blue food coloring. Divide remaining frosting in half; tint one portion red and leave remaining portion plain.
5. Cut a small hole in the tip of a pastry bag or in a corner of a food-safe plastic bag; insert a #1M star pastry tip. Fill bag with plain frosting; pipe over 9 cupcakes. With red frosting, pipe 9 more cupcakes. Pipe the remaining cupcakes blue; top with sprinkles. Arrange cupcakes on a large platter, forming an American flag.

1 cupcake: 220 cal., 13g fat (6g sat. fat), 46mg chol., 139mg sod., 21g carb. (16g sugars, 0g fiber), 4g pro.

🕐 5j

STRAWBERRY WATERMELON LEMONADE

The nutrition department at my local hospital inspired me to create this refreshing summer sipper. I tweaked their recipe slightly to create this drink full of sweet-tart flavor.
—*Dawn Lowenstein, Huntingdon Valley, PA*

Takes: 20 min.
Makes: 12 servings (3 qt.)

- ¼ cup sugar
- 2 cups boiling water
- ½ lb. fresh strawberries, hulled and quartered (about 2 cups)
- 12 cups cubed watermelon (about 1 medium)
- 1 can (12 oz.) frozen lemonade concentrate, thawed
- 3 Tbsp. lemon juice
  Ice cubes

Dissolve sugar in boiling water. Place the strawberries and watermelon in batches in a blender; cover and process until blended. Pour the blended fruit though a fine mesh strainer; transfer to a large pitcher. Stir in lemonade concentrate, lemon juice and sugar water. Serve over ice.

1 cup: 119 cal., 0 fat (0 sat. fat), 0 chol., 7mg sod., 34g carb. (30g sugars, 1g fiber), 1g pro.

GREEN BEAN-CHERRY TOMATO SALAD

My grandmother made a cold green bean salad with potatoes for every family barbecue. Now I bring my own version of the recipe to parties. With added color and taste from the cherry tomatoes, this classic favorite is even better.
—*Angela Lemoine, Howell, NJ*

Prep: 25 min.
Cook: 10 min.
Makes: 12 servings

- 1½ **lbs. fresh green beans, trimmed**
- 1 **pint cherry tomatoes, halved**
- 1 **small red onion, halved and thinly sliced**
- 3 **Tbsp. red wine vinegar**
- 1½ **tsp. sugar**
- ¾ **tsp. dried oregano**
- ¾ **tsp. salt**
- ¼ **tsp. garlic powder**
- ¼ **tsp. pepper**
- ¼ **cup olive oil**

1. In a 6-qt. stockpot, bring 6 cups water to a boil. Add the green beans in batches; cook, uncovered, 2-3 minutes or just until crisp-tender. Remove beans and immediately drop into ice water. Drain and pat dry.

2. Transfer beans to a large bowl. Add the tomatoes and onion; toss to combine. In a small bowl, whisk vinegar, sugar, oregano, salt, garlic powder and pepper. Gradually whisk in oil until blended. Pour over bean mixture; toss to coat.

1 serving: 65 cal., 5g fat (1g sat. fat), 0 chol., 153mg sod., 6g carb. (2g sugars, 2g fiber), 1g pro. **Diabetic exchanges:** 1 vegetable, 1 fat.

PEACH-CHIPOTLE BABY BACK RIBS

My son and I collaborated in the kitchen one day to put our own unique twist on classic baby back ribs. We added a sweet peachy glaze and a little heat with chipotle peppers. It was a great bonding experience, and now we have a keeper recipe for fall-off-the-bone ribs.
—*Rebecca Suaso, Weaverville, NC*

Prep: 15 min.
Bake: 2¾ hours
Makes: 8 servings (2 cups sauce)

- 3 **Tbsp. brown sugar**
- 2 **Tbsp. kosher salt**
- 1 **tsp. pepper**
- ½ **tsp. cayenne pepper**
- 8 **lbs. pork baby back ribs (about 3 racks)**
- 6 **medium peaches, peeled and sliced**
- 2 **Tbsp. olive oil**
- 2 **large sweet onions, finely chopped**
- ⅔ **cup packed brown sugar**
- 4 **finely chopped chipotle peppers in adobo sauce plus 2 Tbsp. sauce**
- 3 **Tbsp. white vinegar**
- 4 **tsp. ground mustard**

1. Preheat oven to 325°. In a small bowl, combine brown sugar, salt, pepper and cayenne. If necessary, remove the thin membrane from back ribs; discard the membrane. Rub brown sugar mixture over ribs. Transfer to large roasting pans. Add 1 in. hot water. Bake, covered, until ribs are tender, 2½-3 hours.

2. Meanwhile, place peaches in a blender; cover and process until smooth. In a large saucepan, heat oil over medium heat. Add onions; cook and stir 12-15 minutes or until tender. Add brown sugar, chipotle peppers, adobo sauce, vinegar, mustard and peach puree; bring to a boil. Reduce the heat; simmer, uncovered, until slightly thickened, 25-30 minutes.

3. Drain ribs. Grill ribs, pork side down, covered, on an oiled rack over medium heat until browned, 5-7 minutes. Turn ribs; brush with 2 cups sauce. Cook 5-7 minutes. Serve with remaining sauce.

1 serving with ¼ cup sauce: 788 cal., 48g fat (16g sat. fat), 163mg chol., 1759mg sod., 43g carb. (37g sugars, 3g fiber), 47g pro.

Get creative with the sauce. Add a few herbs fresh from the garden, replace some of the chipotle peppers with diced green pepper or add a few dashes of hot pepper sauce.

CATCH-A-WAVE
POOL PARTY

Cannonball! Grab a lounge chair and cool off with a poolside party ideal for kids of all ages. Planning is made in the shade with colorful kabobs, refreshing beverages, simple sandwiches and swimmingly cute cookies.

ORANGE LEMONADE

This juice is a favorite at our place. I'll often double the batch and send a jar next door to my mother-in-law. I was looking for a way to sweeten lemonade without using more sugar when I came up with the recipe.
—*Wendy Masters, Grand Valley, ON*

Prep: 15 min. + chilling
Cook: 5 min. + cooling
Makes: 12 servings (3 qt.)

1¾ cups sugar
2½ cups water
2 Tbsp. grated lemon zest
2 Tbsp. grated orange zest
1½ cups lemon juice (about 10 lemons)
1½ cups orange juice (about 5 oranges)
6 cups cold water

1. In a large saucepan, combine sugar and 2½ cups water; cook and stir over medium heat until sugar is dissolved. Cool slightly.
2. Stir in citrus zest and juices. Let stand, covered, 1 hour. Strain syrup; refrigerate, covered, until cold.
3. To serve, fill glasses or pitcher with an equal amount of fruit syrup and water. Add ice and serve.

1 cup: 136 cal., 0 fat (0 sat. fat), 0 chol., 1mg sod., 35g carb. (33g sugars, 0 fiber), 0 pro.

CHICKEN SALAD PARTY SANDWICHES

My famous chicken salad arrives at the party chilled in a plastic container. When it's time to set out the food, I stir in the pecans and assemble the sandwiches. They're always a hit!
—*Trisha Kruse, Eagle, ID*

Takes: 25 min.
Makes: 16 servings

    4   cups cubed cooked chicken breast
    1½   cups dried cranberries
    2   celery ribs, finely chopped
    2   green onions, thinly sliced
    ¼   cup chopped sweet pickles
    1   cup fat-free mayonnaise
    ½   tsp. curry powder
    ¼   tsp. coarsely ground pepper
    ½   cup chopped pecans, toasted
    16   whole wheat dinner rolls
         Leaf lettuce

1. In a bowl, combine first 5 ingredients. Mix mayonnaise, curry powder and pepper; stir into chicken mixture. Refrigerate mixture until serving.

2. To serve, stir in pecans. Spoon onto lettuce-lined rolls.

1 sandwich: 235 cal., 6g fat (1g sat. fat), 30mg chol., 361mg sod., 33g carb. (13g sugars, 4g fiber), 14g pro.

To toast nuts, bake in a shallow pan in a 350° oven for 5-10 minutes or cook in a skillet over low heat until lightly browned, stirring occasionally.

SWEET MACARONI SALAD

A sweet, out-of-the-ordinary dressing makes this macaroni salad special. My aunt gave me the recipe and it has become one of my favorites. I occasionally leave out the green pepper if I know that people don't like it, and it still tastes great.
—*Idalee Scholz, Cocoa Beach, FL*

Prep: 20 min. + chilling
Makes: 16 servings

- 1 pkg. (16 oz.) elbow macaroni
- 4 medium carrots, shredded
- 1 large green pepper, chopped
- 1 medium red onion, chopped
- 2 cups mayonnaise
- 1 can (14 oz.) sweetened condensed milk
- 1 cup cider vinegar
- ½ cup sugar
- 1 tsp. salt
- ½ tsp. pepper

1. Cook macaroni according to package directions. Drain and rinse in cold water; drain well.
2. In a large bowl, combine macaroni and vegetables. Whisk together remaining ingredients until smooth and sugar is dissolved; stir into macaroni mixture. Refrigerate, covered, overnight.

⅔ **cup:** 400 cal., 23g fat (5g sat. fat), 10mg chol., 332mg sod., 43g carb. (22g sugars, 2g fiber), 6g pro.

ITALIAN SUBMARINE

My husband grew up eating this flavorful sandwich, which his mother used to make. This sub can easily be made a few hours ahead and refrigerated, then served with chips, veggies and dip for a delicious meal.
—*Christine Lupella, Fifty Lakes, MN*

Takes: 15 min.
Makes: 8 servings

1	loaf (1 lb.) unsliced Italian bread
2	to 3 Tbsp. olive oil
2	to 4 Tbsp. shredded Parmesan cheese
1	to 1½ tsp. dried oregano
1	medium tomato, thinly sliced
½	lb. thinly sliced deli ham
¼	lb. sliced provolone cheese
¼	lb. thinly sliced hard salami

1. Cut bread horizontally in half. Hollow out bottom half, leaving a ¼-in. shell (save the removed bread for another use or discard). Brush cut surfaces of bread with oil; sprinkle with Parmesan cheese and oregano.
2. Layer bottom half with remaining ingredients. Replace bread top. Cut into 8 slices.

1 slice: 340 cal., 16g fat (6g sat. fat), 40mg chol., 1130mg sod., 30g carb. (2g sugars, 2g fiber), 18g pro.

Going to a pool party instead of hosting one? Make this sandwich the day before. Do not cut into slices, but wrap the entire sandwich tightly in plastic wrap for freshness and easy travel.

FRUIT & CHEESE KABOBS

This fresh and fruity snack is great to make ahead and carry to the pool, beach or even the tailgate. The cinnamon-spiced yogurt dip adds a special touch that easily impresses.
—Taste of Home *Test Kitchen*

Takes: 20 min.
Makes: 12 kabobs (1½ cups dip)

- 1 cup vanilla yogurt
- ½ cup sour cream
- 2 Tbsp. honey
- ½ tsp. ground cinnamon
- 2 cups fresh strawberries, halved
- 1½ cups green grapes
- 8 oz. cubed cheddar or Monterey Jack cheese, or a combination of cheeses

For the dip, mix first 4 ingredients. On 12 wooden skewers, alternately thread strawberries, grapes and cheese cubes. Serve immediately.

1 kabob with 2 Tbsp. dip: 147 cal., 9g fat (5g sat. fat), 22mg chol., 143mg sod., 12g carb. (11g sugars, 1g fiber), 6g pro.

COOL POOL

Here's a party-perfect way to chill drinks. First, fill some water balloons with water, tie them off and place in the freezer until frozen solid. Add the frozen water balloons to a kiddie pool, nestle in the beverages and invite your guests to grab and sip as they please.

SUMMERTIME FUN COOKIES

Use this basic sugar cookie recipe to make the perfect poolside treat. Kids (and adults) won't be able to get enough.
—*Coleen Walter, Bancroft, MI*

Prep: 30 min.
Bake: 10 min./batch + cooling
Makes: about 2½ dozen

- 1 cup butter, softened
- ¾ cup sugar
- 1 tsp. vanilla extract
- ½ tsp. almond extract
- 2 large eggs, room temperature
- 2¼ cups all-purpose flour
- 1 tsp. cream of tartar
- ½ tsp. baking soda
- ¼ tsp. salt
- ¼ tsp. ground nutmeg

FROSTING

- ¼ cup butter, softened
- 3 cups confectioners' sugar
- 1 tsp. almond extract
- 2 to 4 Tbsp. hot water
  Blue food coloring
  Optional decorations: Bear-shaped crackers, fish-shaped graham crackers, Airheads candies, gummy sour rings, white sugar pearls and palm tree party picks

1. Preheat oven to 350°. Cream butter and sugar until light and fluffy; beat in extracts and 1 egg at a time. In another bowl, whisk together the flour, cream of tartar, baking soda, salt and nutmeg; gradually beat into creamed mixture.
2. Drop dough by rounded tablespoonfuls 3 in. apart onto parchment-lined baking sheets; flatten slightly with bottom of a glass dipped in sugar. Bake until the edges begin to brown, 8-10 minutes. Remove from pan to wire racks; cool completely.
3. For frosting, beat butter, confectioners' sugar, extract and enough water to reach desired consistency; tint blue with food coloring. Spread over cookies. Decorate as desired.

1 cookie: 174 cal., 8g fat (5g sat. fat), 33mg chol., 107mg sod., 24g carb. (17g sugars, 0 fiber), 1g pro.

Score big when you load up the car with a cooler, folding chairs and these fantastic bites that offer make-ahead convenience. Perfect party starters at baseball, football and other events, these sweet and savory snacks (and drinks) make for ideal year-round munching.

JEN'S BAKED BEANS

My daughters wanted baked beans, and so I created my own recipe. With mustard, molasses and a dash of heat, this version is absolutely irresistible.
—*Jennifer Heasley, York, PA*

Prep: 20 min.
Bake: 50 min.
Makes: 8 servings

- 6 bacon strips, chopped
- 4 cans (15½ oz. each) great northern beans, rinsed and drained
- 1⅓ cups ketchup
- ⅔ cup packed brown sugar
- ⅓ cup molasses
- 3 Tbsp. yellow mustard
- 2½ tsp. garlic powder
- 1½ tsp. hot pepper sauce
- ¼ tsp. crushed red pepper flakes

1. Preheat oven to 325°. In an ovenproof Dutch oven, cook bacon over medium heat until crisp, stirring occasionally. Remove with a slotted spoon; drain the bacon on paper towels. Discard drippings.
2. Return bacon to pan. Stir in the remaining ingredients; bring to a boil. Place in oven; bake, covered, 50-60 minutes to allow the flavors to blend.
Freeze option: Freeze cooled baked beans in freezer containers. To use, partially thaw in refrigerator overnight. Heat beans through in a saucepan, stirring occasionally and adding a little broth or water if necessary.

¾ cup: 362 cal., 3g fat (1g sat. fat), 6mg chol., 1000mg sod., 71g carb. (39g sugars, 11g fiber), 13g pro.

BIG-BATCH BLOODY MARYS

Tailgates, game-day parties and big brunches call for a Bloody Mary recipe that caters to a bunch. This one has a little bit of a kick—just enough to get the crowd cheering.
—Taste of Home *Test Kitchen*

Takes: 20 min.
Makes: 8 servings

8   cups tomato juice
½   cup lemon juice
¼   cup lime juice
2   Tbsp. Worcestershire sauce
4   tsp. prepared horseradish, optional
1   tsp. celery salt
1   tsp. pepper
1   tsp. hot pepper sauce
2   cups vodka

OPTIONAL GARNISHES
  Celery ribs, pickle spears, green and ripe olives, cucumber slices, pickled mushrooms, cubed cheese, beef sticks, cherry tomatoes, cocktail shrimp

In a pitcher, stir together first 8 ingredients. For each serving, pour about 1 cup over ice with ¼ cup vodka; add the optional garnishes as desired.

1¼ cups: 180 cal., 1g fat (0 sat. fat), 0 chol., 817mg sod., 12g carb. (7g sugars, 1g fiber), 2g pro.

BLOODY MARY TRAVEL TIPS

- Make garnish skewers ahead of time using a variety of classic Bloody Mary fixings, such as cheese cubes, beef sticks, olives, pickled mushrooms and tiny tomatoes. Then guests can just pick up their fave combo and plunk it into their plastic cups.

- Keep a stash of pony-size beer bottles nearby to serve as chasers alongside the drink—the way it's done in bars across the Upper Midwest, especially in Bloody Mary-loving Wisconsin.

- Extra fixings help guests gussy up the drinks to suit their own tastes. Lemon wedges, hot sauce, steak sauce and horseradish are popular add-ins.

THREE-PEPPER COLESLAW

There are never any leftovers when I make this dish for a picnic, barbecue or any social gathering.
—*Priscilla Gilbert, Indian Harbour Beach, FL*

Prep: 20 min. + chilling
Makes: 8 servings

- 1   pkg. (10 oz.) angel hair coleslaw mix
- 1   medium sweet red pepper, finely chopped
- 1   medium green pepper, finely chopped
- 1   to 2 jalapeno peppers, seeded and finely chopped
- 3   green onions, chopped
- ¼   cup white wine vinegar
- 2   Tbsp. lime juice
- 2   tsp. canola oil
- 1   tsp. sugar
- ½   tsp. salt
- ¼   tsp. pepper

Place the first 5 ingredients in a large serving bowl. In a small bowl, whisk the remaining ingredients. Pour over coleslaw mixture; toss to coat. Cover and refrigerate for at least 30 minutes before serving.

Note: Wear disposable gloves when cutting the hot peppers; the oils can burn skin. Avoid touching your face.

¾ cup: 36 cal., 1g fat (0 sat. fat), 0 chol., 158mg sod., 6g carb. (3g sugars, 2g fiber), 1g pro. **Diabetic exchanges:** 1 vegetable.

TAILGATE SAUSAGES

You'll need just a handful of items to put together these incredible sandwiches. Fully cooked sausages are placed in buns with cheese and topped with giardiniera, then wrapped in foil so they're easy to transport and a breeze to grill—anywhere!
—*Matthew Hass, Ellison Bay, WI*

Takes: 20 min.
Makes: 4 servings

- ½ cup giardiniera, drained
- ½ tsp. sugar
- 4 slices provolone cheese
- 4 brat buns or hot dog buns, split
- 4 cooked Italian sausage links
    Additional giardiniera, optional

1. In a bowl, combine giardiniera and sugar; set mixture aside.
2. Place cheese in buns; top with sausages and giardiniera mixture. Wrap individually in a double thickness of heavy-duty foil (about 12x10 in.). Grill, uncovered, over medium-hot heat for 8-10 minutes or until heated through and cheese is melted. Open the foil carefully to allow steam to escape. If desired, serve with additional giardiniera.
Note: Giardiniera, a pickled vegetable mixture, is available in mild and hot varieties and can be found in the Italian or pickle section of your grocery store.

1 sandwich: 584 cal., 33g fat (15g sat. fat), 84mg chol., 1401mg sod., 39g carb. (9g sugars, 2g fiber), 31g pro.

 ⏱ 5i

DIJON-BACON DIP FOR PRETZELS

With just four ingredients that you probably already have in your pantry, this quick appetizer comes together in a snap. If you like the zip of horseradish, start with 1 or 2 teaspoons and add more to your taste.
—*Isabelle Rooney, Summerville, SC*

Takes: 5 min.
Makes: 1½ cups

- 1 cup mayonnaise
- ½ cup Dijon mustard
- ¼ cup bacon bits or crumbled cooked bacon
- 1 to 3 tsp. prepared horseradish
  Pretzels or pretzel crisps

In a small bowl, combine the mayonnaise, mustard, bacon and horseradish. Cover and chill until serving. Serve with pretzels.

2 Tbsp.: 154 cal., 16g fat (2g sat. fat), 8mg chol., 428mg sod., 1g carb. (0 sugars, 0 fiber), 2g pro.

TAILGATE CRATE
Keep a crate or box stocked with tailgate essentials so you're ready to party at a moment's notice.

PEANUT BUTTER CAKE BARS

These cakelike bars are packed with peanut butter and chocolate chips, and they are perfect for any occasion. Kids and adults alike are in for a treat with these tailgate gems.
—*Charlotte Ennis, Lake Arthur, NM*

Prep: 15 min.
Bake: 45 min. + cooling
Makes: 2 dozen

- ⅔ cup butter, softened
- ⅔ cup peanut butter
- 1 cup sugar
- 1 cup packed brown sugar
- 4 large eggs, room temperature
- 2 tsp. vanilla extract
- 2 cups all-purpose flour
- 2 tsp. baking powder
- ½ tsp. salt
- 1 pkg. (11½ oz.) milk chocolate chips

1. Preheat oven to 350°. In a large bowl, cream butter, peanut butter, sugar and brown sugar. Add eggs, one at a time, beating well after each addition. Beat in vanilla. Combine the flour, baking powder and salt; gradually add to creamed mixture. Stir in chocolate chips.
2. Spread into a greased 13x9-in. baking pan. Bake until a toothpick inserted in the center comes out clean, 45-50 minutes. Cool on a wire rack. Cut into bars.

1 bar: 277 cal., 14g fat (6g sat. fat), 52mg chol., 178mg sod., 35g carb. (25g sugars, 1g fiber), 5g pro.

LOW-COUNTRY BOIL

Whether you call it a low-country boil, Frogmore stew, seafood boil or Beaufort stew, it all means the same thing—time to party! Invite the gang over for this change-of-pace bash that gives your grill a break and turns the spotlight on savory southern favorites.

OVEN-FRIED CORNBREAD

Nothing says good southern cooking like crisp cornbread baked in a cast-iron skillet. This is an old family recipe that has been passed down to each generation.
—*Emory Doty, Jasper, GA*

Prep: 20 min.
Bake: 15 min.
Makes: 8 servings

- 4   Tbsp. canola oil, divided
- 1½ cups finely ground white cornmeal
- ¼   cup sugar
- 2   tsp. baking powder
- 1   tsp. baking soda
- 1   tsp. salt
- 2   large eggs, room temperature
- 2   cups buttermilk

1. Place 2 Tbsp. oil in a 10-in. cast-iron skillet; place in oven. Preheat oven to 450°. Whisk together the white cornmeal, sugar, baking powder, baking soda and salt. In another bowl, whisk together eggs, buttermilk and remaining oil. Add to cornmeal mixture; stir just until moistened.
2. Carefully remove hot skillet from oven. Add batter; bake until golden brown and a toothpick inserted in center comes out clean, 15-20 minutes. Cut cornbread into wedges; serve warm.

1 wedge: 238 cal., 9g fat (1g sat. fat), 49mg chol., 709mg sod., 33g carb. (10g sugars, 1g fiber), 6g pro.

BBQ CHICKEN GRITS BITES

I love grits and barbecued chicken, so I decided to combine them into a fun and tasty appetizer. You can also use shredded pork instead of chicken.
—*Jamie Jones, Madison, GA*

Prep: 30 min.
Bake: 15 min.
Makes: 2½ dozen

- 2 **cups 2% milk**
- ¾ **cup quick-cooking grits**
- ¼ **tsp. salt**
- ⅛ **tsp. pepper**
- 4 **oz. crumbled goat cheese, divided**
- ¼ **cup apricot preserves**
- ¼ **cup barbecue sauce**
- 1½ **cups chopped rotisserie chicken**
- 3 **green onions, thinly sliced**

1. Preheat the oven to 350°. Grease 30 mini-muffin cups.
2. In a large saucepan, bring the milk to a boil. Slowly stir in the grits, salt and pepper. Reduce heat to medium-low; cook, covered, until thickened, about 5 minutes, stirring occasionally. Stir in half of the cheese. Spoon 1 Tbsp. mixture into each of the prepared muffin cups.
3. In a bowl, mix the preserves and barbecue sauce; toss with chicken. Spoon about 1 tsp. chicken mixture into each cup; press lightly into grits.
4. Bake until heated through, 15-20 minutes. Top with the remaining cheese; sprinkle with green onions. Cool 5 minutes before removing from pans. Serve warm.

1 appetizer: 56 cal., 2g fat (1g sat. fat), 12mg chol., 76mg sod., 7g carb. (3g sugars, 0 fiber), 4g pro.

5i

SWEET TEA BOYSENBERRY SHANDY

I love an ice-cold beer on a hot summer day. I also love sweet tea, so one day I got the great idea to mix the two. It was absolutely delicious. I experimented with different flavorings, and this combo was my favorite.
—*Kelly Williams, Forked River, NJ*

Prep: 10 min.
Cook: 5 min. + chilling
Makes: 12 servings (2¼ qt.)

- 1½ cups water
- 4 tea bags
- ¾ cup sugar
- ¾ cup boysenberry syrup
- 4 cups cold water
- 3 bottles (12 oz. each) beer or white ale, chilled
- 1 medium orange, sliced, optional

1. In a large saucepan, bring water to a boil; remove from heat. Add the tea bags; steep, covered, 3-5 minutes, according to taste. Discard tea bags. Stir in sugar and syrup until dissolved. Stir in cold water. Transfer to a 3-qt. pitcher; refrigerate until cold.
2. Stir beer into tea mixture; serve immediately. If desired, top individual servings with orange slices.

¾ cup: 137 cal., 0 fat (0 sat. fat), 0 chol., 5mg sod., 29g carb. (26g sugars, 0 fiber), 0 pro.

→

When at the grocery store, look for boysenberry syrup alongside the maple syrup. Stir a tablespoon into marinades for grilled chicken, or use it to give oatmeal a sweet flavor boost. Of course it's also a great way to jazz up waffles and pancakes.

FROGMORE STEW

This picnic-style medley of shrimp, smoked kielbasa, corn and spuds is a specialty of South Carolina cuisine. It's commonly dubbed Frogmore stew or Beaufort stew in recognition of both of the low-country communities that lay claim to its origin. Give it a try! The one-pot wonder never disappoints.
—Taste of Home *Test Kitchen*

Prep: 10 min.
Cook: 35 min.
Makes: 8 servings

16 cups water
1 large sweet onion, quartered
3 Tbsp. seafood seasoning
2 medium lemons, halved, optional
1 lb. small red potatoes
1 lb. smoked kielbasa or fully cooked hot links, cut into 1-in. pieces
4 medium ears sweet corn, cut into thirds
2 lbs. uncooked medium shrimp, peeled and deveined
   Seafood cocktail sauce
   Melted butter
   Additional seafood seasoning

1. In a stockpot, combine water, onion, seafood seasoning and, if desired, lemons; bring to a boil. Add the potatoes; cook, uncovered, 10 minutes. Add kielbasa and corn; return to a boil. Reduce heat; simmer, uncovered, 10-12 minutes or until potatoes are tender. Add shrimp; cook 2-3 minutes longer or until shrimp turn pink.

2. Drain; transfer to a bowl. Serve with seafood cocktail sauce, melted butter and additional seasoning.

1 serving: 369 cal., 18g fat (6g sat. fat), 175mg chol., 751mg sod., 24g carb. (7g sugars, 2g fiber), 28g pro.

BLACK-EYED PEA TOMATO SALAD

Spending time in the kitchen with my late aunt was so much fun because she was an amazing cook and teacher. This black-eyed pea salad was one of her specialties. It's easy to make and is a nice alternative to pasta or potato salad. Add cooked cubed chicken breast to make it a meal on its own.
—*Patricia Ness, La Mesa, CA*

Prep: 20 min. + chilling
Makes: 12 servings

- 4 cans (15½ oz. each) black-eyed peas, rinsed and drained
- 3 large tomatoes, chopped
- 1 large sweet red pepper, chopped
- 1 cup diced red onion
- 4 bacon strips, cooked and crumbled
- 1 jalapeno pepper, seeded and diced
- ½ cup canola oil
- ¼ cup sugar
- ¼ cup rice vinegar
- 2 Tbsp. minced fresh parsley
- 1½ tsp. salt
- ½ tsp. pepper
- ⅛ tsp. garlic powder

1. Combine the first 6 ingredients. In another bowl, whisk together remaining ingredients. Add to the bean mixture; toss to coat. Refrigerate, covered, at least 6 hours or overnight.
2. Stir mixture just before serving.
Note: Wear disposable gloves when cutting hot peppers; the oils can burn skin. Avoid touching your face.

¾ cup: 242 cal., 11g fat (1g sat. fat), 3mg chol., 602mg sod., 29g carb. (9g sugars, 5g fiber), 9g pro. **Diabetic exchanges:** 2 starch, 2 fat.

FAVORITE CHOCOLATE-BOURBON PECAN TART

I grew up in Louisiana, where, as in most of the South, pecan pie is a staple during the holidays. When I tasted my first chocolate pecan pie, it blew my mind! I decided to boost the decadence of this dessert by adding bourbon, a great complement to the chocolate, and by drizzling caramel on top. Store-bought pastry for a pie crust makes it simple, but you can make your own from scratch as well.
—*Amber Needham, San Antonio, TX*

Prep: 15 min.
Bake: 30 min. + cooling
Makes: 12 servings

- Pastry for single-crust pie (9 in.)
- ½ cup semisweet chocolate chips
- 2 large eggs, room temperature
- ¾ cup dark corn syrup
- ½ cup sugar
- ¼ cup butter, melted
- 2 Tbsp. bourbon
- ¼ tsp. salt
- 1 cup pecan halves, toasted
- ¼ cup hot caramel ice cream topping

1. Preheat oven to 375°. On a lightly floured surface, roll dough to a 12-in. circle. Press onto bottom and up sides of an ungreased 11-in. tart pan with removable bottom. Sprinkle with chocolate chips.
2. Beat eggs, corn syrup, sugar, butter, bourbon and salt. Stir in pecans. Pour over chocolate chips. Bake until center is just set and crust is golden brown, 30-35 minutes.
3. Cool on a wire rack. Cut into slices. Serve with caramel topping.
Note: To toast nuts, bake in a shallow pan in a 350° oven for 5-10 minutes or cook in a skillet over low heat until lightly browned, stirring occasionally.

Pastry for single-crust pie (9 in.): Combine 1¼ cups all-purpose flour and ¼ tsp. salt; cut in ½ cup cold butter until crumbly. Gradually add 3-5 Tbsp. ice water, tossing with a fork until dough holds together when pressed. Cover and refrigerate 1 hour.

1 slice: 357 cal., 20g fat (9g sat. fat), 61mg chol., 250mg sod., 43g carb. (32g sugars, 2g fiber), 4g pro.

HOMETOWN POTLUCK

Church suppers, block parties, charity potlucks and bake sales...summer is the perfect time for friendship, fellowship, fundraising and fun! Turn here for easily impressive buffet contributions, but don't be too surprised if you bring home an empty dish!

CHICKEN & SWISS CASSEROLE

Who says you can't enjoy casseroles in the summer? This comforting dish is always a crowd-pleaser. Using rotisserie chicken from the deli makes prep simple.
—*Christina Petri, Alexandria, MN*

Prep: 30 min.
Bake: 10 min.
Makes: 8 servings

- 5½ cups uncooked egg noodles (about ½ lb.)
- 3 Tbsp. olive oil
- 3 shallots, chopped
- 3 small garlic cloves, minced
- ⅓ cup all-purpose flour
- 2 cups chicken broth
- ¾ cup 2% milk
- 1½ tsp. dried thyme
- ¾ tsp. grated lemon zest
- ½ tsp. salt
- ¼ tsp. ground nutmeg
- ¼ tsp. pepper
- 5 cups cubed rotisserie chicken
- 1½ cups frozen peas
- 2 cups shredded Swiss cheese
- ¾ cup dry bread crumbs
- 2 Tbsp. butter, melted

1. Preheat oven to 350°. Cook the noodles according to package directions; drain. In a large skillet, heat oil over medium heat. Add shallots and garlic; cook and stir 45 seconds. Stir in flour; cook and stir 1 minute. Add the broth, milk, thyme, lemon zest, salt, nutmeg and pepper. Stir in chicken and peas; heat through. Stir in noodles and cheese.
2. Transfer to a greased 13x9-in. baking dish. In a small bowl, mix dry bread crumbs and butter; sprinkle over top. Bake 8-10 minutes or until top is browned.

1¼ cups: 551 cal., 25g fat (10g sat. fat), 136mg chol., 661mg sod., 38g carb. (4g sugars, 3g fiber), 41g pro.

GARLIC-DILL DEVILED EGGS

Fresh dill and garlic easily perk up the flavor of these irresistible appetizers. You'll want to serve them all year long.

—*Kami Horch, Calais, ME*

Prep: 20 min. + chilling
Makes: 2 dozen

- 12 hard-boiled large eggs
- ⅔ cup mayonnaise
- 4 tsp. dill pickle relish
- 2 tsp. snipped fresh dill
- 2 tsp. Dijon mustard
- 1 tsp. coarsely ground pepper
- ¼ tsp. garlic powder
- ⅛ tsp. paprika or cayenne pepper

1. Cut eggs lengthwise in half. Remove yolks, reserving whites. In a bowl, mash yolks. Stir in all remaining ingredients except paprika. Spoon or pipe into egg whites.
2. Refrigerate, covered, at least 30 minutes before serving. Sprinkle with paprika.

1 stuffed egg half: 81 cal., 7g fat (1g sat. fat), 94mg chol., 81mg sod., 1g carb. (0 sugars, 0 fiber), 3g pro.

FRUIT WITH POPPY SEED DRESSING

Cool, colorful and easy to prepare, this refreshing, good-for-you fruit salad is a summertime favorite. The simple five-ingredient dressing makes it special.
—*Peggy Mills, Texarkana, AR*

Prep: 20 min. + standing
Makes: 12 servings

- 3 **Tbsp. honey**
- 1 **Tbsp. white vinegar**
- 1 **tsp. ground mustard**
- ¼ **tsp. salt**
- ¼ **tsp. onion powder**
- ⅓ **cup canola oil**
- 1 **tsp. poppy seeds**
- 1 **fresh pineapple, cut into 1½-in. cubes**
- 3 **medium kiwifruit, halved and sliced**
- 2 **cups fresh strawberries, halved**

1. In a small bowl, whisk first 5 ingredients. Gradually whisk in oil until blended. Stir in poppy seeds; let stand 1 hour.
2. In a large bowl, combine fruits. Drizzle with dressing; toss gently to coat.

1 cup: 129 cal., 7g fat (0 sat. fat), 0 chol., 51mg sod., 19g carb. (14g sugars, 2g fiber), 1g pro. **Diabetic exchanges:** 1½ fat, 1 fruit.

ARTICHOKE SHRIMP PASTA SALAD

I have enjoyed this recipe for as long as I can remember. My mom made it famous, and she passed it down to me on my wedding day. It's one of those potluck staples that folks can't get enough of.
—*Mary McCarley, Charlotte, NC*

Prep: 20 min.
Cook: 10 min. + chilling
Makes: 12 servings

1 pkg. (16 oz.) bow tie pasta
2 lbs. peeled and deveined cooked shrimp (31-40 per lb.)
2 cans (7½ oz. each) marinated quartered artichoke hearts, drained
2 cans (2¼ oz. each) sliced ripe olives, drained
2 cups crumbled feta cheese
8 green onions, sliced
½ cup chopped fresh parsley
¼ cup chopped fresh basil
DRESSING
½ cup white wine vinegar
½ cup olive oil
¼ cup lemon juice
2 Tbsp. chopped fresh basil
2 tsp. Dijon mustard
   Fresh ground pepper, optional

1. Cook pasta according to the package directions for al dente. Drain the pasta; rinse with cold water and drain well. In a large bowl, combine the pasta, shrimp, artichokes, olives, cheese, green onions, parsley and basil.
2. In a small bowl, whisk the vinegar, oil, lemon juice, basil, Dijon mustard and, if desired, pepper. Pour dressing over the pasta mixture; toss to coat. Refrigerate, covered, 2 hours before serving.

1⅓ cups: 453 cal., 23g fat (7g sat. fat), 135mg chol., 757mg sod., 34g carb. (2g sugars, 6g fiber), 28g pro.

CHOCOLATE-COCONUT LAYER BARS

I'm a huge fan of Nanaimo bars, the no-bake layered dessert named for the city in British Columbia. For fun, I reinvented this treat with coconut lovers in mind.
—*Shannon Dobos, Calgary, AB*

Prep: 20 min. + chilling
Makes: 3 dozen

- ¾ cup butter, cubed
- 3 cups Oreo cookie crumbs
- 2 cups sweetened shredded coconut
- ½ cup cream of coconut

FILLING

- ⅓ cup butter, softened
- 3 Tbsp. cream of coconut
- ¼ tsp. coconut extract
- 3 cups confectioners' sugar
- 1 to 2 Tbsp. 2% milk

TOPPING

- 1½ cups semisweet chocolate chips
- 4 tsp. canola oil
- 3 Mounds candy bars (1¾ oz. each), coarsely chopped, optional

1. Microwave butter on high until melted; stir until smooth. Stir in cookie crumbs, coconut and cream of coconut until blended (mixture will be wet). Spread onto the bottom of an ungreased 13x9-in. baking pan. Refrigerate until set, about 30 minutes.

2. For filling, beat butter, cream of coconut and extract until smooth. Gradually beat in the confectioners' sugar and enough milk to reach a spreading consistency. Spread over the crust.

3. For topping, microwave chocolate chips and oil until melted; stir until smooth. Cool slightly; spread over filling. If desired, sprinkle with chopped candy bars. Refrigerate.

1 bar: 229 cal., 13g fat (8g sat. fat), 15mg chol., 124mg sod., 28g carb. (23g sugars, 1g fiber), 1g pro.

FROSTED CARROT CAKE COOKIES

I took my favorite carrot cake recipe and tweaked it to make cookies. Just like the cake, the yummy bites are filled with shredded carrot, pineapple and raisins—and topped with a homemade cream cheese frosting.
—*Lawrence Earl, Sumner, MI*

Prep: 30 min.
Bake: 10 min./batch + cooling
Makes: about 4½ dozen

- 1 cup butter, softened
- 1 cup sugar
- 1 cup packed brown sugar
- 2 large eggs, room temperature
- 1 tsp. vanilla extract
- 3 cups all-purpose flour
- 1 tsp. baking soda
- ½ tsp. salt
- 1 medium carrot, shredded
- ½ cup crushed pineapple, drained and patted dry
- ½ cup golden raisins

FROSTING

- 6 oz. cream cheese, softened
- 3¾ cups confectioners' sugar
- 1½ tsp. vanilla extract
- 2 to 3 Tbsp. 2% milk
  Toasted chopped walnuts, optional

1. Preheat oven to 350°. In a large bowl, cream butter, sugar and brown sugar until light and fluffy. Beat in eggs and vanilla. In another bowl, whisk flour, baking soda and salt; gradually beat into creamed mixture. Stir in carrot, pineapple and raisins.

2. Drop dough by tablespoonfuls 2 in. apart onto ungreased baking sheets. Bake until light brown, 10-12 minutes. Remove from pans to wire racks to cool completely.

3. In a small bowl, beat cream cheese until smooth. Gradually beat in confectioners' sugar, vanilla and enough milk to reach a spreading consistency. Frost cookies. If desired, sprinkle with walnuts. Store in an airtight container in the refrigerator.

Freeze option: Drop cookie dough by tablespoonfuls onto waxed paper-lined baking sheets; freeze until firm. Transfer to airtight freezer containers; return to freezer. To use, bake cookies as directed.

1 cookie: 129 cal., 4g fat (3g sat. fat), 18mg chol., 81mg sod., 22g carb. (16g sugars, 0 fiber), 1g pro.

SUMMER'S TOP

CONDIMENTS, PRESERVES & MORE

Few things amp up flavor like savory spice blends and tangy sauces. Take ho-hum dishes over the top with mouthwatering—and easy—jams, sauces and canned delights. They'll help you enjoy summer's bounty for months to come.

BARBECUE SEASONING

I use this rub on country-style ribs, pork chops and chicken. You might have all of the seasonings on hand to make a batch. Whatever you don't use will keep for the next time.
—*Rose Rainier, Sheridan, WY*

Takes: 10 min.
Makes: 1 cup

¼ cup beef bouillon granules
¼ cup chili powder
¼ cup paprika
1 Tbsp. sugar
1 Tbsp. garlic salt
1 Tbsp. onion salt
1 tsp. celery salt
1 tsp. cayenne pepper
1 tsp. pepper
½ tsp. curry powder
½ tsp. dried oregano

In a small bowl, combine all ingredients. Store in an airtight container in a cool, dry place for up to 6 months. Use as a rub for ribs, chicken or pork.

1 tsp.: 6 cal., 0 fat (0 sat. fat), 0 chol., 476mg sod., 1g carb. (0 sugars, 0 fiber), 0 pro.

⑸ⁱ

HOMEMADE LEMON CURD

Lemon curd is a bright, summery spread for scones, biscuits or other baked goods. You can find it in larger grocery stores alongside the jams and jellies or with baking supplies, but we like making it from scratch.
—*Mark Hagen, Milwaukee, WI*

Prep: 20 min. + chilling
Makes: 1⅔ cups

> 3 **large eggs**
> 1 **cup sugar**
> ½ **cup lemon juice (about 2 lemons)**
> ¼ **cup butter, cubed**
> 1 **Tbsp. grated lemon zest**

In a small heavy saucepan over medium heat, whisk eggs, sugar and lemon juice until blended. Add butter and lemon zest; cook, whisking constantly, until the mixture is thickened and coats the back of a metal spoon. Transfer to a small bowl; cool 10 minutes. Refrigerate, covered, until cold.

2 Tbsp.: 110 cal., 5g fat (3g sat. fat), 52mg chol., 45mg sod., 16g carb. (16g sugars, 0 fiber), 2g pro.

Always use fresh lemon juice for lemon curd, not the bottled variety. The results are much tastier. Don't use pans or spoons of aluminum or unlined copper when making curd. They could react with the acid in the lemons, discoloring the curd and leaving an unpleasant metallic aftertaste.

5i
RASPBERRY RHUBARB JAM

I love making and enjoying this jam each summer, but I usually end up giving most of it away! People love receiving it as gift.
—*LaVonne Van Hoff, Rockwell City, IA*

Prep: 5 min. + chilling
Cook: 35 min. + chilling
Makes: 6 cups

6 cups sliced fresh or frozen rhubarb
4 cups sugar
1 pkg. (6 oz.) raspberry gelatin
1 can (21 oz.) raspberry pie filling

1. In a large saucepan, combine rhubarb and sugar; cover and refrigerate overnight.
2. Place saucepan over medium heat; bring to a boil. Reduce heat; simmer, uncovered, 30-35 minutes or until rhubarb is tender. Meanwhile, rinse six 1-cup plastic containers and lids with boiling water. Dry thoroughly.

3. Stir the gelatin and pie filling into the rhubarb mixture. Bring to a boil. Remove from heat; cool.
4. Fill all containers to within ½ in. of tops. Wipe off the top edges of the containers; immediately cover with lids. Refrigerate up to 3 weeks or freeze up to 1 year. Thaw frozen jam in refrigerator before serving.

2 Tbsp.: 108 cal., 0 fat (0 sat. fat), 0 chol., 17mg sod., 27g carb. (23g sugars, 1g fiber), 0 pro.

BEST EVER SWEET PICKLES

When I was a kid, I always looked forward to the homemade jams and jellies my granny made from her farm-grown berries. Our urban backyard doesn't have room for a berry patch, but we do have a trellis for growing cucumbers. I like to pack away jars of these sweet pickles every summer, hoping they'll last the winter—but they are always gone too soon.
—*Ellie Martin Cliffe, Milwaukee, WI*

Prep: 1 hour + standing
Process: 10 min.
Makes: 4 pints

9 cups sliced pickling cucumbers
1 large sweet onion, halved and thinly sliced
¼ cup canning salt
1 cup sugar
1 cup water
1 cup white vinegar
½ cup cider vinegar
2 Tbsp. mustard seed
1 tsp. celery seed
½ tsp. whole peppercorns
4 bay leaves
12 garlic cloves, crushed

1. In a large nonreactive bowl, combine the cucumbers, onion and canning salt. Cover with crushed ice and mix well. Let stand for 3 hours. Drain; rinse and drain thoroughly.
2. In a Dutch oven, combine sugar, water, vinegars, mustard seed, celery seed and peppercorns. Bring mixture to a boil, stirring to dissolve sugar. Add cucumber mixture; return to a boil, stirring occasionally. Reduce heat; simmer, uncovered, about 4-5 minutes or until heated through.
3. Carefully ladle the hot mixture into 4 hot wide-mouth 1-pint jars, leaving ½-in. of headspace. Add 3 garlic cloves and 1 bay leaf to each jar. Remove the air bubbles and, if necessary, adjust headspace by adding hot pickling liquid. Wipe rims. Center lids on jars; screw on bands until fingertip tight.

4. Place jars into canner with simmering water, ensuring that they are completely covered with water. Bring to a boil; process for 10 minutes. Remove jars and cool.

¼ cup: 35 cal., 0 fat (0 sat. fat), 0 chol., 175mg sod., 8g carb. (7g sugars, 0 fiber), 0 pro.

GARLIC-PEPPER RUB

This rub adds a tasty mix of garlic, pepper and lemon to any burger. It's a great way to spice up your grilling experience.
—*Ann Marie Moch, Kintyre, ND*

Takes: 5 min.
Makes: ⅔ cup

6	Tbsp. lemon-pepper seasoning
2	Tbsp. dried thyme
2	Tbsp. paprika
2	tsp. garlic powder
1	tsp. sugar
½	tsp. salt
¼	tsp. ground coriander
⅛	tsp. ground cumin
⅛	tsp. cayenne pepper

In a large bowl, combine all the ingredients; store in a covered container. Rub over meat or poultry; let stand for at least 30 minutes before grilling or broiling.

1 tsp.: 5 cal., 0 fat (0 sat. fat), 0 chol., 296mg sod., 1g carb. (0 sugars, 0 fiber), 0 pro.

LUSCIOUS BLUEBERRY JAM

This perfectly spreadable blueberry jam boasts a beautiful dark color with a sweet, seasonal flavor. Spread it on extra thick!
—*Karen Haen, Sturgeon Bay, WI*

Prep: 20 min.
Cook: 20 min. + standing
Makes: 8 cups

- 8 **cups fresh blueberries**
- 2 **Tbsp. lemon juice**
- 1 **pkg. (1¾ oz.) powdered fruit pectin**
- 7 **cups sugar**

1. Mash the blueberries; transfer to a Dutch oven. Add the lemon juice; stir in pectin. Bring to a full rolling boil over high heat, stirring constantly.

2. Stir in sugar; return to a full rolling boil. Boil for 1 minute, stirring constantly. Remove from the heat; skim off foam. Ladle into jars or freezer containers and cool to room temperature, about 1 hour.

3. Cover and let stand overnight or until set, but not longer than 24 hours. Refrigerate for up to 3 weeks or freeze for up to 12 months.

2 Tbsp.: 95 cal., 0 fat (0 sat. fat), 0 chol., 0 sod., 25g carb. (24g sugars, 0 fiber), 0 pro.

 🕔

QUICK & EASY HONEY MUSTARD

This fast, easy mustard with rice vinegar and honey has more flavor than any other honey mustard dressing I have ever tried.

—Sharon Rehm, New Blaine, AR

Takes: 5 min.
Makes: 1 cup

½   cup stone-ground mustard
¼   cup honey
¼   cup rice vinegar

In a small bowl, whisk all ingredients. Refrigerate until serving.

1 Tbsp.: 28 cal., 1g fat (0 sat. fat), 0 chol., 154mg sod., 6g carb. (5g sugars, 0 fiber), 0 pro.

 CHUNKY PEACH SPREAD

Here's a fruit spread that captures the best tastes of late summer. I like that it's low in sugar and not overly sweet, which lets the fresh peach flavor shine through.
—*Rebecca Baird, Salt Lake City, UT*

Prep: 20 min.
Cook: 10 min. + cooling
Makes: about 3½ cups

- 7 medium peaches (2 to 2½ lbs.)
- 1 envelope unflavored gelatin
- ¼ cup cold water
- ⅓ cup sugar
- 1 Tbsp. lemon juice

1. Fill a large saucepan two-thirds full with water; bring to a boil. Cut a shallow "X" on the bottom of each peach. Using tongs, place peaches, a few at a time, in boiling water for 30-60 seconds or just until skin at the "X" begins to loosen. Remove peaches and immediately drop into ice water. Pull off the skins with tip of a knife; discard skins. Chop the peaches.
2. In a small bowl, sprinkle gelatin over cold water; let stand 1 minute. Meanwhile, in a large saucepan, combine peaches, sugar and lemon juice; bring to a boil. Mash peaches. Reduce heat; simmer, uncovered, 5 minutes. Add gelatin mixture; cook 1 minute longer, stirring until gelatin is completely dissolved. Cool 10 minutes.
3. Pour into jars. Refrigerate, covered, up to 3 weeks.

2 Tbsp.: 25 cal., 0 fat (0 sat. fat), 0 chol., 1mg sod., 6g carb. (5g sugars, 1g fiber), 1g pro.

STRAWBERRY FREEZER JAM

Strawberry season is in early June here in Indiana. A dear friend gave me this recipe, and it quickly became a favorite. It's great on ice cream, too!
—*Mary Jean Ellis, Indianapolis, IN*

Prep: 40 min. + freezing
Makes: 4½ pints

- 2 qt. fresh strawberries
- 5½ cups sugar
- 1 cup light corn syrup
- ¼ cup lemon juice
- ¾ cup water
- 1 pkg. (1¾ oz.) powdered fruit pectin

1. Wash and mash berries, measuring out enough mashed berries to make 4 cups; place in a large bowl. Stir in sugar, corn syrup and lemon juice. Let stand 10 minutes.

2. In a Dutch oven, combine strawberry mixture and water. Stir in pectin. Bring to a full rolling boil over high heat, stirring constantly. Boil 1 minute, stirring constantly. Remove from heat; skim off foam.

3. Carefully pour mixture into jars or freezer containers, leaving ½ in. headspace. Cover and let stand overnight or until set, but not longer than 24 hours. Refrigerate jam up to 3 weeks or freeze up to 12 months.

2 Tbsp.: 79 cal., 0 fat (0 sat. fat), 0 chol., 3mg sod., 20g carb. (20g sugars, 0 fiber), 0 pro.

BASIL & PARSLEY PESTO

Toss this herby pesto with pasta, spread it over sandwiches or stir it into an Italian-style soup, like minestrone.
—*Lorraine Stevenski, Land O' Lakes, FL*

Takes: 15 min.
Makes: 1¼ cups

- 2 cups loosely packed basil leaves
- 1 cup loosely packed Italian parsley
- ¼ cup slivered almonds, toasted
- 2 garlic cloves
- 4 tsp. grated lemon zest
- ⅓ cup lemon juice
- 2 Tbsp. honey
- ½ tsp. salt
- ½ cup olive oil
- ½ cup grated Parmesan cheese

1. Place basil, parsley, almonds and garlic in a small food processor; pulse until chopped. Add the lemon zest, juice, honey and salt; process until blended. Continue processing while gradually adding oil in a steady stream. Add cheese; pulse just until blended.

2. Store pesto in an airtight container in the refrigerator for up to 1 week.

Freeze option: Transfer pesto to ice cube trays; cover and freeze pesto until firm. Remove from the trays and transfer to a resealable plastic freezer bag; return to freezer. To use, thaw cubes in refrigerator about 2 hours.

Note: To toast nuts, bake in a shallow pan in a 350° oven for 5-10 minutes or cook in a skillet over low heat until lightly browned, stirring nuts occasionally.

2 Tbsp.: 148 cal., 13g fat (2g sat. fat), 3mg chol., 195mg sod., 6g carb. (4g sugars, 1g fiber), 2g pro.

MRS. INA'S CORN RELISH

Mrs. Ina attended our church for many, many years. She made an amazing corn relish. Now, I whip up my own batches to give to friends.
—*Brenda Wooten, Dayton, TN*

Takes: 25 min.
Makes: 1½ cups

1	can (11 oz.) whole kernel corn
⅓	cup chopped onion
⅓	cup chopped celery
3	Tbsp. chopped green pepper
3	Tbsp. diced pimientos, drained
1	small garlic clove, minced, optional
⅓	cup sugar
1	tsp. salt
1	tsp. celery seed
1	tsp. mustard seed
¼	tsp. crushed red pepper flakes
⅛	tsp. ground ginger
1	cup white vinegar, divided
1	Tbsp. all-purpose flour
1½	tsp. ground mustard
¼	tsp. ground turmeric

1. Drain corn, reserving 1 Tbsp. liquid. In a small saucepan, combine onion, celery, green pepper, pimientos and, if desired, garlic. Stir in the sugar, salt, celery seed, mustard seed, pepper flakes, ginger and ¾ cup vinegar. Bring to a boil. Boil 5-7 minutes.
2. In a small bowl, mix flour, mustard and turmeric. Stir in reserved corn liquid until smooth. Add to vegetable mixture; stir in remaining vinegar. Cook, uncovered, until slightly thickened, 2-3 minutes. Add the corn; boil 1-2 minutes or until thickened.

¼ cup.: 88 cal., 1g fat (0 sat. fat), 0 chol., 550mg sod., 19g carb. (15g sugars, 2g fiber), 2g pro.

SPICY CHUNKY SALSA

Vinegar adds a refreshing tang to this sweet tomato salsa. It's wonderful as is, but for more heat, leave in some of the hot pepper seeds.
—*Donna Goutermont, Sequim, WA*

Prep: 1½ hours
Process: 15 min.
Makes: 8 pints

- 6 lbs. tomatoes
- 3 large green peppers, chopped
- 3 large onions, chopped
- 2 cups white vinegar
- 1 large sweet red pepper, chopped
- 1 can (12 oz.) tomato paste
- 4 jalapeno peppers, seeded and chopped
- 2 serrano peppers, seeded and chopped
- ½ cup sugar
- ½ cup minced fresh cilantro
- ½ cup bottled lemon juice
- 3 garlic cloves, minced
- 4 tsp. ground cumin
- 1 Tbsp. salt
- 2 tsp. dried oregano
- 1 tsp. hot pepper sauce

1. In a Dutch oven, bring 2 qt. water to a boil. Using a slotted spoon, place tomatoes, a few at a time, in boiling water for 30-60 seconds. Remove each tomato; immediately plunge into ice water. Drain and pat dry. Peel and finely chop the tomatoes to measure 9 cups; place in a stockpot.

2. Stir in remaining ingredients. Add water to cover; bring to a boil. Reduce heat; simmer, uncovered, until slightly thickened, for about 30 minutes.

3. Ladle hot mixture into hot 1-pint jars, leaving ½-in. headspace. Remove air bubbles and adjust headspace, if necessary, by adding hot mixture. Wipe rims. Center lids on jars; screw on bands until fingertip tight.

4. Place jars into canner with simmering water, ensuring that they are completely covered with water. Bring to a boil; process for 15 minutes. Remove jars and cool.

Note: The processing time listed is for altitudes of 1,000 feet or less. For altitudes up to 3,000 feet, add 5 minutes; 6,000 feet, add 10 minutes; 8,000 feet, add 15 minutes; 10,000 feet, add 20 minutes. Wear disposable gloves when cutting hot peppers; the oils can burn skin. Avoid touching your face.

¼ cup: 25 cal., 0 fat (0 sat. fat), 0 chol., 117mg sod., 6g carb. (4g sugars, 1g fiber), 1g pro. **Diabetic exchanges:** ½ starch.

SWEET & SPICY BARBECUE SAUCE

I've never cared that much for store-bought barbecue sauce. I like to make things from scratch—including this spicy, deep red-brown sauce. You'll find it clings well to grilled meats when you slather it on.
—Helena Georgette Mann, Sacramento, CA

Prep: 30 min.
Cook: 35 min.
Makes: 1½ cups

- 1 medium onion, chopped
- 1 Tbsp. canola oil
- 1 garlic clove, minced
- 1 to 3 tsp. chili powder
- ¼ tsp. cayenne pepper
- ¼ tsp. coarsely ground pepper
- 1 cup ketchup
- ⅓ cup molasses
- 2 Tbsp. cider vinegar
- 2 Tbsp. Worcestershire sauce
- 2 Tbsp. spicy brown mustard
- ½ tsp. hot pepper sauce

1. In a large saucepan, saute the onion in oil until tender. Add garlic; cook 1 minute. Stir in the chili powder, cayenne and pepper; cook 1 minute longer.

2. Stir in the ketchup, molasses, vinegar, Worcestershire sauce, mustard and pepper sauce. Bring to a boil. Reduce heat; simmer, uncovered, for 30-40 minutes or until sauce reaches desired consistency. Cool sauce for 15 minutes.

3. Strain sauce through a fine mesh strainer over a large bowl, discarding vegetables and seasonings. Store in an airtight container in the refrigerator for up to 1 month. Use as a basting sauce for grilled meats.

2 Tbsp.: 68 cal., 1g fat (0 sat. fat), 0 chol., 325mg sod., 14g carb. (11g sugars, 1g fiber), 0 pro.

VERY BERRY SPREAD

Two kinds of berries make this easy jam deliciously different. I always keep some of the spread on hand to enjoy not only for breakfast, but also as a treat during the day.
—*Irene Hagel, Choiceland, SK*

Prep: 15 min.
Process: 10 min.
Makes: about 8 half-pints

- 5 **cups fresh or frozen raspberries**
- 3 **cups fresh or frozen blueberries**
- 1 **Tbsp. bottled lemon juice**
- 1 **Tbsp. grated lemon zest**
- 1 **pkg. (1¾ oz.) powdered fruit pectin**
- 6 **cups sugar**

1. In a Dutch oven, combine the berries, lemon juice, zest and pectin. Bring to a full rolling boil over high heat, stirring constantly. Stir in sugar; return to a full rolling boil. Boil for 1 minute, stirring constantly.
2. Remove from the heat; skim off any foam. Carefully ladle hot mixture into hot half-pint jars, leaving ¼-in. headspace. Remove air bubbles; wipe rims and adjust lids. Process for 10 minutes in a boiling-water canner.
Note: The processing time listed is for altitudes of 1,000 feet or less. Add 1 minute to the processing time for each 1,000 feet of additional altitude.

2 Tbsp.: 86 cal., 0 fat (0 sat. fat), 0 chol., 0 sod., 22g carb. (20g sugars, 1g fiber), 0 pro.

SAVORY STEAK RUB

Marjoram stars in this recipe. I use the rub on a variety of grilled beef cuts. It locks in the natural juices of the meat for delectable results.
—*Donna Brockett, Kingfisher, OK*

Takes: 5 min.
Makes: ¼ cup

- 1 Tbsp. dried marjoram
- 1 Tbsp. dried basil
- 2 tsp. garlic powder
- 2 tsp. dried thyme
- 1 tsp. dried rosemary, crushed
- ¾ tsp. dried oregano

Combine all ingredients; store in an airtight container. Rub over steaks before grilling or broiling. Will season 4 to 5 steaks.

1 Tbsp.: 12 cal., 0 fat (0 sat. fat), 0 chol., 2mg sod., 3g carb. (0 sugars, 1g fiber), 1g pro.

HOMEMADE CANNED SPAGHETTI SAUCE

This DIY spaghetti sauce is a tomato grower's dream come true! Use up your summer bounty and enjoy it later in the year.
—*Tonya Branham, Mount Olive, AL*

Prep: 1½ hours + simmering
Process: 40 min.
Makes: 9 qt.

- 25 lbs. tomatoes (about 80 medium)
- 4 large green peppers, seeded
- 4 large onions, cut into wedges
- 2 cans (12 oz. each) tomato paste
- ¼ cup canola oil
- ⅔ cup sugar
- ¼ cup salt
- 8 garlic cloves, minced
- 4 tsp. dried oregano
- 2 tsp. dried parsley flakes
- 2 tsp. dried basil
- 2 tsp. crushed red pepper flakes
- 2 tsp. Worcestershire sauce
- 2 bay leaves
- 1 cup plus 2 Tbsp. bottled lemon juice

1. In a Dutch oven, bring 2 qt. water to a boil. Using a slotted spoon, place tomatoes, one at a time, in boiling water for 30-60 seconds. Remove each tomato and immediately plunge into ice water. Peel and quarter the tomatoes; place in a stockpot.

2. Pulse green peppers and onions in batches in a food processor until finely chopped; transfer to the stockpot. Stir in the next 11 ingredients. Add water to cover; bring to a boil. Reduce heat; simmer, uncovered, 4-5 hours, stirring occasionally.

3. Discard bay leaves. Add 2 Tbsp. lemon juice to each of 9 hot 1-qt. jars. Ladle hot mixture into jars, leaving ½-in. headspace. Remove air bubbles and adjust headspace, if necessary, by adding hot mixture. Wipe rims. Center lids on the jars; screw on bands until fingertip tight.

4. Place jars into canner with simmering water, ensuring that they are completely covered with water. Bring to a boil; process for 40 minutes. Remove jars and cool.

Note: The processing time listed is for altitudes of 1,000 feet or less. For altitudes up to 3,000 feet, add 5 minutes; 6,000 feet, add 10 minutes; 8,000 feet, add 15 minutes; 10,000 feet, add 20 minutes.

¾ cup: 118 cal., 5g fat (0 sat. fat), 0 chol., 614mg sod., 17g carb. (11g sugars, 4g fiber), 3g pro. **Diabetic exchanges:** 1 starch, 1 fat.

When a recipe notes "headspace," it's referring to the area left unfilled between the top of the food in a home canning jar and the bottom of the lid.

SUMMER'S COOLEST

FROSTY TREATS

Top off those lazy hazy days of summer with icy treats from the freezer. From casual to impressive, these frosty favorites tempt everyone's sweet tooth. Homemade ice cream, hand-held pops, colorful sundaes and frozen cakes make any day brighter.

LEMON MERINGUE FLOATS

I dreamed of this float idea one night and woke up knowing I needed to make it. Thank you, Mr. Sandman, for this new family favorite.
—*Cindy Reams, Philipsburg, PA*

Takes: 5 min.
Makes: 6 servings

- 3 **cups vanilla ice cream, softened if necessary**
- 18 **miniature meringue cookies**
- 6 **cups cold pink lemonade**

Place ½ cup ice cream and 3 cookies in each of 6 tall glasses. Top with lemonade. Serve floats immediately.

Note: Make these floats with frozen yogurt for a slimmed-down treat.

1½ cups with 3 cookies: 282 cal., 7g fat (4g sat. fat), 29mg chol., 77mg sod., 51g carb. (48g sugars, 0 fiber), 3g pro.

BLUEBERRY CHEESECAKE ICE CREAM

After sampling this flavor at an ice cream stand, I kept trying to duplicate it until it was just right. I think I nailed it and hope you agree.
—*Melissa Symington, Neche, ND*

Prep: 55 min. + chilling
Process: 20 min. + freezing
Makes: 2 qt.

- ½ **cup sugar**
- 1 **Tbsp. cornstarch**
- ½ **cup water**
- 1¼ **cups fresh or frozen blueberries**
- 1 **Tbsp. lemon juice**

GRAHAM CRACKER MIXTURE
- 2¼ **cups graham cracker crumbs (about 36 squares)**
- 2 **Tbsp. sugar**
- ½ **tsp. ground cinnamon**
- ½ **cup butter, melted**

ICE CREAM
- 1½ **cups sugar**
- 1 **pkg. (3.4 oz.) instant cheesecake or vanilla pudding mix**
- 1 **qt. heavy whipping cream**
- 2 **cups milk**
- 2 **tsp. vanilla extract**

1. In a small saucepan, combine sugar and cornstarch. Gradually stir in the water until smooth. Stir in blueberries and lemon juice. Bring to a boil over medium-high heat. Reduce the heat; simmer, uncovered, for 5 minutes or until slightly thickened, stirring occasionally. Cover mixture and refrigerate until chilled.
2. In a bowl, combine the cracker crumbs, sugar and cinnamon. Stir in butter. Pat into an ungreased 15x10-in. baking pan. Bake at 350° until lightly browned, 10-15 minutes. Cool completely on a wire rack.

3. Meanwhile, in a large bowl, whisk the ice cream ingredients. Fill ice cream freezer cylinder two-thirds full; freeze according to manufacturer's directions. Refrigerate the remaining mixture until ready to freeze. Whisk before adding to ice cream freezer (mixture will have some lumps).
4. Crumble the graham cracker mixture. In a large container, layer the ice cream, graham cracker mixture and blueberry sauce 3 times; swirl. Freeze.

½ cup: 459 cal., 30g fat (18g sat. fat), 101mg chol., 252mg sod., 47g carb. (37g sugars, 1g fiber), 3g pro.

When using frozen blueberries in baked goods, consider reducing the liquid in the recipe and increasing the thickener. Frozen blueberries give off more juice than fresh.

❄️
FROZEN PEACH PIES

A refreshing, peachy filling and a buttery graham cracker crust are the perfect pair. I've found that these pies can be frozen for up to three days.
—*Athena Russell, Greenville, SC*

Prep: 20 min.
Bake: 10 min. + freezing
Makes: 2 pies (8 servings each)

- 2½ cups graham cracker crumbs
- ½ cup plus 2 Tbsp. butter, melted
- ¼ cup sugar
- 1 can (14 oz.) sweetened condensed milk
- ¼ cup lemon juice
- ¼ cup orange juice
- 1 pkg. (16 oz.) frozen unsweetened sliced peaches
- 1 Tbsp. grated lemon zest
- 1½ cups heavy whipping cream
  Sweetened whipped cream, optional

1. In a small bowl, combine the graham cracker crumbs, butter and sugar; press mixture onto the bottom and up the sides of 2 greased 9-in. pie plates. Bake at 350° for 10-12 minutes or until lightly browned. Cool on wire racks.
2. In a blender, combine the milk, lemon juice, orange juice, peaches and lemon zest; cover and process until smooth. Transfer to a large bowl. In a large bowl, beat cream until stiff peaks form; fold into peach mixture.
3. Spoon into crusts. Cover and freeze for at least 4 hours or until firm. Remove from the freezer 15 minutes before serving. Top with whipped cream if desired.

1 piece: 302 cal., 19g fat (11g sat. fat), 58mg chol., 170mg sod., 31g carb. (23g sugars, 1g fiber), 4g pro.

5i ❄

STRAWBERRY-RHUBARB ICE POPS

These cool, creamy pops are a deliciously different way to use up the bounty from your rhubarb patch. They really hit the spot on warm summer days.
—*Donna Linihan, Moncton, NB*

Prep: 10 min. + freezing
Cook: 15 min. + cooling
Makes: 8 pops

- 3 cups chopped fresh or frozen rhubarb (½ in.)
- ¼ cup sugar
- 3 Tbsp. water
- 1 cup strawberry yogurt
- ½ cup unsweetened applesauce
- ¼ cup finely chopped fresh strawberries
- 2 drops red food coloring, optional
- 8 freezer pop molds or 8 paper cups (3 oz. each) and wooden pop sticks

1. Place rhubarb, sugar and water in a large saucepan; bring to a boil. Reduce heat; simmer, uncovered, until thick and blended, 10-15 minutes. Remove ¾ cup mixture to a bowl; cool completely. (Save remaining rhubarb for another use.)
2. Add yogurt, applesauce and strawberries to the bowl; stir until blended. If desired, tint with food coloring. Fill each mold or cup with about ¼ cup rhubarb mixture. Top the molds with holders; top cups with foil and insert the sticks through foil. Freeze until firm.
Note: If using frozen rhubarb, measure rhubarb while it is still frozen, then thaw completely. Drain in a colander, but do not press liquid out.

1 pop: 72 cal., 0 fat (0 sat. fat), 2mg chol., 18mg sod., 16g carb. (14g sugars, 1g fiber), 2g pro. **Diabetic exchanges:** 1 starch.

THOMAS JEFFERSON'S VANILLA ICE CREAM

The third U.S. president is credited with jotting down the first American recipe for this treat. No vanilla bean on hand? Stir in a tablespoon vanilla extract into the cream mixture after the ice-water bath.
—Taste of Home *Test Kitchen*

Prep: 15 min. + chilling
Process: 20 min./batch + freezing
Makes: 2¼ qt.

- 2   qt. heavy whipping cream
- 1   cup sugar
- 1   vanilla bean
- 6   large egg yolks

1. In a large heavy saucepan, combine the cream and sugar. Split the vanilla bean in half lengthwise. With a sharp knife, scrape seeds into pan; add bean. Heat cream mixture over medium heat until bubbles form around the sides of pan, stirring to dissolve sugar.

2. In a small bowl, whisk a small amount of the hot mixture into the egg yolks; return all to the pan, whisking constantly.

3. Cook over low heat until the mixture is just thick enough to coat a metal spoon and the temperature reaches 160°, stirring mixture constantly. Do not allow to boil. Immediately transfer to a bowl.

4. Place bowl in a pan of ice water. Stir gently and occasionally for 2 minutes; discard the vanilla bean. Press waxed paper onto surface of custard. Refrigerate mixture several hours or overnight.

5. Fill cylinder of ice cream freezer two-thirds full; freeze according to the manufacturer's directions. (Refrigerate remaining mixture until ready to freeze.) Transfer ice cream to a freezer container; freeze for 4-6 hours or until firm. Repeat with remaining mixture.

½ cup: 424 cal., 40g fat (25g sat. fat), 182mg chol., 32mg sod., 14g carb. (14g sugars, 0 fiber), 4g pro.

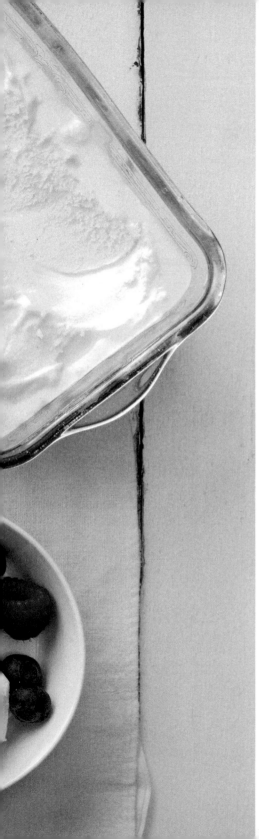

WARM PINEAPPLE SUNDAES WITH RUM SAUCE

Pineapple, rum and sugar are already a flavorful dream together, but adding ginger and butter really takes this dessert to another level.
—*Jamie Miller, Maple Grove, MN*

Takes: 25 min.
Makes: 2 servings

4	fresh pineapple spears (about 8 oz.)
½	cup packed brown sugar
2	Tbsp. dark rum
¾	tsp. ground ginger
4	tsp. butter, cut into small pieces
2	scoops vanilla ice cream or low-fat frozen yogurt
4	gingersnap cookies, crushed

1. Place pineapple in 1-qt. baking dish. In a small bowl, combine the brown sugar, rum and ginger; spoon over the pineapple. Dot with butter.

2. Bake, uncovered, at 425° until pineapple is lightly browned and sauce is bubbly, 8-10 minutes. Divide ice cream between 2 dessert dishes; top with pineapple and sauce. Serve immediately with crushed cookies.

1 serving: 536 cal., 16g fat (10g sat. fat), 49mg chol., 221mg sod., 95g carb. (78g sugars, 2g fiber), 4g pro.

CHOCOLATE FRAMBOISE PARFAITS

Having unexpected company? Make a fabulous dessert in minutes and relieve some of the stress of presenting a beautiful dessert! It doesn't get any easier than these quick, delicious parfaits layered with fresh berries and chocolate wafers.
—*Charlene Chambers, Ormond Beach, FL*

Prep: 15 min. + freezing
Makes: 6 servings

  6 **Tbsp. raspberry liqueur**
1½ **pints vanilla ice cream**
1½ **pints fresh raspberries**
2¼ **cups chocolate wafer crumbs**
     Sweetened whipped cream

Layer each of 6 parfait glasses with 1 tsp. raspberry liqueur, 2½ Tbsp. ice cream, 4 or 5 raspberries and 2 Tbsp. chocolate wafer crumbs. Repeat layers twice. Freeze. To serve, top with whipped cream and the remaining raspberries.

1 parfait: 402 cal., 14g fat (6g sat. fat), 30mg chol., 297mg sod., 59g carb. (38g sugars, 6g fiber), 6g pro.

STRAWBERRY CRUNCH ICE CREAM CAKE

Growing up, I loved treats from the ice cream truck that rolled through my neighborhood. This ice cream cake is inspired by one of those crunchy, strawberry novelties I adored so much.
—*Lisa Kaminski, Wauwatosa, WI*

Prep: 20 min. + freezing
Bake: 10 min. + cooling
Makes: 9 servings

36 **Golden Oreo cookies, divided**
  4 **Tbsp. butter, melted**
  3 **cups vanilla ice cream, softened**
  5 **cups strawberry ice cream, softened**
  1 **carton (8 oz.) frozen whipped topping, thawed**
  1 **pkg. (1 oz.) freeze-dried strawberries, coarsely crushed**
     Fresh strawberries, optional

1. Line a 9x9-in. baking pan with parchment. Preheat the oven to 350°. Finely crush 24 cookies. In a small bowl, mix cookie crumbs and butter. Press onto bottom of prepared pan. Bake until firm, 25-30 minutes. Cool on a wire rack.
2. Spread vanilla ice cream onto the crust; freeze, covered, until firm. Spread with the strawberry ice cream, then whipped topping; freeze, covered, until firm.
3. Coarsely crush the remaining cookies. Combine cookie crumbs and freeze-dried strawberries; sprinkle over the whipped topping. Freeze, covered, until firm, about 8 hours or overnight. Remove cake from freezer 10 minutes before serving. If desired, garnish with fresh strawberries.

1 piece: 584 cal., 30g fat (16g sat. fat), 54mg chol., 280mg sod., 72g carb. (33g sugars, 2g fiber), 6g pro.

If you want even more flavor, stir crumbled freeze-dried strawberries into the strawberry ice cream.

GRILLED BANANA BROWNIE SUNDAES

My niece and I have a lot of fun in the kitchen creating different dishes. One of us will start with a recipe idea and it just grows from there—and so does the mess. That's exactly what happened with our Grilled Banana Brownie Sundaes.
—*Carol Farnsworth, Greenwood, IN*

Takes: 15 min.
Makes: 8 servings

- 2 medium bananas, unpeeled
- 4 oz. cream cheese, softened
- ¼ cup packed brown sugar
- 3 Tbsp. creamy peanut butter
- 8 prepared brownies (2-in. squares)
- 4 cups vanilla ice cream
- ½ cup hot fudge ice cream topping, warmed
- ½ cup chopped salted peanuts

1. Cut unpeeled bananas crosswise in half, then lengthwise in half. Place quartered bananas on an oiled grill rack, cut side down. Grill, covered, over medium-high heat on each side until lightly browned, 2-3 minutes. Cool slightly.

2. In a small bowl, beat the cream cheese, brown sugar and peanut butter until smooth.

3. To serve, remove bananas from peel; place over brownies. Top with the cream cheese mixture, ice cream, fudge topping and chopped peanuts.

1 serving: 505 cal., 28g fat (11g sat. fat), 62mg chol., 277mg sod., 57g carb. (33g sugars, 3g fiber), 10g pro.

Homemade brownies are amazing but to speed things up, go ahead and prepare them from a boxed brownie mix.

5i ❄

PATRIOTIC ICE CREAM CUPCAKES

These frosty cupcakes are practically a fireworks display on their own. The little treats feature red velvet cake, blue moon ice cream, a creamy white topping and star-spangled sprinkles.
—Taste of Home *Test Kitchen*

Prep: 30 min. + freezing
Bake: 15 min. + cooling
Makes: 3 dozen

- 1 pkg. red velvet cake mix (regular size)
- 1½ qt. blue moon ice cream, softened if necessary
- 1 jar (7 oz.) marshmallow creme
- 3 cups heavy whipping cream
  Red, white and blue sprinkles

1. Preheat oven to 350°. Line 36 muffin cups with paper liners.
2. Prepare cake batter according to package directions. Fill the prepared cups about one-third full. Bake until a toothpick inserted in center comes out clean, 11-14 minutes. Cool 10 minutes before removing from pans to wire racks; cool completely.
3. Working quickly, spread ice cream onto cupcakes. Freeze until firm, at least 1 hour.
4. Place marshmallow creme in a large bowl. Add whipping cream; beat until blended and stiff peaks form. Pipe or spread over the cupcakes. Decorate with sprinkles. Serve immediately or freeze until firm.
Note: Vanilla ice cream tinted with blue food coloring may be used in place of blue moon ice cream.

1 cupcake: 220 cal., 13g fat (6g sat. fat), 46mg chol., 139mg sod., 21g carb. (16g sugars, 0 fiber), 4g pro.

5i ❄

WATERMELON CHOCOLATE CHIP SORBET

Summertime and watermelon go hand in hand. My melon sorbet is fresh, fruity and without the gluten and eggs you get in so many other frozen desserts.
—*Rachel Lewis, Danville, VA*

Prep: 15 min. + chilling
Process: 30 min. + freezing
Makes: 1 qt.

1	cup sugar
½	cup water
3	cups chopped seedless watermelon
1	cup orange juice
2	Tbsp. lime juice
½	cup miniature semisweet chocolate chips, optional

1. In a small saucepan, bring sugar and water to a boil. Reduce heat; simmer, uncovered, 5 minutes, stirring occasionally to dissolve sugar. Cool slightly.

2. Place watermelon in a food processor; process until pureed. Add the orange juice, lime juice and cooled syrup; process until blended. Transfer mixture to a large bowl; refrigerate, covered, until cold, about 3 hours.

3. Pour into cylinder of ice cream freezer. Freeze according to manufacturer's directions; if desired, add chocolate chips during the last 10 minutes of processing. Transfer sorbet to freezer containers, allowing headspace for expansion. Freeze until firm, 2-4 hours.

½ cup: 129 cal., 0 fat (0 sat. fat), 0 chol., 1mg sod., 33g carb. (32g sugars, 0 fiber), 1g pro.

❄️

RASPBERRY ICE CREAM DELIGHT

This gorgeous make-ahead dessert is a light, refreshing ending to a summer meal.
—*Nancy Whitford, Edwards, NY*

Prep: 30 min. + freezing
Makes: 15 servings

2 cups crushed chocolate wafers
¼ cup sugar
⅓ cup butter, melted
FILLING
1 cup hot fudge ice cream topping
1 qt. vanilla ice cream, softened
1 pint raspberry sherbet, softened
1 pkg. (10 oz.) frozen sweetened raspberries, thawed and drained
1 carton (8 oz.) frozen whipped topping, thawed

1. In a large bowl, combine chocolate wafer crumbs, sugar and butter; set aside ¼ cup. Press the remaining crumb mixture into a 13x9-in. dish. Cover and freeze crumb crust for 15 minutes.

2. Place hot fudge topping in a microwave-safe bowl; cover and microwave on high for 15-20 seconds. Spread over crust.

3. Spoon ice cream over fudge layer. Place spoonfuls of sherbet over ice cream; cut through sherbet with a knife to swirl. Top with raspberries. Spread with whipped topping; sprinkle with the reserved wafer crumb mixture.

4. Cover and freeze for 2-3 hours or overnight. Remove from the freezer 15 minutes before serving.

1 serving: 342 cal., 14g fat (9g sat. fat), 28mg chol., 192mg sod., 50g carb. (27g sugars, 2g fiber), 4g pro.

❄ FROZEN KEY LIME DELIGHT

In the middle of summer, nothing hits the spot quite like this sublime Key lime dessert.
—*Melissa Millwood, Lyman, SC*

Prep: 50 min.
Bake: 25 min. + freezing
Makes: 8 servings

    1   cup all-purpose flour
    ½   cup salted cashews, chopped
    ½   cup sweetened shredded coconut
    ¼   cup packed light brown sugar
    ½   cup butter, melted
    2   cups heavy whipping cream
    1½ cups sweetened condensed milk
    1   cup Key lime juice
    3   tsp. grated Key lime zest
    1   tsp. vanilla extract
        Optional: Whipped cream and Key
        lime slices

1. Preheat oven to 350°. In a small bowl, combine flour, cashews, coconut and brown sugar. Stir in butter. Sprinkle into a greased 15x10x1-in. baking pan. Bake 20-25 minutes or until golden brown, stirring once. Cool on a wire rack.
2. Meanwhile, in a bowl, combine the cream, milk, lime juice, zest and vanilla. Refrigerate until chilled.
3. Fill the cylinder of the ice cream freezer two-thirds full; freeze according to the manufacturer's directions.
4. Sprinkle half the cashew mixture into an ungreased 11x7-in. dish. Spread ice cream over top; sprinkle with remaining cashew mixture. Cover and freeze 4 hours or until firm. Garnish servings with whipped cream and lime slices if desired.

1 piece: 672 cal., 46g fat (27g sat. fat), 131mg chol., 258mg sod., 60g carb. (42g sugars, 1g fiber), 9g pro.

❄ CREAMY LAYERED BLUEBERRY ICE POPS

These delicious ice-pops can be made with raspberries or blackberries. The rosemary sprig and lemon rind bring another layer of flavor.
—*Gloria Bradley, Naperville, IL*

Prep: 25 min. + freezing
Cook: 10 min. + cooling
Makes: 10 servings

    ⅓   cup agave nectar
    ¼   cup water
    1   fresh rosemary sprig
    1   lemon zest strip (2 in.)
    1   Tbsp. lemon juice
    2   cups fresh or frozen blueberries
    2   Tbsp. sugar
    2¼ cups frozen whipped topping,
        thawed
    10 freezer pop molds or 10 paper cups
        (3 oz. each) and wooden pop sticks

1. For lemon syrup, place first 4 ingredients in a small saucepan; bring to a boil, stirring occasionally. Remove from heat; let stand, covered, 10 minutes. Remove rosemary and lemon zest. Stir in the lemon juice; cool the syrup completely.
2. Place the blueberries and sugar in another saucepan; cook and stir over medium heat until berries pop, 5-7 minutes. Cool berry mixture completely.
3. Add whipped topping to the lemon syrup, whisking to blend. Transfer half of the mixture to a pastry bag. Pipe into molds. Layer with blueberries. Pipe the remaining whipped topping mixture over top. Close molds with holders. For paper cups, top with foil and insert sticks through foil.
4. Freeze until firm, about 4 hours. To serve, dip pop molds briefly in warm water before removing pops.

1 frozen pop: 104 cal., 3g fat (3g sat. fat), 0 chol., 0 sod., 19g carb. (18g sugars, 1g fiber), 0 pro. **Diabetic exchanges:** 1 starch, ½ fat.

Lime flavor would be great in this recipe. Substitute equal parts of lime zest and juice for lemon zest and juice.

BLACKBERRY DAIQUIRI SHERBET

I decided to try making sherbet when blackberries were in season in my mom's garden. I love the flavor of daiquiris, and the two blend together beautifully in this treat.
—*Shelly Bevington, Hermiston, OR*

Prep: 15 min.
Process: 30 min. + freezing
Makes: 1¼ qt.

- 3 **cups fresh or frozen blackberries, thawed**
- 1 **cup sugar**
- ¼ **tsp. salt**
- 1 **can (12 oz.) evaporated milk**
- 2 **Tbsp. lime juice**
- 1 **tsp. rum extract**
- ½ **tsp. citric acid**

1. Place the blackberries, sugar and salt in a food processor; process until smooth. Press through a fine-mesh strainer into a bowl; discard the seeds and pulp. Stir remaining ingredients into puree.

2. Fill cylinder of ice cream maker no more than two-thirds full; freeze according to the manufacturer's directions. Transfer sherbet to freezer containers, allowing headspace for expansion. Freeze until firm, 8 hours or overnight.

½ cup: 147 cal., 3g fat (2g sat. fat), 12mg chol., 96mg sod., 28g carb. (26g sugars, 2g fiber), 3g pro.

Substituting rum for the extract might seem like a fun idea but the alcohol will keep your daiquiri dessert from freezing solid.

 ## FRIED ICE CREAM DESSERT BARS

Fried ice cream is such a delicious treat, but it can be a hassle to make. This recipe gives you the same fabulous flavor in an easy and convenient bar form.
—*Andrea Price, Grafton, WI*

Prep: 25 min. + freezing
Cook: 5 min. + cooling
Makes: 16 servings

- ½ cup butter, cubed
- 2 cups crushed cornflakes
- 1½ tsp. ground cinnamon
- 3 Tbsp. sugar
- 1¾ cups heavy whipping cream
- ¼ cup evaporated milk
- ⅛ tsp. salt
- 1 can (14 oz.) sweetened condensed milk
- 2 tsp. vanilla extract
  Optional: Honey, whipped cream and maraschino cherries

1. In a large skillet, melt butter over medium heat. Add cornflakes and cinnamon; cook and stir until golden brown, about 5 minutes. Remove from heat; stir in the sugar. Cool mixture completely.
2. In a large bowl, beat cream, evaporated milk and salt until it begins to thicken. Gradually beat in condensed milk and vanilla until thickened.
3. Sprinkle half the cornflakes onto bottom of a greased 9-in. square baking pan. Pour filling over crust; sprinkle with remaining cornflakes. Cover and freeze overnight. Cut into bars. If desired, serve bars with honey, whipped cream and cherries.

1 bar: 276 cal., 18g fat (11g sat. fat), 55mg chol., 187mg sod., 27g carb. (18g sugars, 0 fiber), 4g pro.

BANANA SPLIT ICEBOX CAKE

One day a friend showed me how to make a traditional icebox cake with just cream and graham crackers. I make it extra special with fruit. Now you can serve more elegant banana splits at your party!
—*Shelly Flye, Albion, ME*

Prep: 30 min. + chilling
Makes: 10 servings

- 1 carton (16 oz.) frozen whipped topping, thawed
- 1 cup sour cream
- 1 pkg. (3.4 oz.) instant vanilla pudding mix
- 1 can (8 oz.) crushed pineapple, drained
- 24 whole graham crackers
- 2 medium bananas, sliced
  Toppings: Chocolate syrup, halved fresh strawberries and additional banana slices

1. In a large bowl, mix whipped topping, sour cream and pudding mix until blended; fold in pineapple. Cut a small hole in the tip of a pastry bag. Transfer pudding mixture to bag.
2. On a flat serving plate, arrange 4 crackers in a rectangle. Pipe about 1 cup pudding mixture over crackers; top with about ¼ cup of banana slices. Repeat the layers 5 times. Refrigerate, covered, overnight.
3. Just before serving, top icebox cake with chocolate syrup, strawberries and additional banana slices.

1 slice: 405 cal., 15g fat (11g sat. fat), 16mg chol., 372mg sod., 60g carb. (30g sugars, 2g fiber), 4g pro.

5i

RASPBERRY-BANANA SOFT SERVE

When I make this ice cream, I mix and match bananas for their ripeness. Very ripe ones add more banana flavor. Less ripe ones have a fluffier texture.
—*Melissa Hansen, Ellison Bay, WI*

Prep: 10 min. + freezing
Makes: 2½ cups

- 4 **medium ripe bananas**
- ½ **cup fat-free plain yogurt**
- 1 **to 2 Tbsp. maple syrup**
- ½ **cup frozen unsweetened raspberries**
  Fresh raspberries, optional

1. Thinly slice bananas; transfer to a large resealable plastic freezer bag. Arrange slices in a single layer; freeze overnight.

2. Pulse bananas in a food processor until finely chopped. Add the yogurt, maple syrup and raspberries. Process just until smooth, scraping sides as needed. Serve immediately, adding fresh berries if desired.

½ cup: 104 cal., 0 fat (0 sat. fat), 1mg chol., 15mg sod., 26g carb. (15g sugars, 2g fiber), 2g pro. **Diabetic exchanges:** 1 fruit, ½ starch.

ROCKY ROAD FUDGE POPS

These sweet frozen treats are simple to prepare and guaranteed to bring out the kid in anyone. The creamy pops feature a special chocolate and peanut topping.
—*Karen Grant, Tulare, CA*

Prep: 20 min. + freezing
Makes: 12 servings

2½ cups 2% milk
1 pkg. (3.4 oz.) cook-and-serve chocolate pudding mix
½ cup chopped peanuts
½ cup miniature semisweet chocolate chips
12 disposable plastic cups (3 oz. each)
½ cup marshmallow creme
12 wooden pop sticks

1. In a large microwave-safe bowl, whisk milk and pudding mix. Microwave, uncovered, on high for 4-6 minutes or until bubbly and slightly thickened, stirring every 2 minutes. Cool for 20 minutes, stirring several times.
2. Meanwhile, combine chopped peanuts and chocolate chips; divide among plastic cups. Stir marshmallow creme into pudding; spoon into the cups. Insert wooden pop sticks; freeze.

1 serving: 140 cal., 7g fat (3g sat. fat), 7mg chol., 64mg sod., 18g carb. (14g sugars, 1g fiber), 4g pro.

COOL STRAWBERRY CREAM

This dessert makes a wonderful ending to a special dinner. When fresh strawberries are not available, I substitute two packages of the frozen unsweetened kind, thawed and drained.
—*Joyce Cooper, Mount Forest, ON*

Prep: 30 min. + freezing
Makes: 12 servings

2 pkg. (8 oz. each) cream cheese, softened
¾ cup sugar
½ cup sour cream
3 cups fresh strawberries, mashed
1 cup whipped topping
BLUEBERRY SAUCE
1 pkg. (12 oz.) frozen unsweetened blueberries
⅓ cup sugar
¼ cup water

1. Line a 9x5-in. loaf pan with a double thickness of foil; set aside. In a large bowl, beat the cream cheese, sugar and sour cream until smooth. Fold in strawberries and whipped topping. Pour into prepared pan. Cover and freeze for several hours or overnight.
2. In a small saucepan, bring the blueberries, sugar and water to a boil; cook and stir for 3 minutes. Cool slightly. Transfer mixture to a blender; cover and process until pureed. Refrigerate until chilled.
3. Remove dessert from the freezer 15-20 minutes before serving. Use the foil to lift out of pan; remove foil. Cut into slices with a serrated knife. Serve with blueberry sauce.

1 serving: 198 cal., 10g fat (6g sat. fat), 27mg chol., 62mg sod., 26g carb. (23g sugars, 2g fiber), 2g pro.

HERE'S THE SCOOP

What's in a name? A lot, when it comes to frosty treats. Here's a rundown of the most popular icebox sweets.

ICE CREAM

This all-time popular dessert contains about 10% butterfat, but premium brands use a slightly higher percentage for a creamier product.

SHERBET

Made from fruit juice, a milk product, sugar and water, this treat has a lighter texture than ice cream and is often sweeter. Some versions might contain fruit, spices or even chocolate.

SORBET

This freezer sweet is made from pureed fruit, sugar and water. It doesn't contain milk or other diary products. Some are flavored with liqueur or wine.

SUMMER'S MOST

DECADENT DESSERTS

Brilliant berries, juicy fruits, toasted marshmallows, cool and creamy bites, and tangy citrus delights—these are the hallmarks of summer desserts. Cap off backyard barbecues and busy weeknights alike by serving any of these lip-smacking dinner finales.

COMMONLY USED PASTRY TERMS

You don't have to be a professional baker to whip up great desserts this summer. Start here to master your best sweets yet.

MERINGUES

Meringue is sweetened egg white foam shaped into cookies and shells (hard meringues) or used as a topping for pies and baked Alaska (soft meringues).

The amount of sugar used per egg white determines whether the meringue will be hard or soft.

Always make your meringue on dry days. Meringues absorb the moisture in the air, so on humid days they'll become limp or sticky.

Eggs are easier to separate when they are cold, but egg whites obtain a better volume after they have stood at room temperature 30 minutes.

Use perfectly clean, dry beaters and metal or glass bowls. Any specks of egg yolk, oil or grease in the bowl will prevent egg whites from reaching their maximum volume.

After stiff peaks form, check to make sure the sugar is dissolved by rubbing a dab of meringue between your fingers. It should feel silky-smooth.

CREAM PUFFS AND ECLAIRS

Cream puffs and eclairs are airy pastries made from a French dough called *pâté a choux*, or choux pastry. The pastry can be dropped or piped onto greased baking sheets in various sizes and shapes. This simple dough is used for desserts as well as impressive appetizers.

Arrange the oven rack in the lower third of the oven. Preheat the oven 10 to 15 minutes.

When baking cream puffs or eclairs, leave 3 inches of space around each pastry. It's important not to crowd the baking sheet. This dough needs room to expand during baking, and it needs air circulation so the steam can evaporate.

The pastries are done when they are golden brown and have a dry, crisp exterior.

Cream puffs and eclairs are best served the day they're made. If needed, store unfilled pastries in a plastic bag in the refrigerator. Fill before serving.

PHYLLO DOUGH

Phyllo is a tissue-thin dough generally sold in the freezer section of supermarkets. It's used in desserts as well as savory appetizers and main dishes.

Thaw phyllo according to the package directions. It dries out quickly, so always have the other ingredients prepped and measured before unwrapping. Once the dough is unwrapped and unrolled, cover it with a damp kitchen towel to keep it moist.

This fragile dough tears easily; always work it on a smooth, dry surface. Work with just one sheet of phyllo at a time and keep the other sheets covered.

Refrigerate unopened phyllo dough up to 3 weeks or freeze it for up to 3 months. Refrigerate opened dough for up to 3 days. Store baked phyllo dough in an airtight container up to 3 days or freeze it up to 3 months.

Freeze unfilled pastries for up to 2 months. Thaw at room temperature 15 to 20 minutes before using. To recrisp them, heat in the oven for a few minutes.

PUFF PASTRY

Puff pastry is sold in sheets or as shells in the freezer section of supermarkets. With dozens of paper-thin layers of dough that are separated by butter, the result is a crisp, flaky pastry. It's used in desserts, appetizers and main dishes. Puff pastry is impressive, but it's easy to work with.

Thaw puff pastry at room temperature approximately 20 minutes before using. Handle the dough as little as possible to avoid stretching and tearing.

Preheat the oven as directed in the recipe.

Cut pastry with a sharp knife or a cookie cutter for a pretty, clean edge.

Brush egg washes on top of the dough, but not on the edges. If the edges are coated, they will stick together and the pastry won't rise during baking.

Store unbaked puff pastry tightly wrapped in plastic in the refrigerator up to 3 days or in the freezer up to 1 month.

Baked pastries are best served the day they are made, and they don't hold up well in the refrigerator. Baked unfilled pastries may be frozen for up to 6 weeks.

SOUFFLES

Souffles are made from an egg yolk-based custard with beaten egg whites folded in to make them light and help them rise. Souffles bake into impressive, airy desserts.

Eggs are easier to separate when they are cold, but egg whites obtain a better volume after they have stood at room temperature 30 minutes.

Prepare the baking dish as recipe directs. Generally, the dish is dusted with a coating, such as sugar, to give the souffle better traction to rise.

Put oven rack in the middle of the oven. Preheat the oven for 10 to 15 minutes.

Always use clean, dry beaters and metal or glass bowls. Specks of egg yolks, oil or grease in the bowl will prevent egg whites from reaching their maximum volume.

To lighten the batter, fold about a third of the beaten egg whites into the custard base. Then fold in the remaining egg whites and spoon or pour into the baking dish.

Bake the souffle as the recipe directs. It's done when the top is puffed and the center appears to be set.

Serve souffles immediately after baking. They start to fall once they are removed from the oven.

An unbaked souffle may be refrigerated up to 2 hours before baking or frozen up to 3 weeks. If frozen, thaw the souffle in the refrigerator before baking. A previously frozen souffle will rise but not as high as a freshly prepared one.

PUDDINGS AND CUSTARDS

Baked custards are a delicate flavored mixture of sweetened milk and eggs most often baked in a water bath for gentle, even heating. Custards are done when a knife inserted near the center comes out clean and the top looks set.

Unmold cooled custard by running a knife around the edge of the dish to detatch. If possible, lift the bottom edge of the custard with the tip of the knife to loosen. Invert onto a serving plate and lift off the baking dish.

Bread puddings combine a custard mixture with cubes or slices of bread. They may also contain spices, fruits, nuts or chocolate. They can be served warm or cold and often have an accompanying sauce. They're done when a knife inserted in the center comes out clean.

Rice puddings combine a flavored spiced custard mixture with cooked rice. They can be served either warm or cold. Baked rice puddings are done when a knife inserted in the center comes out clean.

Refrigerate baked custard-based puddings up to 2 days.

BERRY-PATCH BROWNIE PIZZA

I just love the combination of fruit, almonds and chocolate that makes this brownie so distinctive. The fruit lightens the chocolate a bit and makes it feel as though you're eating something both decadent and healthy.
—*Sue Kauffman, Columbia City, IN*

Prep: 20 min. + chilling
Bake: 15 min. + cooling
Makes: 12 servings

- 1 pkg. fudge brownie mix (13x9-in. pan size)
- ⅓ cup chopped unblanched almonds
- 1 tsp. almond extract

TOPPING
- 1 pkg. (8 oz.) cream cheese, softened
- 1 Tbsp. sugar
- 1 tsp. vanilla extract
- ½ tsp. grated lemon zest
- 2 cups whipped topping
  Assorted fresh berries
  Fresh mint leaves and coarse sugar, optional

1. Preheat oven to 375°. Prepare brownie batter according to the package directions for fudgelike brownies, adding the almonds and almond extract. Spread into a greased 14-in. pizza pan.

2. Bake until a toothpick inserted in center comes out clean, for 15-18 minutes. Cool completely on a wire rack.

3. Beat first 4 topping ingredients until smooth; fold in whipped topping. Spread over the crust to within ½ in. of edges; refrigerate, loosely covered, 2 hours.

4. To serve, cut into slices; top with berries of choice. If desired, top with mint and sprinkle with coarse sugar.

1 slice: 404 cal., 26g fat (8g sat. fat), 51mg chol., 240mg sod., 39g carb. (26g sugars, 2g fiber), 5g pro.

MANGO RICE PUDDING

Mangoes are my son's favorite fruit, so I was ecstatic to incorporate them into this healthy dessert. You can also use ripe bananas instead of mango, almond extract instead of vanilla, or regular milk in place of soy.
—*Melissa McCabe, Victor, NY*

Prep: 5 min.
Cook: 50 min.
Makes: 4 servings

- 2 **cups water**
- ¼ **tsp. salt**
- 1 **cup uncooked long grain brown rice**
- 1 **medium ripe mango**
- 1 **cup vanilla soy milk**
- 2 **Tbsp. sugar**
- ½ **tsp. ground cinnamon**
- 1 **tsp. vanilla extract**
   Chopped peeled mango, optional

1. In a large heavy saucepan, bring water and salt to a boil; stir rice. Reduce heat; simmer, covered, 35-40 minutes or until water is absorbed and rice is tender.

2. Meanwhile, peel, seed and slice mango. Mash mango with a potato masher or fork.
3. Stir milk, sugar, cinnamon and mashed mango into rice. Cook, uncovered, on low 10-15 minutes longer or until liquid is almost absorbed, stirring occasionally.
4. Remove from heat; stir in vanilla. Serve warm or cold, with the chopped mango if desired.

1 cup: 275 cal., 3g fat (0 sat. fat), 0 chol., 176mg sod., 58g carb. (20g sugars, 3g fiber), 6g pro.

SKILLET BLUEBERRY SLUMP

My mother-in-law made a slump of wild blueberries with dumplings and served it warm with a pitcher of farm cream. We've been enjoying slump desserts for nearly 60 years!
—*Eleanore Ebeling, Brewster, MN*

Prep: 25 min.
Bake: 20 min.
Makes: 6 servings

- 4 **cups fresh or frozen blueberries**
- ½ **cup sugar**
- ½ **cup water**
- 1 **tsp. grated lemon zest**
- 1 **Tbsp. lemon juice**
- 1 **cup all-purpose flour**
- 2 **Tbsp. sugar**
- 2 **tsp. baking powder**
- ½ **tsp. salt**
- 1 **Tbsp. butter**
- ½ **cup 2% milk**
   Vanilla ice cream

1. Preheat the oven to 400°. In a 10-in. ovenproof skillet, combine the first 5 ingredients; bring to a boil. Reduce heat; simmer, uncovered, 9-11 minutes or until slightly thickened, stirring occasionally.
2. Meanwhile, in a small bowl, whisk flour, sugar, baking powder and salt. Cut in the butter until the mixture resembles coarse crumbs. Add milk; stir just until moistened.
3. Drop batter in 6 portions on top of the simmering blueberry mixture. Transfer to oven. Bake, uncovered, 17-20 minutes or until dumplings are golden brown. Serve warm with ice cream.

1 serving: 239 cal., 3g fat (2g sat. fat), 7mg chol., 355mg sod., 52g carb. (32g sugars, 3g fiber), 4g pro.

S'MORES CREME BRULEE

A big bite into a scrumptious s'more brings back sweet campfire memories. This fancy take on the classic is perfect for young and old alike.
—*Rose Denning, Overland Park, KS*

Prep: 30 min.
Bake: 25 min. + chilling
Makes: 6 servings

- 1 **cup 2% milk**
- 3 **large eggs**
- ⅔ **cup sugar**
- ⅓ **cup baking cocoa**
- 2 **Tbsp. coffee liqueur or strong brewed coffee**
- ⅔ **cup graham cracker crumbs**
- 2 **Tbsp. butter, melted**
- ⅓ **cup sugar or coarse sugar**
- 2 **cups miniature marshmallows**
- 1 **milk chocolate candy bar (1.55 oz.), broken into 12 pieces**

1. Preheat oven to 325°. In a small saucepan, heat milk until bubbles form around sides of pan; remove from heat. In a large bowl, whisk eggs, sugar, cocoa and liqueur until blended but not foamy. Slowly whisk in hot milk.
2. Place six 4-oz. broiler-safe ramekins in a baking pan large enough to hold them without touching. Pour egg mixture into ramekins. Place pan on oven rack; add very hot water to pan to within ½ in. of top of ramekins. Bake 20-25 minutes or until a knife inserted in the center comes out clean; centers will still be soft. Remove ramekins from water bath immediately to a wire rack; cool 10 minutes. Refrigerate until cold.
3. In a small bowl, mix cracker crumbs and butter; set aside. To caramelize topping with a kitchen torch, sprinkle the custards evenly with sugar. Hold the torch flame about 2 in. above custard surface; rotate it slowly until the sugar is evenly caramelized. Sprinkle custards with crumb mixture; top with marshmallows. Using torch, heat the marshmallows until browned. Top with chocolate pieces. Serve immediately or refrigerate up to 1 hour.
4. To caramelize topping in a broiler, place ramekins on a baking sheet; let stand at room temperature 15 minutes. Preheat broiler. Sprinkle custards evenly with sugar. Broil 3-4 in. from heat 3-5 minutes or until sugar is caramelized. Sprinkle custards with crumb mixture; top with marshmallows. Broil 30-45 seconds or until marshmallows are browned. Top with chocolate pieces. Serve immediately or refrigerate up to 1 hour.

1 serving: 419 cal., 11g fat (5g sat. fat), 108mg chol., 163mg sod., 74g carb. (59g sugars, 2g fiber), 7g pro.

BLUE-RIBBON APPLE PIE

With its hidden layer of walnuts, this pie won me a blue ribbon at the local fair, and that allowed me to enter it in the state farm show.
—*Collette Gaugler, Fogelsville, PA*

Prep: 45 min.
Bake: 55 minutes + cooling
Makes: 8 servings

Pastry for double-crust pie (9 in.)
WALNUT LAYER
- ¾ cup ground walnuts
- 2 Tbsp. brown sugar
- 2 Tbsp. lightly beaten egg
- 1 Tbsp. butter, melted
- 1 Tbsp. 2% milk
- ¼ tsp. lemon juice
- ¼ tsp. vanilla extract

FILLING
- 6 cups sliced peeled tart apples (4-5 medium)
- 2 tsp. lemon juice
- ½ tsp. vanilla extract
- ¾ cup sugar
- 3 Tbsp. all-purpose flour
- 1¼ tsp. ground cinnamon
- ¼ tsp. ground nutmeg
- ⅛ tsp. salt
- 3 Tbsp. butter, cubed

TOPPING
- 1 tsp. 2% milk
- 2 tsp. sugar

1. Preheat oven to 375°. On a lightly floured surface, roll half of the pastry dough to a ⅛-in.-thick circle; transfer to a 9-in. pie plate. Trim pastry even with rim.

2. In a bowl, mix the walnut layer ingredients until blended. Spread onto bottom of pastry shell. Refrigerate while preparing filling.

3. For filling, in a large bowl, toss apples with lemon juice and vanilla. In a small bowl, mix sugar, flour, cinnamon, nutmeg and salt; add to apple mixture and toss to coat.

4. Pour filling over walnut layer; dot with butter. Roll remaining pastry dough to a ⅛-in.-thick circle. Place over filling. Trim, seal and flute edge. Brush top with milk; sprinkle with sugar. Cut slits in pastry.

5. Place pie on a baking sheet. Bake 55-65 minutes or until crust is golden brown and filling is bubbly. Cover edge loosely with foil during the last 10 minutes if needed to prevent overbrowning. Remove foil. Cool on a wire rack.

Pastry for double-crust pie (9 in.):
Combine 2½ cups of all-purpose flour and ½ tsp. salt; cut in 1 cup shortening until crumbly. Gradually add 4-5 Tbsp. ice water, tossing with a fork until dough holds together when pressed. Divide dough in half and shape into disks; wrap each in plastic and refrigerate dough 1 hour.

1 piece: 611 cal., 36g fat (10g sat. fat), 31mg chol., 234mg sod., 67g carb. (33g sugars, 3g fiber), 6g pro.

BERRY DREAM CAKE

I use cherry gelatin to give a boxed cake mix an eye-appealing marbled effect. It's so festive-looking. Top it with whatever fresh fruit you like!
—*Margaret McNeil, Germantown, TN*

Prep: 15 min. + chilling
Bake: 30 min. + chilling
Makes: 15 servings

- 1 **pkg. white cake mix (regular size)**
- 1½ **cups boiling water**
- 1 **pkg. (3 oz.) cherry gelatin**
- 1 **pkg. (8 oz.) cream cheese, softened**
- 2 **cups whipped topping**
- 4 **cups fresh strawberries, coarsely chopped**

1. Prepare and bake the cake mix batter according to the package directions, using a greased 13x9-in. baking pan.
2. In a small bowl, add boiling water to gelatin; stir 2 minutes to completely dissolve. Cool cake on a wire rack 3-5 minutes. Using a wooden skewer, pierce holes in top of cake to within 1 in. of edge, twisting skewer gently to make slightly larger holes. Gradually pour gelatin over cake, being careful to fill each hole. Cool 15 minutes. Refrigerate, covered, 30 minutes.
3. In a large bowl, beat cream cheese until fluffy. Fold in whipped topping. Carefully spread over cake. Top with strawberries. Cover and refrigerate for at least 2 hours before serving.

1 piece: 306 cal., 16g fat (6g sat. fat), 54mg chol., 315mg sod., 37g carb. (22g sugars, 1g fiber), 5g pro.

TART & TANGY LEMON TART

Our family adores lemon desserts, and I like to make this lemony tart for brunch. For special events, I bake it in my heart-shaped tart pan to show the love.
—*Joyce Moynihan, Lakeville, MN*

Prep: 15 min. + chilling
Bake: 45 min. + cooling
Makes: 14 servings

- ¾ cup butter, softened
- ½ cup confectioners' sugar
- 1½ cups all-purpose flour

FILLING
- ¾ cup sugar
- 1 Tbsp. grated lemon zest
- ¾ cup lemon juice
- 3 large eggs, room temperature
- 3 large egg yolks, room temperature
- 4 oz. cream cheese, softened
- 1 Tbsp. cornstarch
  Sweetened whipped cream, optional

1. Preheat oven to 325°. In a large bowl, cream butter and confectioners' sugar until smooth. Gradually beat in flour. Press dough onto bottom and up sides of an ungreased 11-in. fluted tart pan with a removable bottom. Refrigerate 15 minutes.

2. Line the unpricked crust with a double thickness of foil. Fill with pie weights, dried beans or uncooked rice. Bake until edges are lightly browned, 18-22 minutes. Remove foil and weights; bake until the bottom is golden brown, 5-7 minutes longer. Cool on a wire rack.

3. In a large bowl, beat sugar, lemon zest, lemon juice, eggs, egg yolks, cream cheese and cornstarch until blended; pour into crust. Bake until filling is set, 18-22 minutes. Cool on a wire rack. If desired, serve with whipped cream. Refrigerate leftovers.

Note: Let pie weights cool before storing. Beans and rice may be reused for pie weights, but not for cooking.

1 slice: 254 cal., 15g fat (9g sat. fat), 114mg chol., 125mg sod., 27g carb. (16g sugars, 0 fiber), 4g pro.

RASPBERRY CHOCOLATE PUFFS

This chocolaty, flaky dessert is one of my favorite show-off recipes because it makes a spectacular presentation. The best part? It's actually surprisingly easy and quick to make.
—*Anneliese Deising, Plymouth, MI*

Prep: 25 min.
Bake: 20 min. + cooling
Makes: 8 servings

1 **cup milk chocolate chips**
1 **cup white baking chips**
1 **cup chopped pecans**
1 **pkg. (17.3 oz.) frozen puff pastry, thawed**
1 **pkg. (12 oz.) frozen unsweetened raspberries, thawed**
1 **cup confectioners' sugar**
  Additional confectioners' sugar
  Optional ingredients: fresh raspberries and additional chocolate and white baking chips

1. Preheat oven to 425°. Toss together the chocolate chips, baking chips and pecans. On a lightly floured surface, roll each pastry sheet into a 12-in. square; cut each sheet into quarters, making four 6-in. squares.

2. Place the squares on ungreased baking sheets; top each with about ⅓ cup chocolate mixture. Lightly brush edges of pastry with water; bring together all corners, pinching seams to seal.

3. Bake until golden brown, 18-20 minutes. Remove to a wire rack to cool slightly. Puree frozen raspberries with 1 cup confectioners' sugar in a food processor. Strain to remove the seeds.

4. To serve, dust pastries with confectioners' sugar. Serve with raspberry sauce and, if desired, fresh berries and additional chips.

1 serving: 699 cal., 39g fat (13g sat. fat), 9mg chol., 238mg sod., 81g carb. (40g sugars, 7g fiber), 9g pro.

BERRIES WITH VANILLA CUSTARD

What a simple, delectable way to enjoy fresh raspberries. For a change, try this custard with strawberries or peaches.
—*Sarah Vasques, Milford, NH*

Prep: 20 min. + chilling
Makes: 4 servings

- 1 cup half-and-half cream
- 2 large egg yolks
- 2 Tbsp. sugar
- 2 tsp. vanilla extract
- 2 cups fresh berries

1. In a small heavy saucepan, mix cream, egg yolks and sugar. Cook and stir over low heat until mixture is just thick enough to coat a metal spoon and a thermometer reads at least 160°. Do not allow to boil.
2. Transfer custard to a bowl; stir in vanilla. Refrigerate, covered, until cold. Serve over fresh berries.

½ cup berries with ¼ cup sauce: 166 cal., 9g fat (5g sat. fat), 132mg chol., 34mg sod., 16g carb. (11g sugars, 4g fiber), 4g pro. **Diabetic exchanges:** 1½ fat, ½ starch, ½ fruit.

BOMB POP COOKIES

The sound of the ice cream truck has even my husband running out to the curb with money in hand. Our neighborhood has a big potluck on the Fourth of July, so I decided to make cookies that resemble Bomb Pops. These were a big hit!
—*Darlene Brenden, Salem, OR*

Prep: 30 min. + chilling
Bake: 10 min./batch + cooling
Makes: 40 cookies

- ½ cup butter, softened
- ½ cup confectioners' sugar
- ½ cup sugar
- 1 large egg, room temperature
- ⅓ cup canola oil
- 2¾ to 3 cups all-purpose flour
- ½ tsp. baking soda
- ½ tsp. cream of tartar
- ¼ tsp. salt
  Red and blue paste food coloring
- ½ tsp. each cherry, raspberry and lemon extract

1. Cream butter and sugars until light and fluffy. Add the egg and oil, beating well. In another bowl, whisk 2¾ cups flour, baking soda, cream of tartar and salt. Gradually beat into creamed mixture, adding flour if needed, until dough forms a ball.
2. Divide the dough into 3 portions. Add the red food coloring and the cherry extract to 1 portion. Add the blue food coloring and the raspberry extract to the second portion. Add lemon extract to the untinted portion.
3. Shape each portion into a 10-in.-long block. Place red, white and blue logs side by side. Lightly press blocks together. Wrap and refrigerate until firm, 30 minutes.
4. Preheat oven to 350°. Unwrap and cut dough crosswise into ¼-in. slices. Place 1 in. apart on parchment-lined baking sheets. To create ridges, lightly press cookies with a fork. Bake until set, 10-12 minutes. Cool on pans 2 minutes; remove the cookies to wire racks to cool completely.

1 cookie: 86 cal., 4g fat (2g sat. fat), 11mg chol., 51mg sod., 11g carb. (4g sugars, 0 fiber), 1g pro.

Do not flour the counter, as you don't want to dull the bright colors of these cookies. Since the dough has oil in it, it shouldn't stick to the surface.

PEACH CREAM PUFFS

On a sizzling day, we crave something light, airy and cool. Nothing says summer like cream puffs stuffed with fresh peaches and dreamy whipped cream.
—*Angela Benedict, Dunbar, WV*

Prep: 55 min. + cooling
Bake: 25 min. + cooling
Makes: 16 servings

- 1 cup water
- ½ cup butter, cubed
- ⅛ tsp. salt
- 1 cup all-purpose flour
- 4 large eggs, room temperature

FILLING
- 4 medium peaches, peeled and cubed (about 3 cups)
- ½ cup sugar
- ½ cup water
- ½ cup peach schnapps liqueur or peach nectar
- ½ tsp. ground cinnamon
- ¼ tsp. ground nutmeg

WHIPPED CREAM
- 2 cups heavy whipping cream
- ½ cup confectioners' sugar
- 3 Tbsp. peach schnapps liqueur, optional
  Additional confectioners' sugar

1. Preheat oven to 400°. In a large saucepan, bring water, butter and salt to a rolling boil. Add flour all at once and beat until blended. Cook over medium heat, stirring vigorously until mixture pulls away from sides of pan and forms a ball. Transfer dough to a large bowl; let stand 5 minutes.

2. Add eggs, one at a time, beating well after each addition until smooth. Continue beating until mixture is smooth and shiny.

3. Cut a ½-in. hole in tip of a pastry bag. Transfer dough to bag; pipe sixteen 2-in. mounds 3 in. apart onto parchment-lined baking sheets.

4. Bake on a lower oven rack 25-30 minutes or until puffed, very firm and golden brown. Pierce side of each puff with tip of a knife to allow steam to escape. Cool completely on wire racks.

5. Meanwhile, in a large saucepan, combine the filling ingredients; bring to a boil, stirring occasionally. Reduce the heat; simmer, uncovered, 25-30 minutes or until mixture is slightly thickened and peaches are tender. Cool completely.

6. In a bowl, beat cream until it begins to thicken. Add confectioners' sugar and, if desired, peach schnapps; beat until soft peaks form.

7. Cut top third off each cream puff. Pull out and discard soft dough from inside tops and bottoms.

8. To serve, spoon 2 Tbsp. whipped cream into each bottom; top with 2 Tbsp. filling and 2 Tbsp. additional whipped cream. Replace tops. Dust cream puffs with the additional confectioners' sugar.

1 cream puff with ¼ cup whipped cream and 2 Tbsp. filling: 256 cal., 18g fat (11g sat. fat), 103mg chol., 94mg sod., 21g carb. (14g sugars, 1g fiber), 3g pro.

LEMON PUDDING SOUFFLES

With their tangy lemon flavor, these creamy souffles make the perfect finale for a special meal. It's fun to dress up each dessert with an edible flower.
—*Lily Julow, Lawrenceville, GA*

Prep: 20 min.
Bake: 25 min.
Makes: 2 servings

- 1 large egg, separated
- ⅓ cup sugar
- ⅓ cup 2% milk
- 1 Tbsp. butter, melted
- 1 Tbsp. all-purpose flour
  Dash salt
- 2 Tbsp. lemon juice
- ½ tsp. grated lemon zest
  Coarse sugar, edible pansies and fresh mint leaves, optional

1. In a small bowl, beat egg yolk until slightly thickened. Gradually add sugar, beating until thick and lemon-colored. Beat in the milk, butter, flour and salt. Stir in the lemon juice and lemon zest.
2. In a small bowl, beat egg white until stiff peaks form. With a spatula, stir a fourth of the egg white into lemon mixture until no white streaks remain. Fold in the remaining egg white until combined.
3. Divide the mixture between 2 ungreased 6-oz. ramekins or custard cups. Place in an 8-in. square baking dish; add 1 in. of hot water to dish.
4. Bake at 350° for 25-30 minutes or until tops are golden brown. If desired, sprinkle with coarse sugar, and garnish with pansies and mint. Serve immediately.
Note: Verify that flowers are edible and have not been treated with chemicals.

1 souffle: 255 cal., 9g fat (5g sat. fat), 112mg chol., 175mg sod., 40g carb. (36g sugars, 0 fiber), 5g pro.

MACAROON-TOPPED RHUBARB COBBLER

Crumbled macaroons are a unique addition to this cobbler's topping. Serve hearty helpings alone or with vanilla ice cream.
—Taste of Home *Test Kitchen*

Takes: 30 min.
Makes: 4 servings

- 4 **cups sliced fresh or frozen rhubarb (1-in. pieces)**
- 1 **large apple, peeled and sliced**
- ½ **cup packed brown sugar**
- ½ **tsp. ground cinnamon, divided**
- 1 **Tbsp. cornstarch**
- 2 **Tbsp. cold water**
- 8 **macaroons, crumbled**
- 1 **Tbsp. butter, melted**
- 2 **Tbsp. sugar**
  Vanilla ice cream, optional

1. In a large cast-iron or other ovenproof skillet, combine rhubarb, apple, brown sugar and ¼ tsp. cinnamon; bring to a boil. Reduce heat; cover and simmer until rhubarb is very tender, 10-13 minutes. Combine cornstarch and water until smooth; gradually add to the fruit mixture. Bring to a boil; cook and stir until thickened, about 2 minutes.
2. In a small bowl, combine the crumbled cookies, butter, sugar and the remaining cinnamon. Sprinkle over fruit mixture.
3. Broil the cobbler 4 in. from the heat until lightly browned, for 3-5 minutes. If desired, serve warm with ice cream.
Note: If using frozen rhubarb, measure rhubarb while it is still frozen, then thaw completely. Drain in a colander, but do not press liquid out.

1 serving: 368 cal., 12g fat (7g sat. fat), 8mg chol., 45mg sod., 62g carb. (55g sugars, 5g fiber), 3g pro.

GRAFFITI CUTOUT COOKIES

Talk about playing with your food! Edible color spray lets you create ombre and color blends unlike any other decorating technique. To make ombre lines like I did, hold a sheet of paper over desired sections as you spray to layer the color.
—*Shannon Norris, Cudahy, WI*

Prep: 30 min+ freezing
Bake: 15 min. + cooling
Makes: 15 cookies

- ¼ **cup butter, softened**
- ½ **cup sugar**
- 1 **large egg, room temperature**
- 1 **tsp. vanilla extract**
- 2 **cups almond flour**
- ¼ **tsp. salt**
- ¼ **tsp. baking soda**
ROYAL ICING
- 2 **cups confectioners' sugar**
- 5 **tsp. meringue powder**
- 2 **to 6 Tbsp. water**
  Food color spray, optional

1. In a bowl, cream butter and sugar until light and fluffy. Beat in egg and vanilla. In another bowl, whisk almond flour, salt and baking soda; gradually beat flour mixture into creamed mixture.
2. Preheat oven to 325°. Between 2 pieces of waxed paper, roll dough to ¼-in. thickness. Place on a cutting board in the freezer until firm, about 20 minutes. Remove paper; cut with 3-in. cookie cutters. Place 2 in. apart on parchment-lined baking sheets.
3. Bake until lightly browned on the edges, about 12-15 minutes. Cool on pans about 2 minutes. Remove cookies to wire racks to cool completely. For icing, in a large bowl, combine confectioners' sugar, 2 Tbsp. water and meringue powder; beat on low speed just until blended. Beat on high 4-5 minutes or until stiff peaks form. Add additional water as necessary to reach the desired consistency. Keep unused icing covered at all times with a damp cloth. If necessary, beat again on high speed to restore texture.
4. Frost the cookies and let stand at room temperature several hours or until frosting is dry and firm. Decorate if desired with color spray mist. Store in an airtight container.

1 cookie: 209 cal., 11g fat (3g sat. fat), 21mg chol., 103mg sod., 26g carb. (23g sugars, 2g fiber), 4g pro.

STAR-SPANGLED LEMON ICEBOX PIE

With a little chill time, this no-bake lemon pie turns into a potluck superstar. My kids like to arrange the berries in a star pattern.
—*Lauren Katz, Ashburn, VA*

Prep: 35 min. + chilling
Makes: 8 servings

- 15 pecan shortbread cookies (about 8 oz.)
- 1 Tbsp. sugar
- 3 Tbsp. butter, melted

FILLING

- 8 oz. cream cheese, softened
- ½ cup mascarpone cheese
- 1 Tbsp. grated lemon zest
- ½ cup lemon juice
- 1 can (14 oz.) sweetened condensed milk
- 1 cup sliced fresh strawberries
- 1 cup fresh blueberries

1. Preheat oven to 350°. Place the cookies and sugar in a food processor; process until the cookies are ground. Add melted butter; pulse just until combined. Press mixture onto bottom and up sides of an ungreased 9-in. pie plate. Bake 15-20 minutes or until lightly browned. Cool completely on a wire rack.
2. In a large bowl, beat the cream cheese, mascarpone cheese, lemon zest and lemon juice until smooth; gradually beat in milk.
3. Spread into prepared crust. Refrigerate, covered, at least 4 hours or until filling is set. Top with berries before serving.

1 piece: 591 cal., 41g fat (20g sat. fat), 104mg chol., 310mg sod., 52g carb. (38g sugars, 1g fiber), 10g pro.

ALOHA CUPCAKES

A friend asked me to make a coconut and pineapple cupcake for a gathering she was hosting. Everyone agreed that this beauty took them to the tropics. Because my friend is allergic, I didn't use macadamia nuts, but the cupcakes are fantastic with or without them.
—*Shannon Dobos, Calgary, AB*

Prep: 20 min.
Bake: 15 min. + cooling
Makes: 1 dozen

- 1¼ **cups cake flour**
- 1¼ **tsp. baking powder**
- ½ **tsp. baking soda**
- ½ **tsp. salt**
- 2 **large eggs, room temperature**
- ¾ **cup sugar**
- ½ **cup canola oil**
- 1 **tsp. coconut extract**
- ½ **cup coconut milk**
- ½ **tsp. white vinegar**

PINEAPPLE FROSTING

- ½ **cup shortening**
- ½ **cup butter**
- 4 **cups confectioners' sugar**
- ½ **cup finely chopped fresh pineapple**
- 3 **Tbsp. unsweetened pineapple juice**

TOPPING

- ½ **cup sweetened shredded coconut, toasted**
- ½ **cup coarsely chopped macadamia nuts, optional**

For topping, toast ½ cup sweetened flaked coconut by heating over medium-high heat in a small skillet for 3-4 minutes. Watch it very carefully, however, as it will start to toast quickly once it gets going.

1. Preheat oven to 350°. Line 12 muffin cups with paper or foil liners. Whisk the first 4 ingredients; set aside. Beat eggs and sugar on medium speed for 1 minute. Add oil and coconut extract; beat 1 minute more. Add half the flour mixture; beat on low speed. Combine coconut milk and vinegar. Add half to batter; beat just until combined. Beat in the remaining flour mixture, then remaining coconut milk mixture just until smooth.
2. Fill prepared cups two-thirds full. Bake until cupcakes are golden brown and spring back lightly when touched, 15-18 minutes (do not overbake). Cool on wire rack.
3. For frosting, cream shortening and butter until light and fluffy. Beat in confectioners' sugar a half cup at a time, adding the finely chopped pineapple and pineapple juice after beating in 2 cups of sugar. Add additional confectioners' sugar and pineapple juice to reach desired consistency.
4. Spoon frosting onto cupcakes. Top with toasted coconut and, if desired, chopped macadamia nuts.

1 frosted cupcake: 533 cal., 29g fat (11g sat. fat), 51mg chol., 287mg sod., 67g carb. (55g sugars, 1g fiber), 3g pro.

STRAWBERRY-HAZELNUT MERINGUE SHORTCAKES

In early summer, the strawberry farms in our area open to the public for picking. These shortcakes really show off the big, juicy berries of our harvest.
—*Barbara Estabrook, Appleton, WI*

Prep: 25 min.
Bake: 45 min. + cooling
Makes: 8 servings

- 2 **large egg whites**
- ½ **cup sugar**
- ¼ **cup finely chopped hazelnuts**
- 6 **cups fresh strawberries,
  hulled and sliced**
- 4 **cups low-fat frozen yogurt**

1. Place egg whites in a small bowl; let stand at room temperature 30 minutes.
2. Preheat oven to 250°. Beat egg whites on medium speed until foamy. Gradually add sugar, 1 Tbsp. at a time, beating on high after each addition until the sugar is dissolved. Continue beating the egg whites until stiff glossy peaks form.

3. Using a measuring cup and spatula or an ice cream scoop, drop meringue into 8 even mounds on a parchment-lined baking sheet. With the back of a spoon, shape into 3-in. cups. Sprinkle with hazelnuts. Bake 45-50 minutes or until set and dry. Turn off oven (do not open oven door); leave meringues in the oven for 1 hour. Remove from oven; cool completely on baking sheets. Remove the meringues from paper.
4. Place 3 cups strawberries in a large bowl; mash slightly. Stir in remaining strawberries. Just before serving, top meringues with frozen yogurt and strawberries.

1 serving: 212 cal., 4g fat (1g sat. fat), 5mg chol., 74mg sod., 40g carb. (36g sugars, 3g fiber), 7g pro.

GRILLED FRUIT PHYLLO TART

This tart was a hit at my friend's baby shower. It reminds me of a fruit salad that my mother used to make with cream cheese and whipped topping. Everyone loves the flaky crust, and the bright colors make it a pretty addition to any spread.
—*Laura McAllister, Morganton, NC*

Prep: 30 min.
Grill: 10 min.
Makes: 12 servings

- 3 **Tbsp. butter, melted**
- 4 **tsp. canola oil**
- 8 **sheets phyllo dough (14x9-in. size)**
- 1 **large lemon**
- 3 **medium peaches, peeled and halved**
- 2 **cups large fresh strawberries,
  stems removed**
- 4 **slices fresh pineapple (½ in. thick)**
- ⅓ **cup packed brown sugar**
- ½ **tsp. salt**
- ½ **cup heavy whipping cream**
- 1 **pkg. (8 oz.) cream cheese, softened**
- ⅓ **cup confectioners' sugar**
- 2 **Tbsp. chopped fresh mint**

1. Preheat oven to 400°. In a small bowl, mix butter and oil. Brush a 15x10x1-in. baking pan with some of the butter mixture. Place 1 sheet of phyllo dough into prepared pan; brush with butter mixture. Layer the pan with 7 additional phyllo sheets, brushing each layer. (Keep remaining phyllo covered with a damp towel to prevent it from drying out.) Bake 5-7 minutes or until golden brown (phyllo will puff up during baking). Cool the phyllo completely.
2. Finely grate enough zest from lemon to measure 1 Tbsp.. Cut lemon crosswise in half; squeeze out juice. In a large bowl, toss peaches, strawberries, pineapple, brown sugar, salt, lemon zest and juice. Remove strawberries; thread onto 3 metal or soaked wooden skewers.

3. Place fruit on oiled grill rack. Grill, covered, over medium heat until the fruit is tender, turning once; 8-10 minutes for the pineapple slices and peaches, 4-5 minutes for the strawberries. Remove and set aside.
4. In a small bowl, beat cream until soft peaks form. In another bowl, beat cream cheese and confectioners' sugar until smooth. Fold in whipped cream. Spread over phyllo crust. Slice grilled fruit; arrange over filling. Sprinkle with mint; cut into pieces.

1 piece: 233 cal., 15g fat (8g sat. fat), 38mg chol., 216mg sod., 24g carb. (18g sugars, 2g fiber), 3g pro.

STRAWBERRY LEMON CUPCAKES

My granddaughter Sydney has acquired a love of baking. While I was visiting her in Tampa, we made these light, fluffy cupcakes. She's a natural—they turned out fantastic!
—*Lonnie Hartstack, Clarinda, IA*

Prep: 15 min.
Bake: 20 min. + cooling
Makes: 2 dozen

1   pkg. white cake mix (regular size)
3   large eggs, room temperature
½   cup 2% milk
⅓   cup canola oil
2   Tbsp. grated lemon zest
3   Tbsp. lemon juice
FROSTING
4   cups confectioners' sugar
1   cup butter, softened
¼   cup crushed fresh strawberries

1. Preheat oven to 350°. Line 24 muffin cups with paper liners.
2. In a bowl, combine first 6 ingredients; beat on low 30 seconds. Beat on medium 2 minutes. Fill prepared cups half full. Bake until a toothpick inserted in center comes out clean, 18-20 minutes. Cool in pans for 10 minutes before removing to wire racks to cool completely.
3. For frosting, in a large bowl, combine all the ingredients; beat until smooth. Frost cupcakes. Garnish frosting with additional strawberries. Store in the refrigerator.

1 cupcake: 253 cal., 12g fat (6g sat. fat), 44mg chol., 198mg sod., 35g carb. (27g sugars, 1g fiber), 2g pro.

PEACH & BERRY COBBLER

This is one of my favorite summer recipes because it features peaches and berries that are in season. But it's just as delicious with frozen fruit. The quick biscuit topping brings everything together.
—*Lauren Knoelke, Des Moines, IA*

Prep: 20 min.
Bake: 40 min.
Makes: 8 servings

- ½ cup sugar
- 3 Tbsp. cornstarch
- ½ tsp. ground cinnamon
- ¼ tsp. ground cardamom
- 10 medium peaches, peeled and sliced (about 6 cups)
- 2 cups mixed blackberries, raspberries and blueberries
- 1 Tbsp. lemon juice

TOPPING
- 1 cup all-purpose flour
- ¼ cup sugar
- 2 tsp. grated orange zest
- ¾ tsp. baking powder
- ¼ tsp. salt
- ¼ tsp. baking soda
- 3 Tbsp. cold butter
- ¾ cup buttermilk
  Vanilla ice cream, optional

1. Preheat oven to 375°. In a large bowl, mix sugar, cornstarch, cinnamon and cardamom. Add peaches, berries and lemon juice; toss to combine. Transfer to a 10-in. cast-iron or other ovenproof skillet.
2. In a small bowl, whisk the first 6 topping ingredients; cut in butter until the mixture resembles coarse crumbs. Add buttermilk; stir just until moistened. Drop mixture by tablespoonfuls over peach mixture.
3. Bake, uncovered, until topping is golden brown, for 40-45 minutes. Serve warm. If desired, top with vanilla ice cream.

1 serving: 279 cal., 5g fat (3g sat. fat), 12mg chol., 238mg sod., 57g carb. (38g sugars, 5g fiber), 4g pro.

RECIPE INDEX